Mapping and Analysing Crime Data

Crime mapping and the spatial analysis of crime data are recognised as powerful tools for the study and control of crime. The passing of the 1998 Crime and Disorder Act in England and Wales has driven the emerging demand for more information and detailed crime pattern analysis. It is a topic pursued by every police force and local authority in England and Wales, now that they have a joint statutory duty to produce Crime and Disorder Audits for their areas.

Using a series of case studies this multidisciplinary book highlights the experiences of academics and practitioners to provide a much needed position statement of current practice in the mapping and analysis of crime data in the UK. It covers experiences of crime mapping and spatial analysis of crime data by agencies centrally involved in delivering a partnership approach to crime prevention. There are also examples from the USA, where crime mapping has been an important part of law enforcement and crime prevention efforts for some time.

Very few books have been published on the use of GIS in mapping crime data. This forward-looking and progressive book

- explores the types of problems to which spatial crime analysis can be applied;
- reviews capabilities and limitations of existing techniques and explores future directions and developments of spatial crime analysis;
- addresses questions of direct relevance to practitioners, their involvement in spatial crime analysis, GIS and crime prevention, and the need for training.

Mapping and Analysing Crime Data

Lessons from research and practice

Edited by Alex Hirschfield and
Kate Bowers

London and New York

First published 2001
by Taylor & Francis
11 New Fetter Lane, London EC4P 4EE

Simultaneously published in the USA and Canada
by Taylor & Francis Inc.
29 West 35th Street, New York, NY 10001

Taylor & Francis is an imprint of the Taylor & Francis Group

© 2001 Alex Hirschfield and Kate Bowers

Typeset in Sabon by
Exe Valley Dataset Ltd, Exeter, Devon
Printed and bound in Great Britain by
T. J. International Ltd, Padstow, Cornwall

Every effort has been made to ensure that the advice and information in this
book is true and accurate at the time of going to press. However, neither the
publisher nor the authors can accept any legal responsibilityor liability for any
errors or omissions that may be made. In the case of drug administration, any
medical procedure or the use of technical equipment mentioned within this
book, you are strongly advised to consult the manufacturer's guidelines.

British Library Cataloguing in Publication Data
A catalogue record for this book is available from the British Library

Library of Congress Cataloging in Publication Data
Mapping and analysing crime data: lessons from research and
practice / edited by Alex Hirschfield and Kate Bowers.
     p.   cm.
Includes bibliographical references and index.
     1. Crime analysis – Great Britain – Data processing.   2. Crime
prevention – Great Britain – Data processing.   3. Law
enforcement – Great Britain – Data processing.   I. Hirschfield, Alex.
II. Bowers, Kate.

HV7936 C88 M36 2001
364'.042–dc21   00–060785

ISBN 0–748–40922–X

In Memory of Moss Madden (1946–2000),
Professor of Planning and Regional Science,
Department of Civic Design,
University of Liverpool

Contents

Figures

Tables

Colour plates

Notes on contributors

Kate Bowers is a research associate in the Department of Civic Design at Liverpool University. She recently completed her PhD, which was concerned with crime against non-residential properties. She has been involved in the monitoring, targeting and evaluation of crime prevention schemes on Merseyside over the past four years and has a research interest in the link between crime and deprivation. She is currently working on a Home Office-funded evaluation of the national Burglary Reduction Initiative and a project investigating isomorphic re-victimisation.

Spencer Chainey is a senior consultant for Infotech Enterprises Europe – the UK's leading independent GIS software and services provider. Prior to joining Dataview, Spencer spent three years as Corporate Geographical Information Systems Manager for the London Borough of Hackney and one year as the lead figure for the award winning Brent Crime Mapping Project. Spencer is also an elected Council member of the Association for Geographic Information (AGI) and chairs the AGI Crime and Disorder Special Interest Group. His work in crime mapping and analysis, information sharing, regeneration mapping, housing management systems, social exclusion analysis, and web-based mapping systems is recognised and used as examples of best practice by the Cabinet Office (Social Exclusion Unit), the Department for Environment, Transport and the Regions, the Home Office, the Audit Commission, The Housing Corporation and the United States Department of Justice. Spencer has a BSc degree in Geography (Kingston University) and a MSc degree in GIS (University of Edinburgh).

Andrew Costello is a South Yorkshire Police Authority research fellow, based in the Faculty of Law at the University of Sheffield. His main interests lie in developing the use of geocoded data within the field of environmental criminology. One of the recent focuses of his research has been the analysis of offender journey to crime patterns.

Victor Goldsmith is Professor of Geography and Co-ordinator of Business Incubator Development at Hunter College, City University of New York.

He also directs the Center for Applied Studies of the Environment. He has numerous research publications, most recently focusing on the applications of Geographic Information Science (GIS), especially in the area of crime pattern analysis. He has worked with the New York Police Department (NYPD) and also with the French.

Elizabeth R. Groff is a social science analyst in the Crime Mapping Research Center at the US National Institute of Justice (NIJ). She received both her BSc and MA in Geography from the University of North Carolina at Charlotte. Prior to joining NIJ, Elizabeth was GIS Coordinator at the Charlotte-Mecklenburg Police Department, where she implemented the use of GIS in that agency. Previously, she was a GIS Analyst for a consulting firm. Elizabeth's research interests include the relationship between neighbourhood characteristics and crime, the development of tools to assist law enforcement personnel, and globally, the application of GIS to all facets of criminal justice.

Alex Hirschfield is research co-ordinator of the Urban Research and Policy Evaluation Regional Research Laboratory (URPERRL) and a Reader in the Department of Civic Design at Liverpool University. He has built up a strong portfolio of applied research into the design and implementation of information systems to support the targeting and delivery of resources (especially in relation to crime prevention, fire safety and health care) and the development of approaches for evaluating spatially targeted urban policies. He is currently the principal co-ordinator for the northern evaluation of the Burglary Reduction Programme, funded by the Home Office, which involves assessing the effectiveness of twenty-one Strategic Development Projects in the north of England.

Nancy G. La Vigne is the founder and director of the Crime Mapping Research Center at the National Institute of Justice, U.S. Department of Justice, in Washington, DC. Her research areas include the geographic analysis of crime, situational crime prevention, and community policing. Her previous work experience includes consulting for the Police Executive Research Forum, the National Council on Crime and Delinquency, and the National Development and Research Institute. She also served as Research Director for the Texas Punishment Standards Commission from 1991 to 1993. Ms. La Vigne serves on a number of boards and committees pertaining to the spatial analysis of crime and criminal behaviour, including the advisory board of the National Center for Geographic Information and Analysis, the Center for Spatially Integrated Social Science, and the advisory committee for the Philadelphia Gun Tracking Initiative.

James L. LeBeau is a Professor in the Departments of Administration of Justice and Geography at Southern Illinois University at Carbondale. He received his PhD in geography from Michigan State University in 1978. His research includes studies of the spatial behaviour of serial rapists, the relationships among calls for police service, time, and weather change, and using geographic information systems and spatial analysis for examining police operations.

Michael J. McCullagh is a geographer by training. He lectured in the USA following his PhD for two years at the University of Kansas and the Kansas State Geological Survey: a seat long famed for research into quantitative methods and computer cartography. Returning to the UK and the University of Nottingham he has spent nearly 30 years teaching and researching in the field of GIS, particularly in surface modelling, visualisation and, fleetingly from time to time and most recently, crime pattern analysis. Six years of association with Jerry Ratcliffe has resulted in his contribution to this book.

Philip McGuire is an Assistant Commissioner with the New York City Police Department, where he has been working for twenty-seven years. During his tenure with the NYPD, he has been assigned to the Police Commissioner's staff office and the Office of Management Analysis and Planning (OMAP), where prior to being appointed an Assistant Commissioner in 1995, he held the positions of Research Director and then Director of Crime Analysis and Program Planning. Commissioner McGuire is also a 1989 graduate of the NYPD's Police Management Institute and was a member of the Police Department's Civilian Complaint Review Board (1981–1993). He has also been an adjunct instructor in the City University's Graduate Divisions of Criminal Justice and Public Management. He is a member of the Institute of Electrical and Electronic Engineers, Computer Society and Systems Man and Cybernetics Group and also a member of the American Statistical Association. His professional interests are in public management and information systems that facilitate organisational decision-making.

Sara McLafferty is Professor of Geography at Hunter College of the City University of New York. Her research interests include the use of spatial analysis methods and geographic information systems to analyse health and social problems in cities, and gender and racial differences in geographical access to services and employment opportunities. She is co-author of *Location Strategies for Retail and Service Firms* (with Dr. Avijit Ghosh) and has published in a wide range of geography, epidemiology, and urban studies journals. She currently serves on the editorial boards of 'Economic Geography and Health and Place', and was a member of the Mapping Science Committee of the National Academy of Sciences.

Steven Merrall is a research student in the Department of Civic Design at the University of Liverpool. He graduated with a First Class Honours degree in Geography from the University of Liverpool in 1998. He has been involved in several projects including an evaluation report examining the effectiveness of community safety initiatives within a local authority borough and a national survey of the fire service examining the use of data analysis and GIS for community fire safety planning. Following his involvement in a pilot study examining the distribution of fire incidents across Greater Manchester, he was successful in securing funding from the E.S.R.C. and support from Greater Manchester County Fire Service (GMCFS) to take this work forward in the form of a PhD research studentship. The research examines the relationships between fire incidence and social, economic and environmental risk factors. Preliminary findings from the research have been used in the production of GMCFS's Community Fire Safety plan and are currently informing CFS planning, management and delivery in the GMCFS.

John Mollenkopf is Professor of Political Science and Sociology at the City University of New York Graduate Center and director of its Center for Urban Research. He has authored or edited seven books on urban politics, urban policy, the politics of urban development, and New York City, including *A Phoenix In The Ashes: The Rise and Fall of the Koch Coalition in New York City Politics* (Princeton 1994). He also co-ordinates the graduate center's interdisciplinary program on public policy and urban studies. Some of his current research projects include an assessment of educational attainment, labor market outcomes, and political and civic involvement among second generation immigrant and native minority young adults in the New York metropolitan area and an analysis of the changing spatial patterns of crime incidence in New York City. Other projects include a book on *Rethinking the Urban Agenda*, an edited volume on economic restructuring and social stratification in New York, Tokyo, London and Paris and a volume on historical and contemporary perspectives on the political incorporation of immigrants.

Martin Newton has been a Policy Development Officer for Knowsley Metropolitan Borough Council since the early 1980s and more recently has been the Principal Community Safety Co-ordinator for Merseyside Police Authority (MPA). The MPA is the accountable body for the Safer Merseyside Partnership, which aims to reduce crime and the fear of crime in the Merseyside area. In his role in MPA, Martin co-ordinates crime reduction and community safety initiatives and all external government funding. Since commencing the SMP, he has secured £20 million for community safety in the region.

Richard Nutter is Information Service Manager at Merseyside Information Service (MIS), a Countywide research unit funded by the local authorities and joint boards on Merseyside to provide data, research and GIS services to the funding partners. Richard joined MIS from

Manchester University where he was employed as research officer in the Centre for Urban Policy Studies. A geography graduate with a PhD in geography from Liverpool University, he has substantial experience within the unit having held the post of project manager (services) prior to being appointed to his current position. His main expertise lies in the field of social statistics and analysis – which he taught at both Manchester and Liverpool Universities – survey research and GIS.

Stan Openshaw is Professor of Human Geography in the School of Geography at the University of Leeds. He has been working in the field of spatial data analysis and cluster hunting for many years, in which he has published widely. His particular research interests are in computer modelling, analysis of spatial data, GIS and artificial intelligence. He has also collaborated with Ian Turton on a book on parallel programming for geographers.

Ken Pease is Professor of Criminology at Huddersfield University, currently on secondment to the Home Office. He has previously held chairs at the Universities of Manchester and Saskatchewan. He sits on the crime prevention panel of the DTI's Foresight programme, and has published widely, in recent years primarily about crime prevention.

Steve Quinn is a former police officer with the New York City Police Department. Currently he is employed with the United States Bureau of the Census, working on the Census 2000 project. He holds a Bachelor's degree in geology from Lehman College of the City University of New York, as well as a masters degree in Urban Planning from Hunter College of the City University of New York (CUNY). At present he is a doctoral student at the Graduate Center and University Center also of CUNY. His research interests include crime mapping and internet mapping.

Jerry H. Ratcliffe was a Metropolitan Police officer for eleven years, after which he changed tack from diplomatic protection duties in central London and mounting Raleigh expeditions around the world to take a first class degree in Geography at the University of Nottingham. Following a winter climbing accident resulting in a broken leg he changed his undergraduate dissertation from adventuring in Baffin Island to a more sedentary study of crime patterns in Nottingham. This led on to postgraduate research into crime at Nottingham and a growing interest in GIS and its policing applications. Upon receiving his PhD, Jerry now teaches policing intelligence and crime mapping to the New South Wales Police Service, while holding a lectureship at Charles Sturt University, Goulburn, Australia.

Timothy Ross is a senior research associate at the Vera Institute of Justice, where he directs research projects in the fields of juvenile justice and child welfare. He previously worked at the Center for Urban Research, where he directed research projects involving the New York City Police Department, the Department for Youth and Community Development, and the City Council Finance Division. He edited a book on crime mapping, and authored several reports and book chapters on urban politics and education. He has taught several courses at Hunter and Baruch Colleges, and served as a teacher in the New York City public high schools. Dr Ross has BAs in political science from Williams College and the University of Kent at Canterbury, and a PhD in government and politics from the University of Maryland, College Park.

Ian Turton is director of the Centre for Computational Geography at the University of Leeds. His particular interests are in the field of spatial data analysis. He has been very involved with the implementation of smart spatial pattern detection methods and is currently researching methods of integrating the world wide web and GIS systems as part of an ESRC programme on virtual societies. He has also collaborated with Stan Openshaw on a book on parallel programming for geographers and several undergraduate and masters courses in computational aspects of geography.

Paul Wiles is presently the director of the Research Development and Statistics Directorate at Home Office. At the time the research discussed in his joint contribution with Andrew Costello was carried out, he was Professor of Criminology, at the University of Sheffield. His central and long-term criminological interest continues to be on the spatial patterning of crime and the changes in those patterns in contemporary cities.

Doug Williamson is a PhD candidate at the City University of New York in Earth and Environmental Sciences. He received his BA from Rutgers, the State University of New Jersey in Geography and his MA from Hunter College of the City University of New York in Geography. He has worked as research associate at the Center for Applied Studies of the Environment since 1994. Since 1996 he has worked with the New York City Police Department on number of crime mapping projects including the development of a mapping application for use with their COMPSTAT data. Past projects ranged from 3-D modelling to tax map conversion. His current research interests are spatial statistics, mapping, visualisation and policy evaluation as they relate to law enforcement.

Foreword

Developments within the UK's criminal justice arena within the last five years have provided a favourable context for crime analysis and mapping. In particular the statutory requirement under the Crime and Disorder Act (1998) for the police and local partnerships to undertake crime and disorder audits and produce strategies based on the results of these audits, has provided a powerful stimulus to the mapping and analysis of crime data.

Concurrent with the Crime and Disorder Act, police forces have been encouraged, by Her Majesty's Inspectorate of Constabulary and the Audit Commission, for example, to adopt 'problem-solving' approaches in dealing with incidents brought to their attention by the public. Such an approach, together with the encouragement of 'intelligence-led' policing and the development of the National Intelligence Model, places a heavy emphasis upon the use of analysis, and stresses its centrality in determining police responses and the targeting of police resources. More specifically, aspects of the current government's Crime Reduction Programme, particularly the burglary reduction and targeted policing initiatives, have attempted to foster crime analysis and the use of GIS by the police and other agencies to identify and tackle local problems.

Against this backdrop it is perhaps surprising that so little has been published in the UK in the way of guidance on the analysis and mapping of crime data, particularly high volume crime. While there has been a certain amount published in the United States, this book is the first attempt to provide a comprehensive account of the subject in the UK. Jerry Ratcliffe makes the point in his chapter that the 'recent shift within British policing towards a more decentralised, proactive style has shifted the analytical focus onto analysts and intelligence officers at the police divisional level who are now expected to be the hub of the local intelligence gathering effort. For high volume crime, this has left an analytical void'.

This book is an attempt to fill that void. It brings together work undertaken by leading individuals, both academics and practitioners, mainly from the UK but also from the United States. It provides examples of the application of crime analysis and mapping across a wide range of areas, of relevance, *inter alia*, to those involved in policing, crime and incident analysis, criminological research and evaluation, community safety and crime and disorder work.

Several chapters in this book will be immediately useful to those involved in the analysis of crime in support of partnership work. Spencer Chainey's chapter describes work undertaken by four London Boroughs. His description of attempts to encourage data sharing, and ways in which analysis, and GIS in particular, have been used in the allocation of police resources, to identify hot-spots, to inform the design and implementation of crime and disorder strategies, to site and evaluate CCTV installations, and to assist partnerships in the development of bids for external funding, is particularly important. The chapter also usefully describes some of the problems associated with the spatial analysis of police crime/incident data, expanding on issues raised in the book's introduction.

Alex Hirschfield's account of crime prevention targeting identifies eight interest groups likely to want to scrutinise crime and disorder problems, ranging from the police through community safety co-ordinators, to residents and business managers. Hirschfield describes how different forms of crime data analysis and mapping are needed to meet the varying requirements of these interests, concluding with examples of the way mapping has been used in a variety of contexts in the work of the Safer Merseyside Partnership (SMP). (The book also includes an example of work undertaken for SMP by Kate Bowers, Martin Newton and Richard Nutter in developing a GIS-based system to identify vulnerable targets for domestic burglary). Hirschfield also identifies the skills required by, and training needs of, those involved in the analysis and mapping of crime data for crime prevention and evaluation purposes, information of immediate use to those responsible for the recruitment and training of analysts.

In addition Hirschfield stresses the importance of assembling evidence from a variety of sources to understand the manifestation of problems, obtaining an 'holistic picture' of what is going on. In doing so he addresses some of the concerns expressed in the preceding chapter by Ken Pease who warns about the dangers inherent in any assumption of the paramount importance of mapping. Pease asserts that 'location is almost never a sufficient basis for, and seldom a necessary element in, prevention or detection', and that non-spatial variables can, and should be, used to generate patterns of concentration.

Pease's deductive approach, in turn, contrasts sharply with the inductive approach advocated by Stan Openshaw and Ian Turton in their description of their GAM (Geographical Analysis Machine) and GEM (Geographical Explanations Machine) applications. Taken together the two chapters neatly illustrate the divergence of views on the role of criminological theory in driving mapping.

The book provides other examples of the practical application of crime theory in crime analysis and mapping. Jerry Ratcliffe's chapter examines the phenomenon of repeat victimisation, in particular, the use of GIS to analyse and contextualise locations where repeat victimisation has occurred. Paul Wiles and Andrew Costello's chapter examines the concept of offender travel to crime in relation to patterns of offending in Sheffield. James LeBeau's account of 'mapping out hazardous space for police work' provides a fascinating account of an underused technique. All will be of interest to analysts.

Finally, and perhaps ironically, the section on 'international perspectives' will also be immediately relevant to those involved in crime analysis in the UK. The four spatial analysis techniques (block aggregation, kernel smoothing, Voronoi diagrams, and animation) described in chapter nine will be of interest to analysts keen to go beyond basic automated pin-mapping. Similarly the account by Nancy LaVigne and Liz Groff of the development of crime mapping in the USA provides examples of the use of GIS in a variety of contexts; hot-spot identification, automated pin-mapping, radial analysis, community liaison, inter-agency working and predictive modelling.

The chapter also makes explicit the part played by the Department of Justice's Crime Mapping Research Centre in encouraging the development of crime mapping in the USA, a body without any equivalent in the UK. The references from this chapter, particularly those indicating available mapping software, will be invaluable to those readers keen to pursue the subject in greater detail.

Tim Read
Policing and Reducing Crime Unit,
Research, Development and Statistics Directorate
Home Office

Acknowledgements

The editors would like to thank all the authors for their contributions to this book. They have all been of a very high standard, which has considerably eased our task of producing the volume. They have also widened our knowledge of the various ways in which mapping and analysing spatial data can inform the debate concerning the manifestation of crime from both academic and practical perspectives. We would also like to thank Taylor & Francis for their assistance in the production of this book.

1 Introduction

Kate Bowers and Alex Hirschfield

Since the 1998 Crime and Disorder Act was passed in England and Wales, placing a joint statutory duty on police forces and local authorities to produce Crime and Disorder Audits for their areas, there has been a heightened interest in the techniques, training and technology necessary to perform crime mapping and analysis. This book covers experiences of crime mapping and the spatial analysis of crime data both in academic research and in professional practice. The majority of the chapters in this book are examples of crime mapping and analysis in the UK, although there are some examples from the USA, where crime mapping has been an important part of law enforcement and crime prevention efforts for some time.

The aims of this book are to highlight areas of best practice, explore the types of problems to which spatial crime analysis can be applied, review the capabilities and limitations of existing techniques and explore the future directions of spatial crime analysis. A further objective is to include the perspective of many different user-groups with an interest in spatial analysis, including the police, local authorities, fire brigades, multi-agency crime prevention partnerships and academics.

Crime mapping involves the manipulation and processing of spatially referenced crime data in order for it to be displayed visually in an output that is informative to the particular user. It is, therefore, not surprising that there are many different techniques and technologies that can be instrumental in producing such output. There are numerous different uses for crime mapping, some of the most central are:

- For operational policing purposes. For instance, informing police on the beat of problem areas
- To inform the targeting of resources for crime prevention
- For police investigations
- To inform and interact with the community
- To monitor changes in the distribution of crime over time
- To evaluate the effectiveness of crime prevention initiatives.

In order to put crime mapping to these various ends, users will need access to computer hardware, geographical information systems software, crime analysis software and spatially referenced crime data. In the light of the recent increase in the availability of high performance machines at significantly lower costs, the amount of data that can be handled for crime mapping purposes is virtually limitless, although the production of these maps can sometimes be labour-intensive. There are also many well-established geographical information systems on the market, such as MapInfo or Arcview that have reasonably user-friendly front ends. These factors, coupled with an increase in the number of different crime mapping applications that are available, have made crime mapping more accessible to more users in recent years. Many of the mapping packages that are available are discussed in the following pages. Some examples include the Spatial and Temporal Analysis of Crime (or STAC) developed by the Illinois Criminal Justice Information Authority, which was one of the earliest crime mapping packages to become widely available. Police Forces in the United States have been encouraged to use this package which is free of charge. Since STAC, there have been many other crime mapping packages that have started to be used more widely, including CompStat, first used by the New York Police Department (see Nancy La Vigne and Elizabeth Groff's chapter for details, pp. 203–21), GAM (Geographical Analysis Machines; see Ian Turton and Stan Openshaw's chapter for details, pp. 11–26), adaptations of MapInfo's Vertical Mapper facility, and CrimeStat (developed by Ned Levine; see the chapter by Doug Williamson and colleagues for more details, pp. 187–202). As outlined in many of the chapters in this book, there are further crime mapping packages that are currently under development, several of which are likely to be available to crime mappers worldwide.

The available crime mapping packages vary in terms of their user-interfaces and the level of involvement the user has in the production of the map. For instance, STAC was first developed as a DOS package and the output was not directly connected with a GIS, so there was considerable work involved in importing and exporting data between software packages. More recent versions have been piloted using Microsoft Windows. CrimeStat uses a windows interface, although, resulting hotspots still need to be imported into a GIS for visualisation. Some packages ask the user to define a large number of parameters before processing begins. Some of these parameters can have a significant effect on the resulting maps. For instance, the user can often vary the area of interest – it is technically possible to 'zoom in' on a hotspot produced from an initial analysis and produce a set of further hotspots within it. Many of the programmes ask the user to lay down some conditions a priori concerning what constitutes a hotspot. For instance, a cluster of crimes might only be defined as 'hot' if there are at least ten crimes within it. This ability to manipulate hotspot definition is often very important in the production of clearly interpretable maps, but also means that the user has to have a certain knowledge to produce such maps.

One of the main concerns is the quality of the data that are available for use in crime mapping. First, there is a need to be aware of the type of data that are being used. For instance, there is a significant difference between using recorded crime data from the police and using logs of command and control incidents. Command and control incidents are records of the public getting in touch with the police and, in essence, can be seen as the public's demand for police services, rather than as crime per se. Only when the police have identified that a crime has occurred, will information relating to the offence be input on to the police recorded crime system. There are further concerns with the issue of under reporting of crime – it is obvious that not all incidents are reported to the police. Levels of crime reporting tend to vary with the type of crime that has been committed and the seriousness of the incident. For example, the British Crime Survey has shown that burglary and theft of vehicle is far more likely to be reported than many other types of crime. In fact, 84 per cent of burglaries and 96 per cent of vehicle thefts were reported according to the 1998 British Crime Survey (Budd 1998). This compares with 29 per cent of home vandalism incidents and 37 per cent of all violence incidents. For this reason, the reliability of the data used may vary according to the type of crime being examined.

Another important consideration is the quality of the data that are used. Police recording systems in the UK are not standardised, and although there are now conventions for address referencing (for example, British Standard 7666), these are not often adhered to. It is, therefore, important to audit the quality of crime data before mapping them. Some of the common problems that are found with referencing data include:

- Certain locations being used as 'dumping sites' for records that the system is unable to geocode
- Large amounts of data without an x and y co-ordinate
- Crime incidents being referenced to the midpoint of streets when there is inadequate information to pin them to individual properties
- Duplicate records being entered into a police system due to errors on the first attempt. If not identified these can be incorrectly flagged up as repeat incidents of crime.

Certain types of crime are likely to be more accurately geo-coded than others. Once again, domestic burglary is likely to be one of the more accurate crime types, since by definition the offence takes place within a residential dwelling. However, problems do arise when incidents occur in houses under multiple occupation, flats and high-rise buildings. With other types of crime, especially crimes against the person, the incident does not necessarily take place within a building. For instance, an assault could occur in a park, outside a pub or on a bus; each of these locations will cause particular problems with geo-coding. There is also likely to be a difference in the accuracy of police data held centrally and locally in many police forces. This is because crime analysts who have a more in-depth knowledge of a particular area often clean their data accordingly before conducting further analysis. Unfortunately, the channels of communication which enable local analysts to feed-back such information to the central statistics department are seldom open. The data quality issue is discussed in further detail in Spencer Chainey's chapter (pp. 95–119).

When the data quality has been assessed and the data have been 'cleaned' as and when required, the next decision to be made is the types of output to be produced. Of the techniques that are used in the production of crime maps, as will be reflected by the case studies presented in this book, some are fairly well-established and commonly used, whereas others are more innovative or still at the research stage. Some examples include:

- Pin maps – depicting the location of offences, victims and occasionally, offenders
- Chloropleth maps – shaded maps with colour varying according to the scale of the problem
- Geographical Analysis Machines – that use a search algorithm to find significant clusters of points
- Kernel density estimation- that result in crime 'contour' maps
- Standard deviational ellipses – hotspots created using clustering algorithms
- Voronoi polygons – maps indicating distances between offences
- Offence–offender residential location distance analysis
- Animation – changes in crime distributions over time.

Another key factor with crime mapping is what it can be expected to achieve. It is as important to realise what it does not do as it is to know what it is capable of. Crime mapping can provide information concerning the location of hotspots or high levels of reported crime. It can also assist in putting these hotspots into an environmental (social and physical land use) context which can provide clues about some of the risk factors for certain types of crime. If there is longitudinal information available, changes in the levels of crime can be linked with changes in the environment or crime prevention practice. However, the link between crime mapping, criminological theory and other types of criminological enquiry requires some further thought.

Can crime mapping add to criminological theory? Or is a knowledge of criminological theory necessary to interpret the results of crime mapping? On the one hand, as Ian Turton and Stan Openshaw argue in their chapter (pp. 11–26): 'map detective work may suggest relationships which are . . . of practical utility in applications where no other approach is either feasible or affordable'. In other words, mapping can be used to make useful inferences about the underlying processes that are causing particular types of crime cluster to form. This is not to argue that crime mapping can be used to prove a causal link between environmental factors and certain clusters of crime, only that it can be used as evidence of the likely presence of a particular process. After all, much scientific enquiry begins with observing what is happening and making inferences about possible effects that are generating observed patterns.

On the other hand, in his chapter (pp. 225–36), Ken Pease argues the following about crime maps: 'Their meaning, and hence their memorability and their usefulness, depends on extra knowledge of that which is depicted. A map of player positions on a soccer pitch is informative only if one is aware of the laws and tactics of the game'. Here, he is arguing that some knowledge of the criminological processes at work is required to enable the user to interpret what is at work on the map. This is treating crime mapping as a deductive form of enquiry.

The reality is that crime mapping is likely to be used inductively and deductively in different situations. It will perhaps be a reflection of the experiences of the particular user. For instance, a police officer is likely to use his or her knowledge of general crime trends and correlates and of the area specifically to interpret what is happening in a particular hotspot. An academic might use his or her knowledge of crime theory to interpret the map. A member of the community will see the map in a different light again, with local knowledge of the area playing a major part in its interpretation.

A further point is that crime mapping does not necessarily need to be done in isolation or used as a substitute for other methods of analysis. It is a useful tool for complementing other analysis. An example of this is its use in research into repeat victimisation. Identifying repeat victimisations involves fairly intensive data processing, the end result gives information about how concentrated crime is upon particular individuals or into particular places. Mapping could then be used to examine the spatial distribution of such repeat victims. It is often the case that such victimis-ations are over-represented in particular areas. Other information, such as the social and economic make-up of these areas, the street network or the housing structure can be super-imposed upon the map to search for possible relationships between victimisation and environmental risk factors. Further statistical tests can then be used to assess the significance of any potential relationships.

Another example is the role mapping can play in police investigations. An investigation may use intelligence and MO data to identify that the same offender is likely to be responsible for a series of incidents. Physical mapping of the offences that are linked with the offender can give insights into the possible residential location of the offender which can in turn help to narrow down the list of likely suspects (e.g. Canter and Alison 1997).

A future direction for mapping is an increase in its use as part of a dynamic analysis, which tracks changes in the spatial distribution of crime over time. This is important not only in monitoring how the crime risk of certain properties or areas vary over time, but also in relating these changes to crime prevention interventions in the area. A crime prevention programme might have reduced crime in its area of operation, but without the ability to track the situation in the surrounding areas using spatial data, it is difficult to assess whether the programme has displaced crime to other areas.

Undoubtedly, one of the most important functions of crime maps is their ability to influence people. The human brain devotes much space to visual interpretation and as a result we can perform detailed complex analyses that allow us to see patterns and extract meaning from them. Those with an interest in crime prevention who lack the inclination to conduct complex statistical analysis will find relationships displayed in a visual form more accessible. Maps are, therefore, good tools to use as evidence of the presence of a particular phenomenon.

Chapter outlines

The book is divided into five parts. Part One looks at crime mapping and applied research and contains contributions from three universities that have been active in crime mapping. The first contribution, from Ian Turton and Stan Openshaw, details methods that can be used for automating the spatial analysis of crime data. Specifically, it discusses the use of the GAM and the GEM (respectively, Geographical Analysis Machine and Geographical Explanation Machine). The GAM looks for evidence of clustering in crime data, whereas the GEM goes a step further and investigates potential explanations for these clusters by using other geographical information, such as census data. They point out that the advantage of using these tools is that they include statistical testing which can assess the significance of any clusters of crime or relationships with other geographical information.

Andrew Costello and Paul Wiles demonstrate the use of spatial analysis and crime mapping procedures in analysing patterns in offender behaviour. They use a GIS to help to identify patterns in the journey to crimes that are made by offenders. The analysis uses both recorded crime data and information from the Police National Computer. The results are very informative: the vast majority of journeys to crime (in this case burglary and taking without the owner's consent) are fairly short and tend to depend upon opportunities arising during normal activity rather than being planned.

The third chapter in Part One, written by Jerry Ratcliffe and Michael McCullagh covers a wide range of issues. They review different procedures for identifying the hotspots of crime, examine methods of investigating spatio-temporal changes in crime and they go into considerable depth concerning the phenomenon of repeat victimisation.

Part Two looks at the way crime mapping and data analysis are used in a local authority context. Spencer Chainey describes pioneering work that has taken place in the London Boroughs of Hackney, Brent, Southwark and Harrow. These London Boroughs have active community safety partnerships that have been formed to combat crime and have benefited from particularly effective procedures for sharing information. In particular, these partnerships have been active at using GIS to identify crime and disorder hotspots.

In a second local authority example, Kate Bowers, Martin Newton and Richard Nutter outline the use of geographical information in making resource targeting decisions in crime prevention. Targeting criteria have been developed for prioritising victims of domestic burglary in the Merseyside area. The chapter illustrates how both individual level characteristics (of the victim) and area-level characteristics (where the property is located) can be instrumental in making resource decisions. The rationale behind such a system is to maximise the impact of limited crime prevention resources.

In Part Three, the role of spatial analysis and crime mapping in the police and emergency services is examined. Jim LeBeau describes the use of crime mapping by the police in North America. He illustrates the way that spatial crime data are used to identify hazardous places and inform operational policing decisions. Five types of incident are considered: calls requiring an emergency response, gun assaults and armed robbery, incidents involving officer use of force, incidents resulting in officer injuries and officers requiring immediate help. Density grids are constructed for each type of offence, with grid squares over certain threshold levels being selected. Using this information, areas with particularly high levels of these hazards are identified.

Steve Merrall describes the ways in which GIS analysis is of use to the fire brigade. He uses geocoded information from the Greater Manchester fire brigade on the location of arsons and residential fires to look for patterns in their spatial distribution. These patterns are then cross-referenced with social, economic and environmental variables to identify the risk factors associated with such fires. The implications for fire safety campaigns are discussed.

Part Four contains two North American contributions, which give an international perspective on crime mapping. The US is particularly advanced in the use of crime mapping and spatial analysis tools for informing crime prevention practitioners. Doug Williamson and colleagues describe a software package developed for use by the New York Police Department (NYPD) that offers a number of spatial analysis and mapping techniques that can help inform the Police of emerging crime problems. The techniques described include block aggregation, voronoi diagrams, kernel smoothing and animation.

Nancy La Vigne and Elizabeth Groff outline the evolution of crime mapping in the US from an interest centred around a relatively small user group to becoming a more mainstream activity. Many law enforcement agencies in the US now have a crime mapping capability. The chapter runs through many different uses of the spatial analysis of crime ranging from their use in police operations and command and control decisions to their impact on the community and their ability to enable cross-jurisdictional analysis and to encourage collaboration between different agencies.

Finally, Part Five looks at some of the issues concerning the use of GIS to analyses crime data. Ken Pease compares crime mapping with other types of criminological enquiry. He stresses that it is important to see it as one of a number of different methods that can be used to investigate crime patterns. He also explains why caution should be exercised when producing and interpreting crime maps. In particular, he argues that spatial location is not the only variable that is associated with crime hazard and that there are many other predictors of crime risk.

Alex Hirschfield looks at crime mapping in Britain in the context of recent changes in crime prevention policy due to the Crime and Disorder Act. He looks at skills, data sharing arrangements, crime data and analytical tools required to undertake spatial analysis and mapping and compares this with the current situation in organisations that are required to produce Crime and Disorder audits. He also looks at the rationale of using the results of such analysis for targeting crime prevention initiatives. Some case studies of using spatially geocoded crime information to target such initiatives are described.

References

Budd, T. (1998) *Burglary of Domestic Dwellings: Findings from the British Crime Survey, Issue 4/99*, London: Home Office.

Canter, D.V. and Alison, L.J. (1997) *Criminal Detection and the Psychology of Crime*, Aldershot: Ashgate.

Part I

Crime mapping and applied research

2 Methods for automating the geographical analysis of crime incident data

Ian Turton and Stan Openshaw

This chapter considers ways in which crime analysis can be automated. This allows crime analysts without detailed geographical knowledge to perform geographically sound and rigorous analysis of their data. Two methods are introduced: the geographical analysis machine (GAM) which shows the user where there are clusters or hotspots in their data, and the geographical explanations machine (GEM) which points to geographical data-sets that may explain the clusters found by the GAM. Both these programmes are illustrated by the use of a case study of real crime data.

Introduction

This chapter considers ways of automating the geographical analysis of crime locations. Almost all law enforcement agencies collect crime reports with a form of geocode attached; in the UK this is usually the postcode of the building nearest the incident. By making use of this locational data in conjunction with automated analysis techniques, it is possible for agencies to discover crime hotspots in their data, allowing the targeting of resources to these areas.

The chapter first introduces the reader to the geographical analysis machine (GAM) and then discusses the geographical explanations machine, which makes use of related geographical variables to attempt to 'explain' the patterns found by GAM. The chapter looks at a case study of crime in Baltimore County, USA to show how GAM and GEM can be used to investigate crime data.

The Geographical Analysis Machine

The Geographical Analysis Machine (Openshaw *et al.* 1987, 1988) was an early attempt at automated exploratory spatial data analysis that was easy to understand. The GAM sought to answer a simple practical question: namely, given some point referenced data of something interesting where might there be evidence of localised clustering if you do not know in advance where to look due to lack of knowledge of a possible causal mechanism or if prior knowledge of the data precluded testing hypotheses on the database? More simply put, here is a geographically referenced database, now tell me if there are any crime clusters or hotspots and if so where are they located? It offers a solution to those researchers and users of GIS who want to perform a fast exploratory geographical analysis of their data with a minimum of effort. It is an automated procedure that is designed to yield safe results that are largely self-evident.

GAM reflects the view that useful spatial analysis tools have to be able to cope with both the special nature of spatial data and end-users who do not have degrees in statistics. The results have also to be easily understood and self-evident so that they can be readily communicated to other non-experts. This need has been clearly expressed as follows: 'We want a push-button tool of academic respectability where all the heavy stuff happens behind the scenes but the results cannot be misinterpreted' (Adrian McKeon, Infoshare: email, 1997). There is also a requirement for the results to be expressed as 'pretty pictures' rather than statistics. This allows the analyst to present the results to superiors who have neither the time nor background to understand the results of a complex model or statistical analysis. They are happy that the analysis has been carried out in a rigorous way but do not need to know the details of this process.

The original code required a Cray YMP supercomputer but it will now run on a UNIX workstation or PC. Compute times are a function of the size of data-set; for example, 150,000 points took 700 seconds on a Sun workstation. The latest version of the method dates from 1991, but it was revived in 1997 after the results of a comparison with seven other cluster detectors in a rare disease context. A recent report by the International Agency for Research in Cancer in Lyons (France) concluded that GAM/K was shown to be the best or equivalent best means of both testing for the presence of clustering and for finding the locations of clusters. Alexander and Boyle (1996), authors of the IARC study, concluded: 'The GAM has potential applications in this area if adequate computer resources are available. At the present time, however, the new, more sophisticated version of the GAM is complex, difficult to understand . . .' (p. 157). That was in 1991 and these particular criticisms no longer apply. The key point here is that rare disease data are very hard to analyse. Most of the more general spatial analysis needs in a crime-mapping context are far easier. So a method that works well on rare disease data might be expected to perform even better on crime data.

How does GAM work?

The GAM algorithm involves the following steps:

Step 1:   Read in X,Y data for population at risk and a variable of interest (crimes) from a GIS

Step 2: Identify the rectangle containing the data, identify starting circle radius and degree of overlap

Step 3: Generate a grid covering this rectangle so that circles of current radius overlap by the desired amount

Step 4: For each grid-intersection generate a circle of radius r

Step 5: Retrieve two counts for the population at risk and the variable of interest

Step 6: Apply some 'significance' test procedure

Step 7: Keep the result if significant

Step 8: Repeat steps 5 to 7 until all circles have been processed

Step 9: Increase circle radius and return to step 3 or else go to step 10

Step 10: Create a smoothed density surface of excess incidence for the significant circles using a kernel smoothing procedure and aggregating the results for all circles

Step 11: Map this surface

Note that the original GAM/1 consisted of steps 1 to 9. Steps 10–11 are the GAM/K version.

The choice of significance test is not considered as being too critical. The aim is not to test conventional hypotheses, but merely to determine whether or not an observed positive excess incidence is sufficiently large to be unusual and hence of interest. It is more a measure of unusualness or surprise than a formal statistical significance test. A number of different measures of 'unusualness' can be applied depending on the rarity of incidence of interest, e.g. Poisson, bootstrapped z-scores, and Monte Carlo tests based on rates. The aim here is not a formal test of significance, instead 'significance' is being used only as a descriptive filter employed to reject circles. It is the map created by the overall distribution of significant circles that is of most interest.

The 'significant' circles are converted into a smooth excess incidence density surface using a kernel estimation procedure. An Epanechnikov (1969) kernel is used with a bandwidth set at the circle radius and the excess incidence is smoothed out over this region. The effects are then aggregated and stored as a raster density surface. These raster surfaces can be produced as maps for each radius examined or more usually they are added together to give a single map of all circles examined. The resulting accumulation of evidence is used as the basis for conclusions about the existence, strength and locations of possible clusters. In most instances, simply eye-balling these results will be sufficient to inform about the existence, strength and locations of any apparent clusters.

Finally, some of the critics of GAM argue that any clusters found on the output map could well be the consequence of testing multiple hypotheses. The argument is as follows: if you set some arbitrary significance threshold, e.g. alpha=0.05, and if you test 100 hypotheses then 5 will be false positives (i.e. they will appear as being incorrectly significant). If you test 1,000,000 hypotheses, then on average 50,000 will appear as false positives. There are two problems with this argument: it assumes that the hypotheses are independent whereas in a GAM search they are clearly not (because the circles overlap) and it ignores the geography of the problem as it is surely quite different if all the significant circles occur around one or two locations rather than be scattered randomly all over the map. These effects can be studied by Monte Carlo simulation and this feature is now built into GAM. Quite simply, you re-run the entire process on 500 or 1000 randomly generated crime distributions and compare the results with the observed ones.

The Geographical Explanations Machine

GAM is purely a pattern detector and no explanation is provided that can help the user understand what variables may be geographically correlated with any clusters it may find. The vague hope is expressed that it will sometimes be possible to develop some degree of understanding by mapping the clusters against this or that background coverage. Location is being used as a surrogate for other missing explanatory variables and it is hoped that the mapping will be insightful and suggest possible hypotheses for subsequent examination elsewhere. However, performing this search for explanation by manual means is likely to be a very hit or miss affair. The advent of GIS helps only a little. The search for explanation using a GIS reduces to multiple spatial queries to find out what appears to be geographically associated with the clusters. There is nothing wrong with this approach but it would be better if the procedure could be automated so that it could be made far more comprehensive and thus rigorous.

It is also possible that the apparent patterns being uncovered by GAM merely reflect confounding variables and that they are, therefore, of no real consequence. There is also a risk that a good understanding of what the patterns of clusters mean will be greatly hindered by missing information. Indeed, there are many different possible variables that may be considered important. Some of these could well be related more to individual behaviour, others to geographical location, and some to both. This is particularly the case in studies of disease, where some important variables relate to the unmeasured individual exposure to allegedly harmful chemicals. Yet many of these 'thought to be important' variables in developing a better understanding of a disease may well be missing from the available spatial databases. However, they may still be represented implicitly by map location and a geographer may well be able to make useful inferences from an understanding of geographical association. Clearly this stops far short of proof or evidence of causality. This is simultaneously a major restriction on the power of all types of geographical inquiry and also a strength in that map detective work may suggest relationships which are nonetheless of practical utility in applications where no other approach is either feasible or affordable.

The basic idea is very simple, having found an interesting circle (in GAM terms); take M geographic coverages and examine the 2^{M-1} coverage permutations for the data contained within the circle. There are now two different approaches to processing the point coverage permutations. (1) Subsets of the data can be defined which are homogeneous with respect to a particular permutation of coverages and each is analysed separately for evidence of clustering (a kind of disaggregated GAM). (2) The coverages act as covariates, which are used to 'correct' the expected number of cases, which is essentially the approach of a conventional epidemiologist.

Again there is no suggestion that patterns are 'caused' by what may be termed 'GIS variables' only that if 'strong' or 'significant' or localised or 'recurrent' geographical associations can be found then this may well be of interest to cluster or pattern hunters as an indicator of where to look further. It serves two seemingly contradictory objectives: (1) (mode 2) to find significant localised excesses that can only be ascribed to what might be regarded as mystery locational factor X because they cannot be made to go away no matter how hard the attempt using covariates based on a wide range of map (and any other) spatial data-sets; and (2) (mode 3) to find significant localised excesses that are (perhaps locally) spatially associated with particular sets or combinations of geographical variables in a sufficiently strong way to offer a form of geographical explanation of them and hence appear as worthy of further study.

How does GEM work?

The GEM algorithm involves the following steps.

Step 1:   Read in X,Y data for population at risk and a variable of interest from a GIS. Also read in the X,Y data classified by values for each of M coverages

Step 2:   Identify the rectangle containing the data-set a starting circle radius r, and the degree of circle overlap

Step 3:   Generate a grid covering this rectangular map area so that circles of current radius overlap by the desired amount

Step 4:   For each grid intersection generate a circle of radius r

Step 5:   Retrieve two counts for the population at risk and the variable of interest

Step 6:   Apply some 'significance' test procedure

Step 7:   If the result is not significant go to step 5 and investigate another location, or store summary of results to permit later identification of recurrent or important coverage permutations

Step 8:   Repeat steps 5 to 7 until all circles have been processed

Step 9:   Increase circle radius and return to step 3 or else go to step 10

Step 10: Create smoothed density surface of excess incidence for the significant circles for selected combinations of coverage permut-

ations using a kernel smoothing procedure and aggregating the
results for all circles

Step 11: Map this surface

Again the choice of significance test in step 6 is not considered as being too
critical. The secret of GEM is how to build in these geographical covariates
used in modes 2 and 3 outlined above. The idea is to adjust expected rates
for the incidence of a variable within a GAM circle to allow for local
geographical covariation. In a GIS there are often additional levels of
contextual information that may provide useful surrogates for missing
variables. For example, points can be classified by their location with
respect to various data layers, namely geological type and membership of a
point or line based buffer region around a chemical works or a road.

This standardisation for geographical covariates can be done as follows.
Consider a single coverage C that has five categories. The adjusted
incidence rate is

$$\sum_j^5 P_j \, C_j \tag{1}$$

where P_j is the population at risk inside the circle in the jth category of the
coverage and C_j is the average rate for this category in the coverage. This
readily generalises to two-way interactions by adding subscripts so if a
second subscript K is used to represent the effects of a second coverage,
this time with eight categories then equation (1) becomes

$$\sum_j^5 \sum_k^8 P_{jk} \, C_{jk} \tag{2}$$

where P_{jk} is now the population at risk inside the circle in the jth category
for coverage 1 and in the kth category on coverage 2, and C_{jk} is the
associated incidence rate. Note that the composition of C_{jk} and P_{jk} now
depends on which of the two from M coverage permutations are being
considered. For example if there are ten coverages then there are forty-five
unique permutations of two-way interaction effects to be considered. This
approach can be extended to consider three and four or higher order
interaction effects. However, there may be little merit in going beyond
three-way interactions unless the database is extremely large because of
small number effects. Compute times also explode exponentially so this
GEM is living on the edge of a combinatorial precipice.

Table 2.1 gives some relevant counts. Note that for each of the circles
being examined the number of coverage permutations given in this table
have to be considered. The use of supercomputers merely gains you a few
hundred thousand more permutations before compute times will again
become impossibly large. So this technology has hard limits to the degree
of searching it can do. However it is thought that these should not present
any significant practical constraints because the principle of parsimony and

Table 2.1 Number of coverage permutations

Coverages (M)	Interactions (k)						
	1	2	3	4	5	6	7
1	1	–	–	–	–	–	–
5	5	10	10	5	1	0	–
10	10	45	120	210	252	210	120
15	15	105	455	1,365	3,003	5,005	6,435
20	20	190	1,140	4,845	15,504	38,760	77,520
25	25	300	2,300	12,650	53,130	177,100	480,700
30	30	435	4,060	27,405	142,506	593,775	*
40	40	780	9,880	9,1390	658,008	*	*
50	50	1,225	19,600	230,300	2,118,760	*	*
60	60	1,770	34,220	487,635	5,461,512	*	*
70	70	2,415	54,740	916,895	12,103,014	*	*
80	80	3,160	82,160	1,581,580	24,040,016	*	*
90	90	4,005	117,480	2,555,190	43,949,268	*	*
100	100	4,950	161,700	3,921,225	75,287,520	*	*
150	150	11,750	551,300	*	*	*	*
200	200	19,900	1,313,400	*	*	*	*

data sparsity sets in well before the combinatorial explosion becomes critical. The counts in Table 2.1 are theoretical maximum limits and in reality only a small fraction would be relevant (because there are data) to any particular search circle. Parsimony also suggests that the number of overlaid maps K is best kept small, in which case large numbers of coverages can be examined. For example, there are only 3,160 permutations of eighty maps into two overlays, compared with 24,040,016 if five overlays are considered. The latter is feasible but only on fast parallel machines whilst the former is possible even on a cheap workstation.

Altogether there are three ways of running GEM depending on the purpose:

Mode 1: Pure GAM

This is a GAM run with no coverage information being used and will only detect patterns. If some patterns are found then modes 2 and 3 are worth considering.

Mode 2: GAM with geographical covariates

The aim now is to include one-two-three-way interaction effects with M available geographical covariates. When a circle is found which GAM would regard as having significant excess, then the combinations of coverages are examined to try and remove the significance and thus 'explain away' the clustering. Surviving circles should be examined further for possible related variables or at the very least mapped because they cannot so easily be made to go away. However, there may also be a case for looking at the circles that GAM found significant but which in whole or in part have been explained away to try and establish the reasons and the coverages responsible.

Mode 3: GAM as a 'GCEM'

Another way of running GAM is to change the mode 2 operation so that it replicates the intention inherent in the original 'GCEM' (the Geographical Correlates Exploration Machine outlined in Openshaw *et al.* (1990)). It was to try and exploit the latent potential of the map (and the associated GIS databases) as a source of 'geographical explanation' that the GCEM of Openshaw *et al.* (1990) was developed. The original GCEM examined polygons formed by permutations of overlays for excess incidence. These polygons are homogenous with respect to the GIS overlays that defined them so note could be made of the GIS data most associated with an excess value. Here this process is modified so that a circle and its interaction with the implicit but invisible underlying map polygons define the area being examined. Not all the polygons may lie completely within the circle or the circle may contain fragments of several different ones. It is necessary, therefore, to classify the cases inside each circle being examined into homogenous subsets (so their GIS features can be unambiguously defined) and then perform analysis on all subsets large enough to be considered safe to use. All circles with map permutations that yield significant results are now output together with their associated map features. This replicates the type of spatial query that GIS users would do when presented with evidence of a clusters, except that the computer search for potentially interesting results is automated and far more comprehensive than could be performed manually.

Case study: residential and street crime in Baltimore

Data-set used

The dataset used in the case study are crime data from Baltimore County, the area surrounding the Baltimore metropolitan area. Two offences were chosen: residential burglaries and street robberies. In the data there are 6,054 burglaries and 1,188 street robberies (see Figure 2.1). Clearly the residential burglaries are more densely concentrated than the street crimes. Street crime occurs mostly in areas near to the metropolitan area whereas property crime occurs even in the rural areas to the north of the city.

The original data were converted to 1-metre grid references. GAM has a mechanism for handling data uncertainty, namely the search circles overlap so there is a constant sensitivity analysis being performed as an integral part of the analysis.

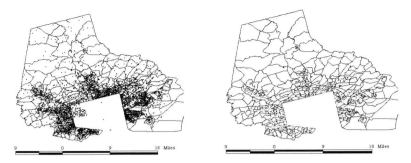

Figure 2.1 Residential burglaries (left) and street robberies (right) in Baltimore
county.
Source: Phil Canter, Baltimore County Police Department.

GAM seeks to identify localised hotspots, which are defined as an
accumulation of excess crimes over and above what might have been
expected from the population at risk data. These hotspots are mapped
providing a visual feel and clue to the location and strength. The more
extreme the values the more unusual the result. Simulation can be used to
identify whether the observed hotspots could have occurred by chance.
GAM is quite sophisticated in that the population at risk can be modified
to handle any covariates believed to be important.

Residential crimes

The data were analysed at street block scale as GAM can cope with very
large data sets and the supplied data were reasonably small. The best
results will come from using the finest spatial resolution of the data. The
obvious population at risk is the census population although this could be
adjusted to reflect socio-economic covariates.

Figure 2.2 shows the hotspots detected by GAM in the residential crime
data. There are two large hotspots (labelled A and B in the figure). Hotspot
B is the larger while hotspot A is strong, its location in a 'peninsular'
means that edge effects may be responsible for some of the excess, circles
located near the edge of the zones may take in crimes located in the edge
zones, but attempt to draw population from the missing areas of the map
leading to false excesses. It may be interesting in the future to repeat the
analysis with central Baltimore included in the study area since this
boundary is clearly not a low crime area as with the outer boundaries of
the study area.

Street crimes

For the analysis of the street robberies there are two available populations
at risk: census night time population and the length of street in each

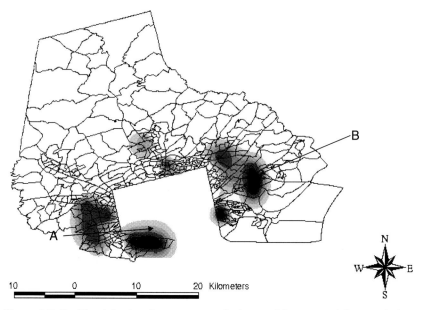

Figure 2.2 Residential crime hotspots, population at risk census night population.

polygon. Obviously a population at risk based on pedestrian flows along streets would have been best but these were not available. We investigated both, since it is relatively easy to calculate the length of street in each block group using an intersect command in the GIS.

Figure 2.3 shows the hotspots detected if resident population is used as the population at risk. Again there are two large hot spots detected, however in this case they are both situated well back from the edges of the map.

Figure 2.4 shows the pattern of hotspots detected by GAM when the length of street in each block group is used to define the population at risk, here only a single hotspot in the south west of the map is detected.

Explaining the patterns found

Once GAM has been run to discover clusters in a data-set, the analyst can consider the task completed. However, if driven by curiosity or a need to determine reasons for the patterns detected they can proceed to attempt to explain the patterns discovered by using GEM to explore the factors that are associated with the hotspots.

In this case three 'explanatory' coverages were chosen: house value (Plate 1), ethnicity (Plate 2) and proportion of elderly residents (Plate 3). All three variables were available on the US Census Bureau's world wide web site for public download. Agencies working in the UK also have access

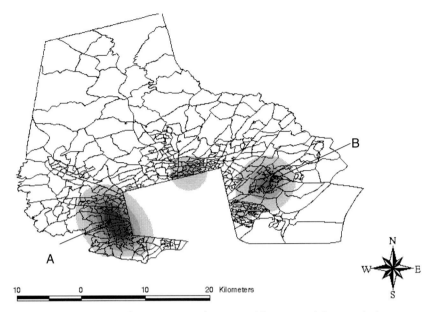

Figure 2.3 Street crime hotspots, population at risk census night population.

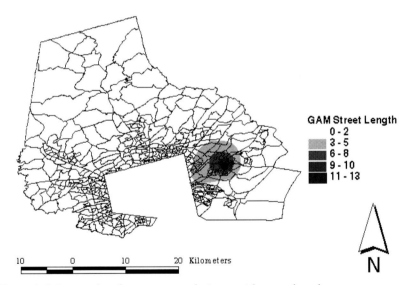

Figure 2.4 Street crime hotspots, population at risk street length.

to similar census variables though not income at present. In some cases the council tax register could be used as an income proxy. These three variables were chosen as they were felt to be the most useful in explaining the types of crime under investigation, though that is the opinion of a pair of geographers not criminologists. For different crimes or areas a different set of explanatory variables could be chosen depending on the view of the analyst.

Each of the data-sets used was loaded into a GIS and the raw values were converted to a percentage (except for house price). These values were then reclassified into quintiles to reduce the number of combinations of classes that needed to be examined by GEM.

Residential crime patterns explained

Both GEM modes 2 and 3 were run. Mode 2 which is attempting to explain the clusters by the use of the geographical covariates produced a map with very few significant circles left unexplained. This shows that there is sufficient 'explanatory' power in the variables used to account for the crime hotspots found in the GAM run.

Figure 2.5 shows the results of a GEM mode 3 run for the residential crimes. This map can be seen as a more sensitive GAM run (Figure 2.2). The GEM results show that residential burglaries are associated with areas of high house value and higher than average concentrations of older people.

Street crime patterns explained

Again both mode 2 and 3 of GEM were used to investigate the patterns of street robberies and as with the GAM runs two populations at risk were

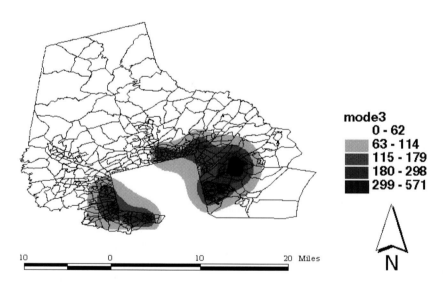

Figure 2.5 Results of GEM mode 3 for residential crime.

considered. Mode 2 succeeded in removing almost all the significant circles by the use of the explanatory variables. The results of the mode 3 run are shown in Figure 2.6. The two clusters previously detected by GAM (Figure 2.6) can be seen, GEM reports that these clusters are related to high proportions of white residents and high house values, suggesting that street robberies tend to occur in richer areas of the study region.

The results of the mode 3 run with street length as the population at risk (Figure 2.7) is very similar to the results found in the GAM run for the same population at risk (Figure 2.4). This cluster is located in a similar area to crime hotspots found for the residential burglaries and one of the other street crime clusters found with the residential population being the population at risk. This indicates that this new cluster is very likely to be a real cluster and worthy of the assignment of resources to the area. In fact, local knowledge gained after the analysis was complete, suggests that the area in the east highlighted by all three GEM runs is the site of a major drug-dealing area.

Using GAM and GEM to do more sophisticated crime data analysis

The data used here are less than adequate. GAM is a cluster detector. It will happily search for clusters in any kind of crime data. The results would probably be most useful if they related to particular time periods, particular times of day, particular modus operandi, if the population at risk had relevant covariates included in it, if the full data-set were being

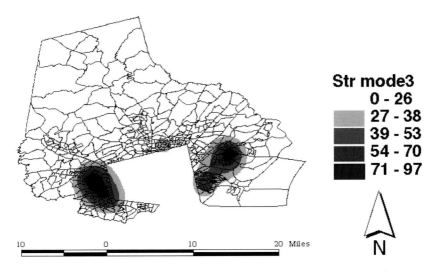

Figure 2.6 GEM mode 3 analysis of street crime, with resident population as population at risk.

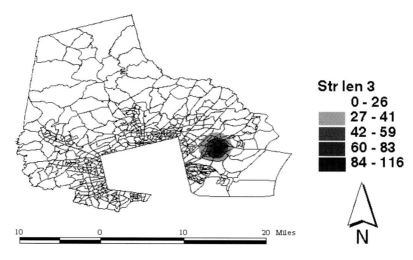

Figure 2.7 GEM mode 3 analysis of street crime, with street length as population
at risk.

analysed rather than a subset with potentially large edge effects. GAM can
be used to monitor crime patterns. If you used last year's (or last time
period's) crime data to define a population at risk you could then measure
changes from it. Also because GAM is automatic then it can be used to
spot hotspots as they emerge in real-time. Most computer runs take only a
few minutes.

A residual question is how do you know when a hotspot which appears
on the map is not a real hotspot at all? There are four possible answers.
One is to feed randomised crime data (that is data the have the same
average incident rates as the data under investigation but where the cases
are randomly assigned to zones, GAM can automatically generate this data
for you) into GAM and see what sorts of hotspots are found. Typically,
they will be weak pathetic things that are not 'highly peaked'; but how
high does a peak have to be before you get excited about it? The answer is
data-dependent and qualitative. It also depends on what you plan to use
the results for. The safest and simplest strategy is merely to look for the
highest peaks. The second answer is to expend lots more compute time on
multiple testing by Monte Carlo simulation. This will indicate how easy it
is to obtain results as extreme as those being observed by running GAM on
multiple sets of randomly generated crime data-sets with similar incidence
to the observed data (see Figure 2.8). The third solution is to keep for
training purposes the results for differing degrees of clustering and use
them to train the user to discriminate between the massively interesting
and the rubbish. The strength of GAM is that it is a visual method of
analysis. It is meant to suggest and create new insights in an almost artistic

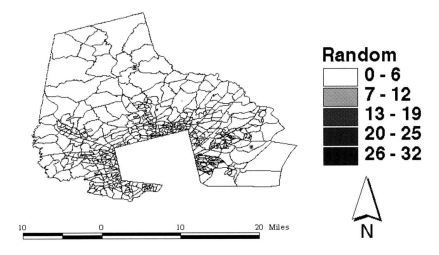

Random
- 0 - 6
- 7 - 12
- 13 - 19
- 20 - 25
- 26 - 32

10   0   10   20 Miles

N

Figure 2.8 Results of a random GAM run.

and qualitative kind of way. The fourth solution is to use GAM purely as an automated procedure and re-install the simple expert system that GAM/K had in 1990, before it was decided to use the human eyeball instead. It is important to remember that there are many different causes of hotspots, many of which are related to the quality of the data being analysed. No machine-based procedure can at present detect 'bad data' for you. You have to do it and 100 per cent automation would so reduce the value of human inputs as to render these spurious causes of clustering totally invisible to the end-user.

Getting a copy of GAM and GEM

An on-line test facility and considerable help documentation can be found at http://www.ccg.leeds.ac.uk/smart/intro.html. The on-line versions of GAM and GEM allow users to upload their data, view results in their browser and download the results for later analysis in a GIS.

Conclusion

This chapter has demonstrated that with a little effort and very little GIS know-how it is possible for an analyst to produce maps of crime hotspots in their area using the geographical analysis machine. The discussion of GEM has shown how with a little more data from their GIS it is possible to start to look for 'explanatory' geographic variables that may well assist police officers on the ground to deal with the hotspots found.

coalfield we were given details of every domestic burglary in the period September 1996 to August 1998. This provided a data-set of 19,085 offences, of which 5,381 (28 per cent) were cleared up.

The Sheffield data were geocoded using a MapInfo Geographical Information System (GIS).[16] A GIS is a computer programme which enables the geographical location of any data to be mapped using x and y co-ordinates and then to be analysed against topographical or other digitised maps, or other data-sets which are also geographically referenced. We geocoded the Sheffield offences by where they occurred; complainants by their home address; and offenders by their home address. We did this initially by using computer software which automatically geocodes any location which has a recognisable address. However, we found that this method was capable of geocoding less that half of our data accurately and geocoding the rest involved cleaning up the police data (so that the software could recognise it) and geocoding items by hand when the software could not geocode the location (for example, when an offence had occurred in a park and, therefore, had no 'address' as such). We eventually geocoded almost all of the data, but a proportion had to be geocoded to the nearest postcode or approximate postcode level.[17]

The Coalfield data were initially sorted into 'cleared'[18] and 'uncleared' offences. From the cleared offences we created a database of offenders and then identified the most prolific. For the purpose of our research, prolific was defined as 40 or more offences in the two year period. This gave us a database of 26 offenders. This group was then refined by excluding those who had not crossed borough boundaries to offend which left only twelve 'travelling' offenders whose offences were geocoded. We then requested their residential address data from South Yorkshire Police. This led to a further two offenders being excluded because of incomplete address data. The home addresses[19] of the remaining ten prolific 'travelling' offenders were then geocoded to allow hypotheses testing.

The advantage of geocoded data for this study was three-fold. First, it allowed distances between a large number of geographical locations to be measured very quickly using x/y co-ordinates. Throughout this paper, distance measures are all 'straight-line' (i.e. the shortest distance between two points). Some researchers (often American, where many cities are laid out in a regular grid pattern) have used other measures of distance such as 'cab route distance' to try and reflect the most likely route between two points. However, in many British towns and cities it is not always easy to identify one likely route between two points and therefore we have settled for the straight-line distance as the best available standard measure. The data were analysed with particular reference to the distance between the home address of known offenders and the address of offence commission (offender movements[20]) and for the Sheffield data the home address of complainants; all of which could be linked via each offence's unique crime number. Second, it also meant that underlying socio-demographic data could easily be linked to our crime data. Finally, by geocoding the data, we achieved a flexible geography so that our analysis was not limited by the boundaries of police beats or basic command units.

As geocoding becomes routine for police data then the kind of analysis reported here will be able to be quickly and easily replicated elsewhere.

Other data-sets

In order to test the findings based upon our geocoded data we were fortunate to have access to a number of additional data-sets:[21]

1 The Police National Computer (PNC)
2 Interviews carried out with a stratified sample of recently convicted burglary and TWOC offenders
3 Victimisation surveys on two Sheffield council estates
4 The national DNA database.

PNC data

One problem with using police force data is that they do not include information about offenders who live in the force area but who commit their offences elsewhere (exported offenders). In order to examine this problem we used Police National Computer (PNC) records. We extracted from PNC the details of all convicted offenders for the period July 1995–June 1996 who gave a Sheffield home address but who, on arrest, had been taken to a police station outside the city.[22] This gave us details of a further 2,534 offender movements by Sheffield-based offenders. Whilst the home addresses of these offenders were geocoded, we were unable to geocode precisely the offence location for two reasons. First, the data only came with police station codes for the offence and, second, we would have required digital maps for the whole of the country. Because of this we were only able to calculate approximate distances travelled so we could not be sure if the travel associated with offending in places adjoining the city boundary was only a mile or less, or up to and above ten miles.

DNA database 'hits'

The National DNA database was established in 1995 by the Forensic Science Service (FSS). Any police force can send DNA samples to the FSS for analysis.[23] Each sample sent is given a unique reference on the FSS database and a code to indicate which police station has sent the sample. Each sample is automatically compared with all other samples held on the database. Samples relate either to a stain found at a crime scene or a DNA sample taken from a crime suspect. The latter are taken from suspects arrested for recordable offences and are deleted if no conviction follows. In the period January 1995 to December 1997, a total of 398,147 samples were received and 229,355 retained. The vast majority of samples related to either burglary or auto crime.

We were provided with data on all cases between June 1997 and December 1997 inclusive where comparison showed that the same person was responsible for two stains or DNA samples. This gave us a database where there was prima facie evidence of offender mobility, although we had no idea where the offender lived. Our data-set consisted of 7,820 matched samples, of which 6,246 related to burglary and 1,133 to auto crime. Again the geographic reference was a police station code so we could only approximately calculate the distance between sample points.

Offender interviews

One potential weakness with the data described so far is that offender addresses in police records may be inaccurate, or out of date, and more generally the records cannot provide more qualitative information about why and how offenders travel to crimes in the way shown by police data. In order to gather such qualitative data, we interviewed sixty Sheffield-based burglary and TWOC offenders. The offenders were mainly interviewed whilst in prison immediately after sentencing although some of the youngest offenders were not in custody at the time of interview (because of the much lower rates of imprisonment for juvenile offenders).

Victim survey

As part of a PhD study looking at territoriality and victimisation Aldrin Abdullah (1999) conducted a victimisation survey on two Sheffield council estates. Both have poor reputations in the city but, on the basis of police recorded crime data, contrasting crime rates.[24] Whilst the surveys showed much higher rates of victimisation than officially recorded crime data, the police data were correct in that one estate showed a much higher victimisation rate than the other. From the point of view of our research, the important aspect about the survey was that it asked victims where their victimisations took place.

The remainder of this chapter describes how these diverse data-sets were investigated and the findings that emerged.

Results from recorded crime data analysis

Offender travel within Sheffield

Travel to crime distances, for offences committed in the city of Sheffield (Table 3.1), are fairly short and are similar to the findings of previous research. The great majority of the offenders are young males, with only shoplifting producing a sizeable proportion of female offenders (44 per cent).

Table 3.1 Average distance travelled and age of offender for selected offences within Sheffield 1995

Offence	Average distance (miles)	Average age (years)	Number of cases
All offences	1.93	22.5	11,179
A.B.H.	1.49	25.9	607
Shoplifting	2.51	22.5	2,065
Theft from vehicle	1.97	19.2	984
Domestic burglary	1.88	21.3	1,401
Non-domestic burglary	1.83	21.8	983
TWOC	2.36	18.8	1,326

The data in Table 3.1 count all movements made by offenders, including joint offending. The average journey from home to place of offence for domestic burglary is 1.88 miles. However, for solo offending the average distance travelled is 1.73 miles, whilst for joint offending the average of the shortest offender journeys is 1.35 miles and the average of longest offender journeys is 3.17 miles. If we take solo journeys, and the shortest distance travelled to a joint offence, we find the average journey overall falls to 1.73 miles. For TWOC, the same process reduces the average journey to crime from 2.36 miles to 2.10 miles.

One of the most consistent findings from previous research has been that young offenders do not travel as far as older offenders. However, our more recent findings for Sheffield suggest that this relationship may be changing (see Table 3.2).

Only theft from a motor vehicle now shows a statistically significant positive correlation between age and distance to crime. Yet car ownership has increased and so the need to travel to find a vehicle to victimise ought,

Table 3.2 Age vs distance correlation coefficients: selected offences, Sheffield 1995

Offender movements	Age vs distance correlation	No. of cases
All offences	−0.0912[a]	11,179
A.B.H.	−0.0790[b]	607
Shoplifting	−0.1699[a]	2,065
Theft from a vehicle	+0.0910[b]	984
Domestic burglary	+0.0327 ns	1,401
Non-domestic burglary	+0.0446 ns	983
TWOC	−0.0488[b]	1,326

Notes:
[a]Significant at the 0.1% level.
[b]Significant at the 5% level.
ns, not significant

All the above correlations based upon Pearson correlation coefficient one-tailed test.

if anything, to be less not more. Burglary shows no correlation and TWOC shows a statistically significant negative correlation. Therefore, for Sheffield-based offenders, offending in the city, there is no longer a positive correlation between travel to crime and age. This is in contrast to Sheffield data from 1966 which showed a significant positive correlation between distance and crime for TDA and breaking and entering (see Baldwin and Bottoms 1976: 83, Table 12).

Sheffield recorded crime data: offender movements into and out of the city

Police force recorded offence and offender data will always give the appearance that a force is a net importer of offenders because the data will include information about offences committed in the force area by those who live elsewhere, but not about those who live in the force area, but commit their offences elsewhere. For example, the 1995 data for Sheffield showed that of cleared up offences, 12,538 were committed by offenders living in Sheffield but 1,849 by offenders living elsewhere (13.6 per cent of all offenders involved in cleared up offences in the city). In order to correct this impression of Sheffield being an importer of offenders, we extracted from the Police National Computer the details of all convicted offenders for the period July 1995–June 1996, who gave a Sheffield home address but who on arrest had been taken to a police station outside the city.

This gave us details of a further 2,534 offender movements by Sheffield-based offenders. We, therefore, had 2,534 offender movements out of the city and 2,127 movements in, making Sheffield a net exporter of known offenders. The offences committed by offenders who travel are different from those who commit their offences near to home: travellers are more likely to commit shoplifting, rather than burglary or car crime (Table 3.3). However, there are significant differences between offenders travelling into Sheffield and those that move out of the city. This relates particularly to shoplifting which is by far the most common offence of those who move into Sheffield.

Table 3.3 Comparison of offender movements: selected offences within, into and out of Sheffield 1995

Offender movements	Within Sheffield (% of total)		Into Sheffield (% of total)		Out of Sheffield (% of total)	
Shoplifting	2,758	(19)	980	(46)	574	(23)
Domestic burglary	1,955	(14)	37	(2)	167	(7)
Non-domestic burglary	1,349	(9)	56	(3)	183	(7)
Theft from a vehicle	1,143	(8)	78	(4)	76	(3)
TWOC	1,648	(12)	87	(4)	304	(12)

Table 3.4 shows the destination of exported offenders and the origin of imported offenders. For both exports and imports over 50 per cent of movements are between Sheffield and places closely linked with the city (57 per cent of exports and 73 per cent of imports). As can be seen, the strongest single link is between Sheffield and Rotherham. This is unsurprising since Sheffield and Rotherham share a long boundary which in many places is effectively meaningless as the two places merge; industry and employment has traditionally been shared in the Don Valley; Sheffield has long attracted shoppers from Rotherham; and the Meadowhall shopping mall, whilst in Sheffield, is right on the border between the two places. Both imports and exports differ from the within city offender movements in the type of offences which dominate.[25]

When we examine the distances travelled out of Sheffield to offend we find that not only is the average distance travelled not very great but even this is distorted by a few long-distance travellers (as can be seen by comparing the average (mean) with the mid-point of the distances travelled (median) in Table 3.5). The greater distances recorded for out of city

Table 3.4 Origin of imported offenders and destination of exported offenders: Sheffield 1995

Place	No. of offenders out of city (%)		No. of offenders into city (%)	
Rotherham	528	(21)	981	(46)
N.E. Derbyshire	455	(18)	102	(5)
Doncaster	210	(8)	191	(9)
Barnsley	156	(6)	235	(11)
Leeds	64	(3)	51	(2)
London	64	(3)	25	(1)
Skegness	52	(2)	0	(0)
Worksop	48	(2)	51	(2)
Other	957	(38)	492	(23)
Total	2,534		2,127	

Table 3.5 Average distance by offence (miles)

	All areas(i.e. all Sheffield -based offender movements)	Mean out of city	Median out of city
All offences	6.86	35.05	18
A.B.H.	3.78	55.16	48.5
Shoplifting	7.93	34.52	18
Theft from vehicle	3.37	22.67	9
Domestic burglary	4.66	31.92	16
Non-domestic burglary	5.94	32.85	18
TWOC etc.	7.11	30.81	11

violent crimes is because many of the offences are committed at seaside resorts, whereas each of the other medians fall directly within Sheffield's normal day-to-day sphere of influence

The impact of Meadowhall

Meadowhall is a very large out-of-town shopping mall built on the site of what was the centre of Sheffield's steel industry. It is interesting because it is the largest attractor of visitors to the city[26] and also the main attractor of imported offenders. Table 3.6 sets out the origin of offenders and victims at Meadowhall, compared with the city as a whole. As can be seen, 41 per cent of known imported offender movements occur at Meadowhall, whereas only 13 per cent of Sheffield-based offenders' movements that take place within the city, occur there.[27] Meadowhall (and other edge of town facilities) has also impacted upon the distribution of offences in the city; in 1966, 25 per cent of offences in the city took place within half a mile of Sheffield city centre, by 1995 this had fallen to just 10 per cent (in particular shoplifting had declined from 69 per cent in 1966 to just 34 per cent in 1995; TWOC from 22 per cent to 8 per cent and theft from motor vehicles from 33 per cent to 10 per cent).

The same pattern holds with victims of crime at Meadowhall, with a much greater proportion of non-Sheffield residents victimised at this location, in fact the highest proportion for anywhere in the city.

Offender travel within Sheffield: different area patterns

So far we have looked at the general situation with regard to Sheffield, however very different offender travel patterns emerge if we examine different types of small residential areas. A consistent pattern in our Sheffield data is that the offence rate in most residential neighbourhoods of the city is driven by the local offender rate. This can be illustrated if we look at patterns of offending in a series of residential districts. The neighbourhoods are briefly described in Table 3.7 and the findings with regard to these areas are set out in Table 3.8.

When we look at offenders offending in the areas we find, not surprisingly, that offenders travel the greatest distance to offend in the low

Table 3.6 Comparison of offending and victimisation at Meadowhall: Sheffield residents and non-residents

	Sheffield residents (% of total)	Non-residents (% of total)
Offender movements:		
all offences	2,204 (13)	876 (41)
Victimisations (excluding		
commercial victims)	1,092 (2)	692 (11)

Table 3.7 Sheffield neighbourhoods: characteristics

Area	Characteristics	Lifestyle	Recorded crime pattern
A	An exclusive middle-class suburb on the edge of the city, 6 miles from the city centre	8 and 9	low offender and offence rates
B	An exclusive middle-class suburb, 2.5 miles from the city centre	9 and 10	low offender and offence rates
C	A working-class/lower middle-class suburb, 6 miles from the city centre, mainly consisting of owner-occupied housing, but with a substantial minority of council housing.	3 and 7 and 10	medium offence and offender rates
D	An area of turn of the century terraced, owner-occupied housing, with a substantial minority of private rented student accommodation and a mixed class structure; 1.5 miles from the city centre	5 and 6	medium offence and offender rates
E	A terraced housing area with a substantial student population but more middle-class structure than area D; generally considered a desirable residential suburb 1 mile from the city centre	5 and 6	high offence and low offender rate
F	Three fairly small and deprived council estates 3 miles from the city centre; one of the estates has long had a very poor reputation in the city	2	high offender and offence rates
G	A council estate 2 miles from the city centre; it has a poor reputation in the city and is one of its most deprived neighbourhoods	2	high offender and offence rates
H	An area 1 mile from the city centre with a sizeable ethnic minority population (about 25%) mainly Asian, but also Afro-Caribbean. A deprived area which has a poor reputation in the city. The housing is a mix of modern public housing (mainly flats) cheap owner occupied terraces and private renting, some in multi-occupation.	1 and 2 and 4	high offender and offence rates
I	An area of mainly system built 1960s housing with the shortest waiting list of any public housing in the city. A mile from the city centre, the area is characterised by poverty and a poor reputation	1 and 2	high offender and offence rates

Notes:
The lifestyle analysis utilised is GB Profiler developed by Stan Openshaw at Leeds University, it can be downloaded from http://www.geog.leeds.ac.uk/software/gbprofiles/

1 Struggling: Multi-ethnic areas, pensioners and single parents, high unemployment, LA rented flats.
2 Struggling: Council tenants, blue collar families and single parents, LA rented terraces.
3 Struggling: Less prosperous pensioner areas, retired blue collar residents, LA rented semi's.
4 Struggling: Multi-ethnic areas; less prosperous private renters, young blue collar families with children, privately renting terraces and bedsits.
5 Aspiring: Academic centres and student areas, young educated white collar singles and couples, privately rented bedsits and flats.
6 Aspiring: Young married suburbia, young well-off blue collar couples and families, mixed tenure terraces.
7 Climbing: Well-off suburban areas, young white collar couples and families, buying semi's and detached houses.
8 Established: Rural farming communities, mature well-off self-employed couples and pensioners, owning or privately renting large detached houses.
9 Prospering: Affluent achievers, mature educated professional families, owning and buying large detached houses.
10 Established: Comfortable middle agers, mature white collar couples and families, owning and buying semi's.

Table 3.8 Travel to offend in selected residential areas: Sheffield 1995

Area	Total offender movements in area	From within area (%)	From elsewhere in Sheffield (%)	From outside Sheffield (%)	Average distance of Sheffield-based offenders (miles)
A	135	33 (24)	101 (75)	4 (3)	3.96
B	95	8 (8)	75 (79)	12 (13)	3.51
C	256	107 (42)	123 (48)	26 (10)	2.85
D	118	15 (13)	90 (76)	13 (11)	2.32
E	237	9 (4)	217 (92)	11 (5)	2.27
F	438	261 (60)	157 (36)	20 (5)	0.81
G	375	205 (55)	158 (42)	12 (3)	0.97
H	399	200 (50)	178 (45)	21 (5)	1.09
I	339	187 (55)	134 (40)	18 (5)	0.77

offender/offence rate areas – on average over 3.5 miles (see Table 3.8). The shortest distances to offend are all found in the high offence/offender areas: again confirming our earlier finding that most offender travel is small-scale.

Offender interviews: evidential support[28]

To what extent did our offender interviews support the findings of the police recorded data? First, with regard to travel outside the city 38 per cent of interviewees claimed to make no regular visits beyond the city boundaries; of the remaining 37 interviewees 68 places were mentioned some of which are set out in Table 3.9. As can be seen, it bears a remarkable resemblance to the places that police data show Sheffielders offend, as set out in Table 3.4. Second, with regard to offending within the city, we found that police data gave a broadly accurate picture of offender travel, with offenders offending generally close to home. If anything, police data overestimate travel because what appears like a journey to crime from the offender's home address is in fact not a journey because they were staying at a friend's (or girlfriend's or parents', etc.) flat when they committed the offence. Offending was concentrated in areas the offenders lived in, had lived in or knew well. This was not because offenders avoided wealthier middle-class areas where they feared they might stand out, they simply did not know them to any extent. During the interviews we divided the city into 23 neighbourhoods and we found that 41 (68 per cent) of the offenders had lived in or did live in just six of these. All were unpopular social housing estates.

DNA database: evidential support

The DNA database provided us with 7,820 'movement' hits for the period June–December 1997, out of a total of 15,536 hits where DNA samples

Table 3.9 Places regularly visited by Sheffield offenders

Place	No. (%) visiting regularly
Rotherham	21 (31)
Chesterfield/NE Derbyshire	15 (22)
Doncaster	10 (15)
Barnsley	4 (6)
Skegness	5 (7)
Leeds	4 (6)
Other	9 (13)
Total *n*	68

matched. However, a number of hits have had to be excluded and this left us with a total of 7,745 'movement' hits and 15,451 hits overall. This produces the pattern of matches set out in Table 3.10.

As can be seen, the vast majority of matches are within force, and half of all matches are within the same police division. Even if we examine matches involving apparent movement we find that the overwhelming majority are within force. Furthermore, movement between adjoining divisions (whether this also involves cross force boundary movement or not) could involve no more than crossing a road. The importance of these results is that they appear to confirm our findings based upon police data and our interviews that the majority of offender movements are relatively short. Also, given the over-representation of burglary in the DNA database, we are particularly able to suggest that offence type, which forms the main element of this study appears to be a localised phenomena.

The journey to victimisation

As was noted earlier, journeys to victimisation are a largely ignored aspect of criminological research. However, as we investigated the journey to offend and began to look at victimisation patterns in different residential areas of Sheffield, we began to realise that where people were victimised was an important aspect of the journey to crime question. In particular there are significant differences between contrasting types of residential

Table 3.10 DNA matches by inter-divisional movement

DNA matches	No. (%)	% Movement matches
Non-adjoining force	1,067 (7)	14
Adjoining force	1,144 (7)	15
Within force (movement, different BCU)	5,534 (36)	71
Within force (no movement, same BCU)	7,706 (50)	na
Total	15,451	

area. Table 3.11 sets out the average distance to victimisation (home address to place of offence commission) for a range of offences in Sheffield.[29] As can be seen the average distances are generally shorter than journeys to offend and appear quite similar for a range of offences.

However, these averages disguise important area differences. These can be illustrated by dividing the city into deciles based upon victimisation rates.[30] Table 3.12 shows the average distance to victimisation for a number of deciles.

As can be seen, there are considerable differences between high, medium and low victimisation areas, which broadly replicate our findings for offender travel into different types of area (see Table 3.8). Now it could reasonably be argued that two potential factors make the findings in Table 3.12 unreliable:

1   Victimisations in decile 10 are dominated by offences such as domestic burglary which by definition have to take place at home, whereas victimisations against residents of the wealthier decile 1 tend to be car crime which can occur anywhere in the city.
2   The areas included in decile 10 are closer to the city centre than those in decile 1 and therefore most journeys around the city by residents of decile 1 may, on average, be longer, which would therefore cause the journeys that result in victimisation to be longer.

When we look at the breakdown of victimisation types by each decile we do find important differences, as set out in Table 3.13. As can be seen,

Table 3.11 Average distance to victimisation: Sheffield 1995

Offence	Number of cases	Average distance (miles)
Theft from motor vehicle	8,258	1.2
TWOC	8,151	1.1
Criminal damage	8,041	0.6
Violence	1,538	1.1
Robbery	765	1.4
Other theft	2,958	1.1

Notes:
Sheffield residents only are included in this analysis.
The figure for criminal damage may be somewhat misleading as we were unable to differentiate between damage to dwellings and damage to vehicles.

Table 3.12 Average distance to victimisation (selected victimisation deciles)

Decile	Number of cases	Average distance
1	1,776	1.4
5 and 6	7,722	0.9
10	7,392	0.4

Table 3.13 Victimisation type by decile (selected offences, selected deciles)

Offence	Decile 1 (%)	Deciles 5 and 6 (%)	Decile 10 (%)
Domestic burglary	19	22	37
TWOC	24	20	15
Theft from motor vehicle	21	23	12

generally as victimisation rates increase the importance of car crime decreases whilst the importance of domestic burglary increases.

However, when we look at the average distance to victimisation by offence for deciles we find the results set out in Table 3.14. As can be seen, considerable differences emerge between deciles so we can say that the average journey to victimisation does differ in areas with different victimisation rates. To what extent can we blame these differences on the location of areas in relation to the city centre? If we take areas B and F (see Table 3.7), then both are approximately equal distances from the city centre and yet have contrasting journey to victimisation patterns and victimisation rates. For area B the victimisation rate per 1,000 households is 178 whilst for area F it is 414; journey to victimisation findings are set out in Table 3.15. As is clear the differences in journey are real even when allowing for distance from the city centre

One further objection to our findings could perhaps be made: that a few victimisations well away from home are skewing the findings for our low victimisation areas. One way to look at this is to examine the victimisation patterns for the areas described in Table 3.7. As Table 3.16 illustrates for the two wealthiest areas, A and B, almost 50 per cent of victimisations of

Table 3.14 Average distance to victimisation (selected offences, selected deciles)

Offence	Decile 1 (miles)	Deciles 5 and 6 (miles)	Decile 10 (miles)
Violence	1.6	1.1	0.8
TWOC	1.7	1.3	0.6
Theft from motor vehicle	1.9	1.2	0.7
Criminal damage	1.3	0.8	0.3
Other theft	1.5	1.4	0.8

Table 3.15 Average distance to victimisation (selected offences) areas B and F

Offence	Area B (miles)	Area F (miles)
TWOC	1.6	0.5
Theft from motor vehicle	1.8	0.9
Criminal damage	1.5	0.2
Violence	1.9	1.0

Table 3.16 Distance to victimisation by home area: Sheffield 1995

Area	Resident complainants	In area victimisation (%)	Out of area victimisation (%)	Average distance: home to victimisation (miles)
A	984	514 (52.2)	470 (47.8)	2.01
B	933	511 (54.8)	422 (45.2)	1.73
C	1,986	1,456 (73.3)	530 (26.7)	1.35
D	694	479 (69.0)	215 (31.0)	0.47
E	1,043	713 (68.4)	330 (31.6)	0.55
F	1,225	1,034 (84.4)	191 (16.6)	0.31
G	1,243	1,106 (89.0)	137 (11.0)	0.23
H	1,415	1,195 (84.5)	220 (15.5)	0.30
I	881	7,228 (2.0)	159 (18.0)	0.29

residents take place outside the area they reside in; for the poor, high crime areas F, G, H and I this figure falls to below 20 per cent. Furthermore, in area B almost 22 per cent of offences take place three or more miles from the victims place of residence. In general terms we can say that for residents of high offence/high offender areas the chance of victimisation is at its highest at or close to home. In contrast, in low offence/low offender areas victimisation is as likely well away from area of residence as it is close to home. Figures 3.1 and 3.2 show the relationship between victimisation and offender movement in contrasting crime areas of the city.

We were able to identify further evidence for the claim that victimisation of residents of poor, high crime areas takes place very close to home by drawing on victimisation surveys conducted on two Sheffield council estates (Abdullah 1999). The survey showed that of 240 victimisations (a count that excludes burglary), only two occurred off the estates. It would be very interesting to conduct similar surveys in middle-class areas to compare findings.

Identifying travelling burglars in the Yorkshire coalfield

The data from Sheffield on offender travel patterns suggested that most burglary in the city was committed by residents, and that Sheffield burglars did not, as a rule, offend to any extent outside the city. The PNC data we had did not allow us to examine whether the burglars who offended outside the city were a subset of our city offenders or a separate group, although the interview data suggested they were not a separate group. This section uses police data on 'cleared'[31] burglaries committed in the metropolitan boroughs of Barnsley, Doncaster and Rotherham over a two-year period. These three adjoining areas formed the main part of the Yorkshire coalfield and they each contain a large town surrounded by small towns and large villages which usually developed around a mine or

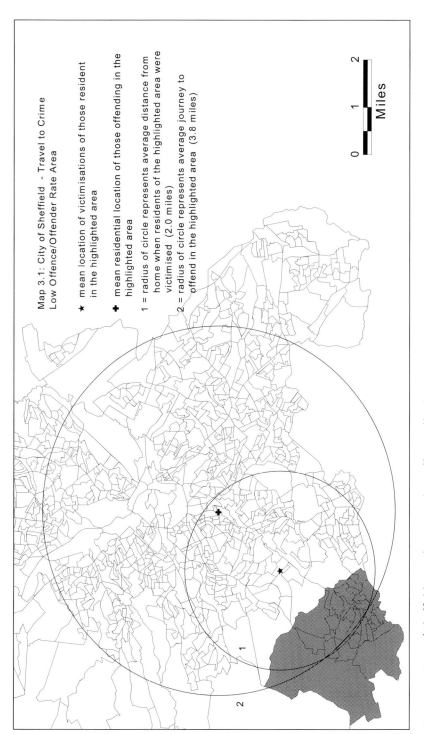

Miles

0   1   2

Figure 3.1 City of Sheffield: travel to crime, low offence/offender rate area.

important point for policing and GIS; as all forces begin to geocode data there is no reason why forces should have 'fixed' internal borders and, where necessary, they can simply share spatial data with adjoining forces.

How localised is offending?

The first sign that offending is extremely localised is provided by calculating the average distance between home address[33] and place of offence commission for all the offences the ten offenders were involved in, this came to only 1.5 miles which is even lower than the average journey to domestic burglaries we found within Sheffield (1.9 miles). For the individual offenders the average distances are set out in Table 3.17. As was predicted the offenders generally lived close to borders between boroughs and more specifically most lived and offended in the Dearne Valley[34] which covers parts of all three boroughs and journeys across borough boundaries are 'normal' in the routines of everyday life.

As can be seen, only four of the ten could in any way be designated 'travellers'[35] on the basis of the average distance travelled. The pattern of travel is not so different from the pattern of the ten most prolific burglars within Sheffield in 1995, where the average distance travelled was also 1.5 miles and the individual averages as set out in Table 3.18. Again we could argue that four of the ten offenders are 'travellers' even though all offences are committed within a single city. The extremely localised nature of offending is confirmed when we look at the journeys carried out by our offenders in terms of distance bands as set out in Table 3.19.

As can be seen over three-quarters of journeys to offend are of less than two miles which seems to suggest that our travelling burglars follow the basic journey to offend pattern of burglars generally. For example, if we examine the travel patterns of offender 5 who committed twenty-seven burglaries in Barnsley and sixteen burglaries in Rotherham we find the pattern as set out in Figure 3.3, with him living in both boroughs, very

Table 3.18 Average distance travelled by 'prolific' Sheffield burglars (1995)

Offender	Age	No. of offences	Distance (miles)
1	19	40	0.6
2	23	68	0.9
3	18	56	0.6
4	24	30	2.7
5	31	41	0.9
6	19	33	3.8
7	20	26	3.0
8	27	24	2.8
9	23	44	0.8
10	18	20	0.8

Table 3.19 Travel patterns : Yorkshire coalfield burglars

Offender	0–0.9 miles (%)	1–1.9 miles (%)	Two or more miles (%)
1	39	52	2
2	45	21	33
3	54	42	4
4	9	30	61
5	49	51	0
6	36	0	64
7	86	7	7
8	47	28	24
9	9	39	52
10	74	7	20
All	48	28	24

close to where he offended, during the period under question. Even an apparent traveller such as offender 6 produces a highly localised pattern as set out in Figure 3.4. The vast majority of his offences are close to home or in one particular Rotherham small town. So even when he travels he mainly travels in one direction and to one particular place.

With regard to our original hypotheses we believe that all three are confirmed by our analysis. A further point to note is that the individual offence patterns of the offenders were the same as those produced by 'prolific' council estate burglars in Sheffield, even though one group was offending in a large city and the other group in an area of small towns and villages. However, the short distances travelled in the coalfield areas comes as no surprise; traditionally mining communities are relatively isolated and self-sufficient with little tradition of commuting to work beyond nearby mines.

Summary

On the basis of the evidence gathered we believe a number of conclusions can be drawn about the offender and victim movement patterns involved in high volume crimes.

First, the vast majority of offender movements are relatively short: for Sheffield-based offenders (regardless of offence location), police crime data show that over a third of crime trips are less than one mile; over 50 per cent consist of less than two miles and only 11 per cent involve travel greater than ten miles. This finding is not surprising given the short travel to crime journeys found in earlier research in more mobile North American cities (see first section). Our Sheffield findings are confirmed by those from the Yorkshire coalfield, where we were unable to identify substantial travel.

Second, our research indicates that much travel associated with crime is not primarily driven by plans to offend. The offenders we interviewed did not travel to the offence location in order to offend in well over 50 per cent of instances (70 per cent for burglary and 62 per cent for TWOC). Offending appeared to be much more dependent upon opportunities presenting themselves during normal routines, rather than as a result of instrumental long range search patterns. This is further supported by the fact that the strongest correlation we found between offence location and other factors was the current residence of the offender.

Third, when offenders do travel to offend it is overwhelmingly local in nature. Even if we look at all trips over three miles by Sheffield-based offenders, 55 per cent were wholly within the city. Even when offending crossed local authority borders most offence locations of Sheffield-based offenders had strong connections with the city. When coalfield burglars crossed borough boundaries generally they were only travelling short distances, to adjoining towns and villages.

Fourth, even when longer range travel was involved in offending elsewhere, this was mainly in places which had strong traditional connections with Sheffield (such as Skegness) or were obvious destinations for leisure trips (such as southern seaside resorts or London).

Fifth, the localised nature of offending meant that victimisation was largely concentrated in areas with high resident offender rates or in 'shared' parts of the city such as the city centre. For residents of low offender/low offence rate areas their chances of being a victim of crime were dependent to a significant degree on the extent to which they chose, or needed to travel into high offender or shared parts of the city.

Overall, there was little evidence that offenders' travelling to offend was significantly increasing compared with the past or that new travel opportunities were changing traditional travel patterns used by offenders. Indeed, an overwhelming impression was just how traditional the travel behaviour of the offenders was. Theories of late modernity, or post-modernism, have argued that various global forces are undermining traditional social structures and culture and this will ultimately affect crime patterns (see, for example, Bottoms and Wiles 1995). As far as the travel patterns of our offenders were concerned there is little sign of such changes. Whilst the more successful inhabitants of South Yorkshire have moved to other more long-range and exotic travel, the world of persistent offenders remains firmly rooted in this earlier tradition. Given what we know generally about persistent and repeat offenders, these limited travel patterns are not surprising. Long range travel, like much other human activity, requires knowledge, confidence, skills, resources, etc.[36] However, one of the risk factors associated with offending behaviour is the lack of such skills. Offenders generally do not travel long distances because they are drawn from those groups in the population who lack the personal and material resources to learn to travel and sustain such travel thereafter.

Whilst these findings were confirmed by interview data, the general patterns could all be identified from police recorded crime data. In fact, if anything, police data tend to overestimate travel. This is because using home address and offence location to measure travel distance produces noticeably larger figures than using offence location and where the offender spent the night prior to the offence. Again this finding illustrates that offender travel is not primarily about offending, but is mainly due to routines such as staying at a friend's or a girlfriend's house, thus the location of the offence is not determined by instrumental search patterns except over short ranges. Earlier research has discussed the extent to which patterned routine activities produce 'anchor points' (such as home, place of work, place of leisure, etc.) around which offending is carried out. Our persistent offenders had little contact with a world of regularised work and lacked the resources for stable leisure pursuits. The one clear anchor point which emerged, therefore, was their home. However, since their lives were largely irregular, spontaneous and unstructured, alternative and temporary 'anchor points', such as a girlfriend's home, came and went. However, even these anchor points are not simply related to non-criminal routines. For example, Figure 3.5 shows the pattern of burglaries committed by a single Sheffield offender relative to his home. As can be seen there are two clusters of burglaries: the larger cluster is around the offender's home but a secondary cluster is further to the south. In this case we know (from interview) that this secondary cluster is around the place where the offender regularly goes to buy drugs. Offending patterns may be largely driven by routine activities but offenders do not inhabit a world in which offending and non-offending behaviour is dichotomised and so offending fits in with other routines as opportunities, needs or temptations present themselves and routines themselves can include both deviant and non-deviant behaviour.

The behaviour of the known offenders who committed the high volume crimes we have been investigating is dominated by opportunistic offending during routine and limited travel patterns.

Given the foregoing and other research we have conducted into crime patterns, particularly in Sheffield, we feel confident in asserting that, generally, high volume crime is a highly localised phenomenon, especially for offences such as domestic burglary and criminal damage. Residential areas with high offence and victimisation rates are generally found on poorer social housing estates, and some mixed inner-city areas (and in South Yorkshire, in ex-pit villages). We can suggest this highly localised pattern holds for a number of reasons:

1   Even poor areas contain plenty of suitable targets such as videos, televisions and cars, etc. Recent Home Office research into car crime, for example, appears to support the notion of localised victimisation as it shows the highest rates of theft for older cars of the type that predominate in poorer areas of Britain (see Houghton 1992).
2   Offenders tend to live in these areas and also, on the whole, tend to offend close to home rather than conduct long range instrumental

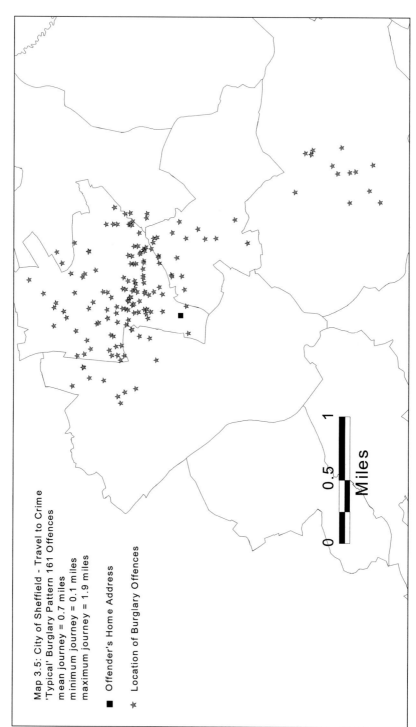

Map 3.5: City of Sheffield - Travel to Crime
'Typical' Burglary Pattern 161 Offences
mean journey = 0.7 miles
minimum journey = 0.1 miles
maximum journey = 1.9 miles

■ Offender's Home Address

✶ Location of Burglary Offences

0   0.5   1
Miles

Figure 3.5 City of Sheffield: travel to crime 'typical' burglary pattern.

searches across a city. Our Sheffield interviewees generally lived in a restricted number of the poorer social housing areas of the city.

3 The other areas the offenders we interviewed knew (other than the city centre) were similar in character to the one they currently lived in and usually they had either lived in them previously or had friends or family in the area. The result is that even if offending is carried out away from home it tends to be in areas where offenders have contacts, not unknown middle-class parts of the city.

These factors mean that a city's broad crime patterns tend to be stable and predictable in the short term. High offence and victim rate areas are the parts of cities, towns and even some villages where offenders tend to live and are generally those areas which are considered least desirable in terms of residential location. Such patterns will be self-reinforcing through mechanisms such as the housing market and allocation systems unless other macro policy or market factors disrupt them.

Notes

1 Geographical Information Systems. Our initial research into the journey to crime was supported by the Home Office Policing and Reducing Crime Unit and we are very grateful for their help (see Wiles and Costello 2000). We would also like to acknowledge the help of many colleagues in South Yorkshire Police.

2 South Yorkshire Police Authority Research Fellow, Faculty of Law, University of Sheffield.

3 Presently, Director, Research Development and Statistics Directorate, Home Office, but at the time when this research was mostly carried out Professor of Criminology at the University of Sheffield.

4 As the section on data and methods makes clear, other data were available to allow us to check the validity of our GIS findings.

5 1991 Census.

6 See the *Financial Times* (24 November 1999), which discusses the relative decline in the fortunes of South Yorkshire compared with the rest of the Yorkshire and Humberside region.

7 According to a recent report by the Yorkshire and Humberside Regional Development Agency, South Yorkshire is expected to have the slowest jobs growth of any English sub-region over the next decade (see the *Financial Times* 25 January 1999).

8 To qualify for Objective 1 status a region must have gross domestic product per capita of only 75 per cent or less of the EU average. A recent survey by CACI suggests that South Yorkshire is the third poorest county in Britain with an average household income of only £17,500 compared with the national average of £21,365. Furthermore, Sheffield income levels are in the bottom five of towns and cities nationally (the CACI findings were available on the CACI website at: http://www.caci.co.uk).

9 Taking Without the Owners' Consent; in this chapter TWOC also includes Aggravated TWOC and Theft of a Motor Vehicle.

10 In the spirit of Weber, these are conceptually pure and are unlikely to be found so neatly in the 'real world'; also the characterisations of previous research findings are simplified to assist explanatory clarity; the various explanations given are by no means mutually exclusive.

11 This research was based upon offence location data with no analysis of any offender data. There was an implicit assumption that criminals are generated in the urban core. However, notwithstanding this weakness it exemplifies the use of an 'economic man' model of human behaviour.

12 Davidson's findings regarding tenure appear to be consistent with our current findings in Sheffield where, on some poorer council estates, offending and victimisation is extremely localised.

13 For references to this field see Bottoms and Wiles 1997: 307, note 7.

14 Only about 3 per cent of crime recorded by the British Crime Survey (basically household and personal crime) result in a court conviction or caution.

15 This is expensive because it either involves using a general population sample to find the (relative) few who have committed burglary or TWOC, or snowballing from known offenders in the hope of contacting non-known offenders.

16 MapInfo was chosen for its ease of use, but any other GIS would have been equally suitable.

17 Offender and victim data are relatively straightforward to geocode as they generally contain a recognisable address. Offence data are slightly more problematic as offences such as TWOC, violence, robbery, etc., often take place away from a residential/business address. Overall we were able to geocode over 98 per cent of domestic burglary data to its exact address, with car crime this fell to around 75 per cent of offences.

18 Cleared offences included all primary and secondary detections.

19 When we were given address details of the selected offenders, a number came with more than one address for the two-year period.

20 Throughout, we refer to offender movements; this is because each offender can be involved in more than one offence and one offence can be committed by more than one offender.

21 Access to data-sets 1, 2 and 4 was provided through the Home Office Police and Reducing Crime Unit for a research project we were carrying out looking specifically at offender mobility in Sheffield and North Yorkshire (see Wiles and Costello 2000). We are grateful to the Policing and Reducing Crime Unit for all the assistance they have provided in our recent research. Data-set 3 was provided by Aldrin Abdullah and we are grateful for access to his data (Abdullah 1999).

22 Unfortunately PNC data could not be provided for the whole of 1995 because of the recent implementation of the new Phoenix system, so we took the closest possible dates. This meant we were unable to ascertain if offenders who travelled out of the city were a subset of those who offended in the city or a separate group.

23 One problem with this database is that since police forces have to pay for each sample they submit then the rate at which samples are sent may not reflect police forces, populations or crime rates. See further comments later in the report.

24 By crime rates we mean offence, offender and victimisation rates.

25 Imports, in particular, differ because of the level of shoplifting by non-Sheffielders at Meadowhall.

26 As we write, the new National Centre for Popular Music based in the city is technically insolvent because it has failed to attract expected visitor numbers, a fact which is blamed on the city not being a tourist attraction (the *Guardian* 19 October 1999).

27 It could be argued that this is unrepresentative because shoplifting is an offence which is identified at the same time as the offender is identified. Nevertheless, the difference between the importance of shoplifting for locals and non-locals is illuminating.

28 A full discussion of the interview data can be found in Wiles and Costello (2000).

29 All offences not directed at individuals or households have been excluded, for example shoplifting as an offence or robbery when the victim is a bank.

30 The city's enumeration districts (excluding those dominated by non-residential use) were ranked on the basis of their household victimisation rate and then divided into deciles, this gave a total of 1032 EDs. Decile 1 is the lowest ranked in terms of victimisation up to decile 10 the highest.

31 'Cleared' in this instance means both primary and secondary detections.

32 For example, population density in the former metropolitan county of Merseyside is three times greater than South Yorkshire.

33 Where an offender had two addresses we calculated the distance between the offence location and the closest of the two addresses.

34 The Dearne Valley is centred on the small towns of Mexborough and Wath upon Dearne.

35 Average journeys above two miles.

36 One area there does appear to be anecdotal evidence of travel is 'bootlegging' although this is currently an area requiring research.

References

Abdullah, A. (1999) 'Crime landscape: the relationship of victimisation and fear of crime with residents' territorial functioning in high and low crime rate estates in Sheffield', unpublished PhD thesis, University of Sheffield, Department of Landscape Aechitecture.

Baldwin, J. and Bottoms, A. (1976) *The Urban Criminal: A Study in Sheffield*, London: Tavistock.

Bottoms, A.E. and Wiles, P. (1995) 'Crime and insecurity in the city', in C. Fijnaut *et al.* (eds) *Changes in Society, Crime and Criminal Justice in Europe*, two vols, The Hague: Kluwer.

—— (1997) 'Environmental criminology', in M. Maguire, R. Morgan and R. Reiner (eds) *The Oxford Handbook of Criminology*, 2nd edn, Oxford: Clarendon.

Brantingham, P.J. and Brantingham, P.L. (1984) 'Burglar mobility and crime prevention planning', in R. Clarke and T. Hope (eds) *Coping with Burglary*, Boston, MA: Kluwer Nijhoff.

Carter, R.L. and Hill, K.Q. (1979) *The Criminal's Image of the City*, New York: Pergamon.

Cromwell, P., Olson, J.N. and Avary, D'Aunn Wester (1991) *Breaking and Entering*, Newbury Park, CA: Sage.

Davidson, R.N. (1984) 'Burglary in the community: patterns of localisation in offender-victim relations', in R. Clarke and T. Hope (eds) *Coping with Burglary*, Boston, MA: Kluwer Nijhoff.

Donnelly, P.G. and Kimble, C.E. (1997) 'Community organizing, environmental change, and neighbourhood crime', *Crime and Delinquency* 43(4): 493–511.

Gabor, T. and Gottheil, E. (1984) 'Offender characteristics and spatial mobility: an empirical study and some policy implications', *Canadian Journal of Criminology* 26: 267–81.

Hakim, S. (1980) 'The attraction of property crimes to suburban locations', *Urban Studies* 17: 265–76.

Houghton, G. (1992) *Car Crime in England and Wales: The Home Office Car Theft Index*, Crime Prevention Unit Paper 33, London: Home Office.

Phillips, P.D. (1980) 'Characteristics and typology of the journey to crime', in D.E. Georges-Abeyie and K.D. Harries (eds) *Crime: A Spatial Perspective*, New York: Columbia University Press.

Porter, M. (1996) *Tackling Cross Border Crime*, PRG Crime Detection and Prevention Series Paper 79, London: Home Office.

Pyle, G.F. (ed.) (1974) *The Spatial Dynamics of Crime*, Department of Geography Research Paper 159, Chicago: University of Chicago Press.

Rand, A. (1986) 'Mobility triangles', in R. Figlio *et al.* (eds) *Metropolitan Crime Patterns*, Monsey, NY: Criminal Justice Press.

Reiss, A.J. and Farrington, D.P. (1991) 'Advancing knowledge about co-offending: results from a prospective longitudinal survey of London males', *Journal of Criminal Law & Criminology* 82(2): 360–95.

Rengert, G. (1989) 'Spatial justice and criminal victimisation', *Justice Quarterly* 6(4): 543–64.

—— (1992) 'The journey to crime: conceptual foundations and policy implications', in D. Evans, N. Fyfe and D. Herbert (eds) *Crime, Policing and Place*, London: Routledge.

Rengert, G. and Wasilchick, J. (1985) *Suburban Burglary*, Springfield, Ill: Charles Thomas.

Reppetto, T.A. (1974) *Residential Crime*, Cambridge, MA: Ballinger.

Rhodes, W.M. and Conly, C.C. (1981) 'Crime and mobility', in P.J. Brantingham and P.L. Brantingham (eds) *Environmental Criminology*, Beverly Hills: Sage.

Shaw, C. and McKay, H. (1969) '*Juvenile Delinquency and Urban Areas*', revised edition, Chicago: University of Chicago Press.

White, R.C. (1932) 'The relations of felonies to environmental factors in Indianapolis' *Social Forces* 10: 498–509.

Wiles, P. and Costello, A. (2000) *The Road to Nowhere: The Evidence for Travelling Criminals*, Home Office Research Study, London: Home Office.

Zendner, L. (1997) 'Victims', in M. Maguire, R. Morgan and R. Reiner (eds) *The Oxford Handbook of Criminology*, 2nd Edition, Oxford: Clarendon.

4 Crime, repeat victimisation and GIS

Jerry H. Ratcliffe and Michael J. McCullagh

Repeat victimisation is a difficult concept in terms of definition. There is a strong argument for considering two types of repeat, based on either the conventional definition of numerous incidents at a single location over a period of time or, less traditionally, a closely grouped set of events in a defined homogenous area. Much research has concentrated on the former temporal definition, but little on spatially defined repeats. Identification of these two forms of victimisation needs to include analysis of both the temporal and spatial nature of crime data. Aoristic principles can improve the selection of data prior to analysis. Statistical tests within a GIS can be used to detect significant clusters both in time and space. Where these are temporally related a hotspot of pinpoint form will be found on the resulting analytical map. In the spatial case the result will be a hotbed of crime of indeterminate but compact shape, that defines the zone of areal repeat. LISA statistics can be used to outline the points or areas of concern for later investigation.

Spatial hotpoints may be examples of repeat victimisation. Analysis of the crime trail, however, may show a variation in the modus operandi of the crime set over time suggesting not a repeat by the same offender, but merely a spatial coincidence owing to other social or environmental factors. An exploration of the relationship between repeats and social indices might indicate whether victimisation is correlated with, for example, deprivation. Repeat victimisation locations are not distributed according to the standard census boundaries that supply much of a researcher's basic socio-economic data. A close vicinity relationship calculated using GIS techniques can be used to aggregate social and other variables at a specific location on the basis of census tract data, resulting in an improved estimation of the relationship between crime and deprivation.

Preface

The purpose of this chapter is to determine how far GIS (Geographical Information Science/Systems) techniques have progressed in attempting to pick the lock that is the conundrum called repeat burglary victimisation. This requires that all the analytic tools to be used be examined carefully to see how they could contribute to the task. In addition, before any analysis can take place it is vital to ensure that the data are correctly interpreted in both space and time. This requires investigation of the time stamps of crimes and of the spatial precision with which they have been recorded. Another problem that will be addressed is to know when is there a significant level of crime in an area. Research has attempted to locate these hotspots, but frequently without thought of a statistical basis, and usually without being able to modify the shape of a hotspot to the local map. One must be able to detect hotspots correctly before one can tell whether areas liable to repeat victimisation have been detected. Once data are correct and the definition of meaningful crime areas has been made then analysis of repeat burglary victimisation may be undertaken. This chapter will attempt to take these themes and show how they can be fused to form the key to recognition, if not solution, of the repeat victimisation problem.

Introduction

Geographical Information Systems have been adopted quickly by police forces for their use in a variety of different operational situations, though their use has not yet been fully utilised for crime mapping or analysis. There has recently been a flood of publicity as police forces in Britain and the United States have invested in GIS technology (see Berkeley Police Department 1997; Campbell 1992; Clegg and Robson 1995; Fox-Clinch 1997; Grescoe 1996; Hirschfield *et al.* 1995a; ICL 1995; MapInfo 1997; Mitchell 1997; Nagle 1995; Page 1997; Salinas Police Department 1997; Tempe Police Department 1997). These systems have been used mainly for mapping live incident data, occasional crime mapping, and for describing incident scenes to a court. GIS has also been applied to other emergency services (Smith 1997).

Campbell (1992) identified a number of areas in which GIS can contribute to the efficiency of police services. During the early 1990s, the first research papers began to appear which utilised the geocoding of police reported crime information (examples include Berry and Jones 1995; Campbell 1992; Ekblom 1988; Grogger and Weatherford 1995; Wrighton 1987). The majority of examples were drawn from North America (Berkeley Police Department 1997; Grogger and Weatherford 1995; Maltz *et al.* 1991; Salinas Police Department 1997; Tempe Police Department 1997), where the usage of GIS for crime mapping has been quite significant. Berry and Jones' article (1995) carries an excellent discussion of police and crime census statistics using the postcode address file (PAF) and ARC/INFO to develop a crime-based GIS.

Hirschfield and others (1995a) have developed a GIS-based crime analysis and mapping system for use in the analysis of crime incident data recorded by Merseyside police. Like most of the applications mentioned above, the system is a crime mapping system, and not an analysis tool. The crucial difference in all these systems is that they produce maps of crime distribution, but then require the user to perform the analysis themselves. The knowledge of where the highest crime concentrations are located is important to policing and crime prevention strategies, yet once a mapping system produces a number of maps, the human operator must still interpret the images and look for clusters or 'hotspots' of crime. One of the landmark papers in the area of crime mapping with GIS is the account of a failed early attempt to introduce a GIS system to Northumbria constabulary in the late 1980s (Openshaw *et al.* 1990). Maltz and others describe in great detail some of the problems of implementing a GIS crime mapping system for the Chicago police force (Maltz *et al.* 1991).

Read and Oldfield (1995) identified eight different forms of crime analysis of which two are relevant here. *Comparative Case Analysis* seeks to detect similarities between crimes that point to the same perpetrator or groups of perpetrators, and *Crime Pattern Analysis* forms a picture of the nature and scale of crime in a particular area. Commercial examples of pattern analysis systems – albeit non-spatial for the most part – include the Harlequin Criminal Intelligence System (Harlequin 1997) and ProQuest by i2 software (i2 1997).

Crime prevention and repeat victimisation

Repeat victimisation is a recent target area for crime prevention. Most of the related work has been published in criminology journals. A review of recent quantitative criminology in the UK is given by David Farrington (Farrington 1996). The benefit to crime prevention of identifying repeat victimisation has been widely recognised (Anderson *et al.* 1995; Ellingworth *et al.* 1995; Farrell and Pease 1993), but the process of accurately distinguishing the repeat locations has always been difficult. A number of articles highlight the difficulties posed by police crime data in identification of repeat victims in addition to the authors above (Hope 1995; Read and Oldfield 1995; Sampson and Phillips 1995; Ratcliffe and McCullagh 1998a).

The majority of repeat victimisations occur within one month of previous (or the first) victimisation (Pease 1997). Once a repeat victim has been identified, crime prevention resources have to be mobilised rapidly to prevent further attacks on the same target.

Aoristic data extraction

Temporal data

An application of crime data which has not been discussed in depth in the literature is the use of temporal data to plot changes over time. Temporal GIS (TGIS) has been proposed (Peuquet 1994) as a way of introducing a temporal element to spatial analysis. A number of different conceptual frameworks for temporal GIS have been suggested (see Peuquet and Niu

1995; Raafat *et al.* 1994) but a defining standard has yet to be agreed. The problems of how much historical information to retain and in what format are also discussed in Langran (1989) and Langran (1993). These papers contain some of the more thorough reviews of recent temporal analysis and temporal database storage.

One of the more comprehensive descriptions of the variety of possible temporal combinations comes from Peuquet (1994) and is applicable if the passage of time can be viewed as a fixed line and events are fixed to this line in some manner. Time stamping crime is difficult as the time of occurrence of a crime event, for instance burglary and motor vehicle theft, may not be known exactly. Therefore when describing crime events, they must be viewed as singularities of variable length along the time line shown in Figure 4.1. Although field names vary from force to force, variations on *on_date, at_time, from_date, from_time, to_date* and *to_time* allow the crime record sheet to incorporate a range of possible incident times. This creates problems when it is desired to search a crime database for events that occurred during a specific time period. A number of solutions to this problem are possible, however each has limitations on its functionality. Three different methods of temporal search could be envisaged: an averaging temporal search which averages the date and time fields; a rigid temporal search which only contains definite records within the search criteria, and an aoristic[1] search which considers all records which might have occurred within the search criteria time

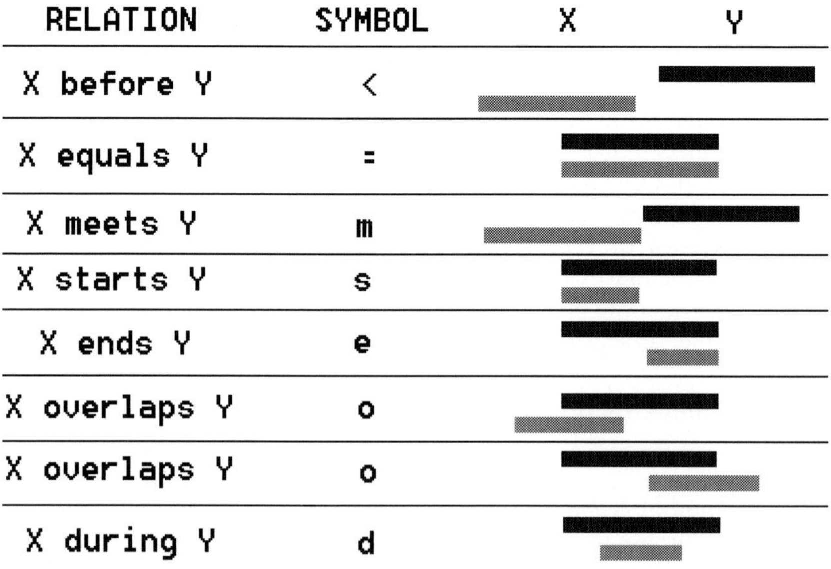

RELATION	SYMBOL	X	Y
X before Y	<		
X equals Y	=		
X meets Y	m		
X starts Y	s		
X ends Y	e		
X overlaps Y	o		
X overlaps Y	o		
X during Y	d		

Figure 4.1 Temporal topological relationships.
Source: Peuquet 1994: 455.

These processes are summarised in Figure 4.2. Horizontal bars (labelled a–d) represent crime incidents which have a start time, a duration (the length of the bar) and an end time. The search criteria similarly has a start and end time shown by the vertical long arrows. The small triangular markers in the middle of each event represent the location of the average along the time line. One of the limitations of averaging methods is visible in the second incident from the top (b) where, although a considerable amount of the second incident might have taken place within the search parameters, it is not included because the location of the average is just outside the search criteria. Unfortunately averaging the date field has been used frequently in studies of burglary repeat victimisation (Johnson *et al.* 1997). Another possibility is to record only those incidents that fall rigidly within the search period. Only the fourth incident is returned by the rigid search method. This type of search method results in generally lower numbers of crimes than the originating database, but with a higher degree of accuracy in the temporal search. The aoristic search method records crime incidents that might have occurred within the search time. An incident will be recorded when the possibility exists that it might have occurred in a search block. The result shows a larger number of crimes each registering the possibility of an incident rather than a definite incident as in the previous method. Every potential instance of a crime can be weighted according to the probability of its occurrence, thus removing the unreasonable dominance of crimes of very uncertain but extensive temporal coverage. The aoristic method allows for the exploration of all possible events from the originating database, either as a standard aoristic search or through the probabilistic aoristic process. The more accurate are the temporal fields in the database, the less an aoristic search becomes necessary.

An example where aoristic analysis has proved its worth is a study of car crime (Ratcliffe and McCullagh 1998) where an average or rigid analysis of six months of data showed no significant daily or weekly temporal pattern. The subsequent aoristic analysis showed a well-developed pattern, significant at 99 per cent level, of Monday night peaks in crime.

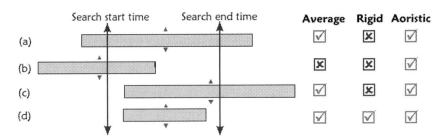

Figure 4.2 Summary of averaging, rigid and aoristic temporal search processes.

No other day showed similar peaks of any significance. These Monday peaks were obscured by all other crime recording methods.

Analysis of mixed spatial and temporal studies

Once data has been extracted from a crime database in a meaningful manner it is possible to consider whether there is any trend in the data over time. This traditionally has been done using some form of trend line, often a linear regression. The rising or falling nature of the line is considered to indicate whether an increase or decrease in crime has taken place in the area concerned. The temporal data are often not amenable to this form of treatment owing to its periodic nature or general distribution. A solution may be to adopt a temporally weighted adaptive thresholding technique such as that in Figure 4.3 proposed in Ratcliffe and McCullagh (1998) where a record of all crime in a grid square area for a year is displayed. The calculation of a standard deviation of crime over a temporally weighted window allows peaks or troughs in the general crime level to be seen.

The choice of a suitable event threshold depends on the type of data. Where weekly peaks can be proven to exist, such as in the motor vehicle crime example given earlier, the weekly frequency could be used as the basis for an adaptive thresholding process through time. For repeat victimisation studies a longer time period would be necessary to show changes in trends. In a spatial sense, the thresholds will vary from area to area as they depend on local crime characteristics.

Mapping the results of the temporal thresholding based on aoristic data can be very prone to data misrepresentation. Figure 4.4 shows two gridded

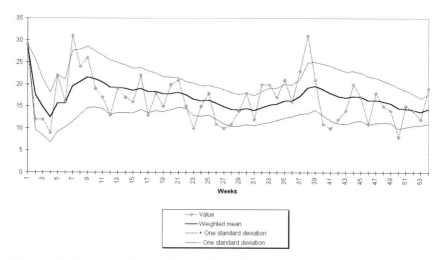

Figure 4.3   Linear weighting adaptive threshold process with 15-week window.

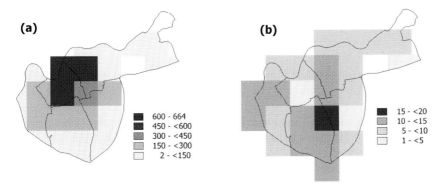

Figure 4.4 Police beats overlaid with one-kilometre square grids to show general crime and temporal analysis. (a) Standard mapping practice. The aoristic search using weighted threshold results is shown in (b). Here the number of times the upper threshold has been exceeded during the year is mapped.

crime maps. Figure 4.4a gives a summary of all crimes and is the type of map commonly employed in police work which can mislead the user as to changes in more complex crime patterns. Figure 4.4b depicts the number of times over the year that a grid square's aoristic temporal count exceeded the threshold. Note that the traditional approach to policing would be to increase resources to the north-westerly squares in Figure 4.4a, whereas Figure 4.4b shows that crime is rising fastest in the more south-easterly squares.

Hotspot analysis

Crime events can be thought of as a continuous flow of discrete events over a study area. The heaviest clusters signify areas with spatial clusters of criminal activity. The search for the heaviest crime clusters has been termed hotspot analysis (Hirschfield *et al.* 1997). Most of the literature relating to spatial crime analysis techniques share similarities and origins with aspects of medical geography and the search for clusters of rare diseases within medical epidemiology, research that goes back to the classic research of Knox and Mantel in the 1960s (Knox 1964; Mantel 1967; Openshaw *et al.* 1988). One of the seminal works in the literature has been provided by Openshaw and Charlton (Openshaw and Charlton 1987), in the form of the 'Mark 1 Geographical Analysis Machine' which sought to provide a fully automated process for the complex analysis of point pattern data using isodensity interpolation techniques based on circular search regions, the traditional geometry used in epidemiological studies, and sometimes as hexagons in other studies (Hirschfield *et al.* 1997). Testing of the significance of discovered hotspots has been based on Monte Carlo simulations by Openshaw and Charlton (1987) or, in epidemiology, on quartic kernel intensity patterns (Gatrell *et al.* 1996).

The use of georeferenced data in digital mapping packages and Geographical Information Systems (GIS) has vastly simplified the process of mapping crime incident data. A number of authors have been involved in creating these types of crime-based mapping systems (Berry and Jones 1995; Grescoe 1996; Hirschfield *et al.* 1995). Crime-specific systems implementing these ideas have been few and far between. The Illinois Department of Justice 'Spatial and Temporal Analysis of Crime' software (STAC) is used extensively for crime profiling in the USA, and outlines the boundaries of crime clusters as standard deviational ellipses. Two major problems of STAC are a lack of correspondence between the shape of the hotspot and the underlying patterns of land use, and that STAC is susceptible to the Modifiable Areal Unit Problem (MAUP) (Hirschfield *et al.* 1997). The ubiquity of STAC and rather few other methods can be seen through the dominance of STAC in a number of recent books (for example, LaVigne and Wartell 1998; Weisburd and McEwen 1998).

The Spatial Crime Analysis System (SCAS) was made available during 1998 as an add-on for ArcView and was offered freely over the Internet by the Crime Mapping Research Center, a department of the US Department of Justice (http://www.usdoj.gov/criminal/gis/scashome.htm). It was intended to be a Windows technology form of STAC analyser working on a modern GIS base. The ArcView Spatial Analyst extension was used to develop the spatial crime analysis modules (Nulph *et al.* 1997). The single standard deviational ellipse generated is rather too crude to elicit any useful information and SCAS has now been withdrawn from the CMRC web site.

Two less widely known systems have been tested: SPAM and Vertical Mapper. SPAM (the Spatial Pattern Analysis Machine) was developed (Ratcliffe 1999) to embrace the good features of the Openshaw GAM, but to extend the result much further by adding a LISA (Local Indicators of Spatial Association) analysis module to determine the significant boundary to hotspot areas (Ratcliffe and McCullagh 2000). Vertical Mapper (Northwood Geoscience 1998) and MapInfo have been used by the Brent Crime Mapping Project in a study of Wembley in North London (BCMP 1997), but it is very difficult to determine significance of the output.

Evaluation of current crime-specific hotspot programs

The example data set used in Figure 4.5a is drawn from 2,524 non-residential burglaries in Nottingham over the period April 1995 to April 1997. Crime events merge into one as the graphical resolution deteriorates, but whenever there is repeat victimisation the subsequent symbols are placed in exactly the same place as the preceding points. One symbol position may indicate either one crime or a number of incidents. The

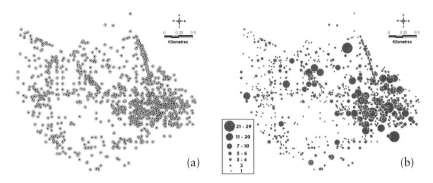

Figure 4.5 (a) Non-residential burglary locations (April 1995 to April 1997); and (b) the same but using a circle proportional in size to the number of repeats.

repeat victimisation effect is shown in Figure 4.5b where the number of reported burglaries occurring at each location is indicated by symbol size.

In the STAC hotspot area search mode an isodensity surface is defined. The locations of the most dense 25 cells in the resulting surface are retained as potential centre points for later ellipses. Adjacent high-density regions are defined from these cell positions and combined to form 'hot clusters' and for each hot cluster a standard deviational ellipse calculated. This ellipse is termed a hotspot area and is the final display medium for the crime hotspots (ICJIA 1996). Although STAC is able to define a limit to the size of a hotspot, the hotspots are always displayed as standard deviational ellipses (Figure 4.6a), a shape which generally bears little resemblance to the underlying crime morphology.

The equivalent analysis for the vertical mapper is presented in Figure 4.6b. The generated surface follows the flow of the crime patterns more accurately than the standard deviational ellipses produced by STAC because the hotspots are not delimited in any way, and placing a limit on the extent of a hotspot from the total surface would be entirely subjective.

The SPAM results in Figure 4.7a illustrate the first stage in a two-stage process aimed at generating a simple binary classification of hotspots. This system recognises that there can be sharp distinctions in the crime level between two adjacent parts of a city and the intensity calculation reflects this in recognising the influence of distance within the search circle. The second stage, shown in Figure 4.7b, is to determine where the limit of hotspot boundaries might lie using spatial statistics. Global statistics such as Moran's I and Geary's c act, according to Unwin (1996), as subsets of global statistical methods including nearest neighbour analysis and k-functions. Both statistics require a null hypothesis of stationarity and of close to zero spatial autocorrelation; unlikely for crime data. Edge effects and the MAUP can also cause problems (Bailey and Gatrell 1995;

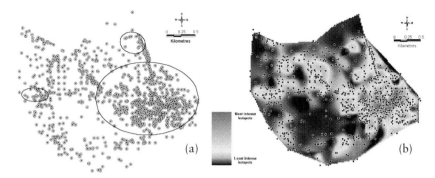

Figure 4.6 (a) Non-residential burglaries with STAC hotspot areas, and (b) the Vertical Mapper hotspot surface, with individual crimes plotted as dots.

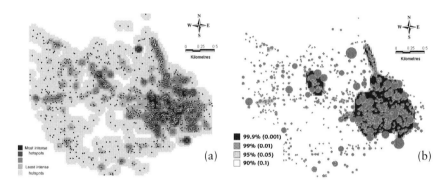

Figure 4.7 (a) SPAM isodensity map generated for non-residential burglaries with absolute crime locations, and (b) SPAM derived significant hotspots with repeat crime locations. Hotspot surface generated by Getis and Ord G_i^* statistic at varying confidence levels, shown in different colours.

Openshaw 1984). A distinction has been drawn between general and focused tests (Ord and Getis 1995), using the class of tests referred to by the term LISA, Local Indicators of Spatial Association (Anselin 1995). LISA statistics allow for the decomposition of global statistics and provide an additional tool in Exploratory Spatial Data Analysis (ESDA). They can measure dependence in one area of the study region and are particularly adept at: (1) indicating regions of spatial non-singularity, and (2) identifying the existence of local spatial clustering around an individual location, or 'hotspots' (Anselin 1995; Getis and Ord 1996). The statistics G_i and G_i^*, also written as $G_i(d)$ and $G_i^*(d)$, introduced by Getis and Ord (1992) for the study of local patterns in spatial data, were extended and rewritten in 1995 to redefine G_i as a standard variate and to allow for non-binary classifications of the distance d (Ord and Getis 1995). The calculation of G_i^* used in this study was derived from Getis and Ord (1996) and a detailed account is given in Ratcliffe and McCullagh (2000). Ord and Getis (1995) suggest a Bonferroni test to overcome problems of overlap between samples leading to inflated correlation between adjacent statistics and hence false hotspot extent. The result in Figure 4.7b shows confidence level surfaces for hotspot area determination. Interestingly the definition of the hotspots is very constant over the 90 to 99 per cent limits.

Identifying repeat victimisation

The crime prevention benefits of accurately identifying repeat victimisation are undeniable. The introduction outlined the general background to the subjects of crime prevention and repeat victimisation and the gains that could be accrued if a system of rapidly identifying repeats were developed. It also described the manifest problems of identifying repeat victimisation locations from text-based police crime records. Until recently most attempts at identifying repeat victimisation locations have focused on searching address fields in police records. Problems with inaccurate data entry and variation in address format make this method fraught with difficulty and time consuming to correct. The use of British Crime Survey results has highlighted the deficiencies in police crime records, and while the under-reporting of crime to the police is well-documented (Hough and Lewis 1989; Mayhew *et al.* 1993), it remains a reality that the police recorded crime data are still one of the best sources of information on local crime distribution in the UK. Computerised systems for recording police crime data have been set up within forces but usually the extraction of data pertinent to the geographical crime distribution and the identification of repeat victims is not a priority, or is often extraordinarily difficult (Ellingworth *et al.* 1995: p 360; Anderson *et al.* 1995; Johnson *et al.* 1997).

The time course of repeat victimisation

In the results of the repeat victimisation analyses, most studies in the field drew similar conclusions. Anderson *et al.* (1995) found that 40 per cent of all repeats happen within a month of the preceding one, while Burquest *et al.* (1992) found an even greater figure of 79 per cent of revictimisations occurring within one month for school burglaries in Merseyside. The generally accepted pattern is of an initial high rate of repeat victimisation that decreases rapidly after the first six to eight weeks. Many of the studies in the literature cover shorter periods of between six months and a year. Longer study periods raise questions regarding the interpretation of repeat victimisation. Repeats, by definition, have a relationship with the initial incident. This might be because the same burglar returns to the location, or the burglar informs associates that the address is particularly vulnerable. At what point, therefore, do repeat incidents become unconnected with the initial occurrence? Is the burglary just another one, which happens to be at an address where a previous incident once took place? Polvi *et al.* (1991) conducted a four-year study (one of the longest studies in the literature) but failed to address this point, finding 'repeats' which occurred over three years from the initial incident. The drop in risk decreased in the Polvi data from an initial high until six months after the initial incident at which point the level of risk returned to the same as for the rest of the study area, demonstrating the absence of any elevated risk after six to seven months. This correlates with general findings from other studies (Anderson *et al.* 1995; Burquest *et al.* 1992; Farrell and Pease 1993; Hope 1995; Polvi *et al.* 1990; Spelman 1995).

Identifying a repeat with geo-referenced co-ordinates

A study by Ratcliffe and McCullagh (1998a) focussed on burglary in an area of varied inner-city and suburban Nottingham housing. A myriad of small passageways and paths between cul-de-sacs provides ample opportunity for burglars to access the rear of properties undetected. The area stretches from poor inner-city council housing to mixed council and privately owned housing to leafy affluent. Each of these different types of housing and social mix is within a few miles of each other and they are often uneasy neighbours. Although the inner-city regions are short of space, Nottingham has resisted the urge to construct large numbers of tower blocks in this area. This allows easy geo-referencing of individual properties in two dimensions.

In 1997 Nottinghamshire constabulary were in the process of changing from the postcode address file (PAF) to address-point data. Some addresses in the county were still referenced in the crime data with PAF 100 metre resolution geo-references rather than 1 metre address-point co-ordinates. This meant that sometimes the PAF reference could have applied to more than one property. Records where the same PAF reference was given, but the address field implied that they were, in fact, different properties were removed from the analysis. About a dozen errors were detected, but only two of these were errors in address-point.

Correcting for edge effects in the study time period

In some studies which have looked at burglary figures, the researchers have been able to examine only a limited number of months data (e.g. Anderson *et al.* 1995). If, for example, burglaries repeat uniformly within one month, the events that happen at the very beginning and very end of the study time period are at a statistical disadvantage. Events at the beginning are denied the possibility of being repeats to crimes that happened just before data recording commenced. For example, if a study time of one calendar year is used, events in the first week of January are denied the possibility of being a repeat of an incident in December, because the December incidents are not included. Similarly crime events towards the end of the time-frame are denied possible repeats in the next period. The Nottingham data-set covered a two-year time period, and a minor correction for edge effects was therefore necessary. For the majority of the data-set the greatest repeat time between burglary events was found to be twenty-six weeks. There were seventy-eight weeks where a repeat burglary half a year later could be included in the data available. A correction suggested by Anderson (1995: 47) was used to prevent the time-course graph declining artificially rapidly: $(\alpha\eta)/(\eta-\beta)$, where: α is the number of events, β is the number of weeks repeat time, and η is the total number of survey weeks. The longer than usual time-frame used in this study lead to some over-compensation in the final months following the application of the correction. This effect became more pronounced still if applied to the full two years of the study.

Figure 4.8 shows the distribution of victimisation for all burglaries across the study area. During the two years' data 1,987 burglaries were recorded committed against 1,600 properties. Just over two thirds of these properties were burgled only once during the study period. Seventy per cent of the rest were burgled twice. This leaves 70 of the 1,600 properties victimised more than twice. These heavily burgled properties account for under 4 per cent of

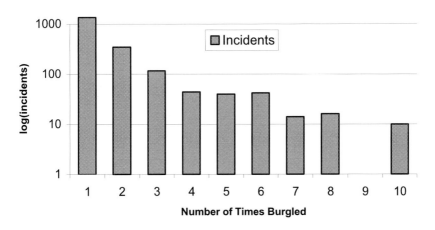

Figure 4.8 Distribution of burglary victimisation for 'C' sub-division: April 1995 to April 1997.

the number of victimised properties, but they account for 14 per cent of the number of burglary events. Burglaries which did not have a clear event date and could have occurred over a number of days, such as a weekend, were allocated the average of the starting and ending date to be comparable with other studies (Johnson *et al.* 1997). The repeat time between burglaries showed the greatest risk of a repeat to be the month immediately after a burglary around 25 per cent, which was lower than Anderson *et al.* (1995) at 40 per cent and Burquest *et al.* (1992) at 79 per cent for school burglaries in Merseyside. There could be a number of reasons for this difference. Anderson *et al.* (1995) examined domestic burglaries exclusively while Burquest *et al.* (1992) were looking only at school burglaries. This study did not differentiate between types of burglary and examined all burglaries, domestic or otherwise. When the GIS was employed to select locations which had been revictimised twice or more frequently, it was found that over 80 per cent of the premises were non-residential. These included sports centres, schools and building sites. Police experience would suggest that thefts from building sites have an extremely high reporting rate and are reported as burglaries owing to the financial liability of the contractors. Similarly schools and sports centres tend to have set guidelines for reporting burglaries.

Identification of repeat victimisation would improve if a fuzzy area, rather than an exact location were used to identify crimes. Vehicle crimes such as theft from motor vehicles and theft of vehicles tend to occur in the street. Identifying a particular point on a street where a vehicle crime occurred from police recorded crime data is nearly impossible. The few studies that have identified repeat vehicle crimes have had difficulty in describing a repeat vehicle crime.

Visualisation of repeats

Many texts identify problems of integrating GIS and other technology into police forces (Hirschfield *et al.* 1995a; Maltz *et al.* 1991; Openshaw *et al.* 1990). The examples given here shows a typical software application (Ratcliffe and McCullagh 1998a).

There is a high incidence of burglary across the study area, and the accurate targeting of crime prevention resources is a local priority. A large number of repeats appear concentrated around a busy road junction (Figure 4.9), approximately in the centre of the map, but in some areas of the map repeat burglaries are almost unknown. Possible reasons for this are that the residents took it upon themselves to improve their home security or other more complex social factors. Curiously, one of the largest circles in the study (not present in the Figure) marks a works depot that suffered seven burglaries over the two-year period, and demonstrates the addressing problems discussed earlier. At the time of the study the depot was not included within the Nottinghamshire constabulary address database and crimes at the location were assigned to the nearest property, a

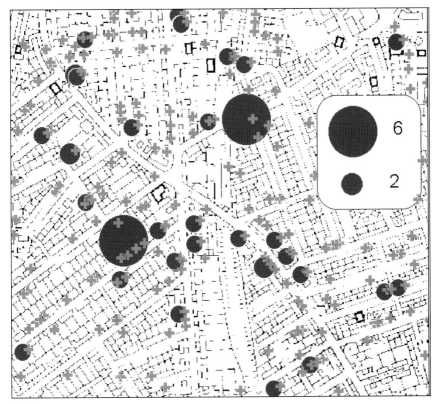

Figure 4.9 Location of all burglaries near a busy road junction (detail inside the study area). Crosses denote locations burgled, circles those premises burgled more than once. Reproduced from the Ordnance Survey map by permission of Ordnance Survey on behalf of the Controller of Her Majesty's Stationery Office, © Crown Copyright ED 275514.

dwelling house in the same street. This gives the inaccurate indication of a high number of repeats at a domestic property.

When is a repeat not a repeat?

Repeat victimisation studies often have covered periods of between six months and a year. This two-year study period raised questions regarding the interpretation of repeat victimisation. The concept of a 'repeat' is that there is a connection of some description with a previous event. With burglaries this can be because the same modus operandi is employed, or the same criminal is responsible. Alternatively, the premises might be particularly vulnerable by default and this vulnerability is obvious to a number of different opportunist thieves. This is often the case with end-of-terrace properties or houses which back on to railway lines, both of which offer easy access and escape routes to the criminal. The question exists, therefore, as to when an event becomes unconnected from any previous incident.

Polvi *et al.* (1991) has fitted regression curves to repeat victimisation data that show a decrease in risk of repeat victimisation to a stable level after about six months. A legitimate question that must be asked in a two-year study is whether repeats that occur a year or more after the initial incident can truly be considered repeats, or are they new initial events, unrelated to the original (or previous) event?

Recognition of genuine repeats

The original data were re-examined to identify whether criminals committed the repeat incident with a similar modus operandi to the original event. Nottinghamshire constabulary record the point of entry (POE) where the burglar gained entry to the location (for example, upper first floor sliding window, or roof skylight), the method of entry (MOE) employed (for example, using a glass cutter, or bodily pressure), and the times between which the offence was committed. A crude index of crime similarity could be produced from these data. Repeat incidents were considered matched if they had an identical POE, if they had an identical MOE, or could be identified as both being burglaries committed at similar times of day. Out of 631 incidents in the original repeat examination 244 were 'originator' events leaving 387 repeat events to compare with a previous incident. The crime data recording system relied on the reporting officer accurately describing the burglar's method and point of entry (if known), which was by no means the case. Similarly there is also the problem of consistent (from 169 available POEs) interpretation of the burglary crime scene by the officer. One hundred and thirteen crimes exhibited a match between occurrence and repeat in terms of either time of day, MOE or POE from the 236 complete records in the data. Where a match existed it was assumed there was a reasonable probability that the repeat was directly related to the previous incident. However, in 123 cases no match was found. Here it was possible that the apparent relationship between the incident and the repeat did not exist. From this evidence it would appear likely that the longer the repeat interval the higher the probability that a repeat is not a genuine repeat but a fresh incident.

The central factor in determining whether an incident is truly a repeat victimisation is whether or not the initial event and the subsequent incident were carried out by the same individuals. However, the similarity between different crime events can also be determined by other factors. Environmental change, such as improved crime prevention measures or different policing patterns might be reflected in a different modus operandi. Figure 4.10 shows the calculated similarity ratios up to a six-month limit. A similarity value of 1.0 indicates that all repeats have at least one aspect of commonality with their predecessors. The decline in similarity over time suggests that the number of genuine repeats detected within the data declines as lag-time increases.

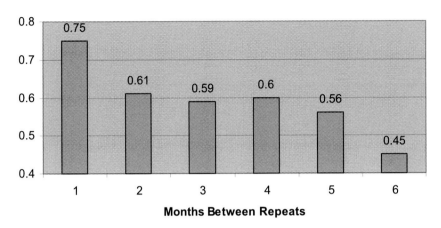

Figure 4.10 Similarity between probable and total cases of repeat victimisation over time.

Taking the hypothesis further

A reasonable conclusion from the previous section could be that the similarity between a repeat burglary and a previous incident decreases with time between the events. The analysis was repeated to see if the similarity decay phenomenon existed for larger data-sets. Instead of using a small suburban area as a data-set, the exercise was repeated for two complete divisions of Nottinghamshire constabulary for burglary data from April 1995 to April 1997. In 'A' division, 3,741 burglaries were detected of which 2,557 were repeats. Of these, 2,338 burglary repeats took place within a year of the previous incident. On 'B' division, there were 1,880 burglaries, of which there were 1,254 repeats without their primer crime, and 1,131 were re-occurrences within a year. This is about an order of magnitude more data than that used in the previous sub-divisional example. The similarity indices were calculated for 'A' and 'B' divisions and are plotted in Figure 4.11 alongside the small data-set results for 'C' sub-division. The histograms in Figure 4.11 show that the 'C' sub-division data demonstrated the most noticeable decline in similarity as the time between burglary incidents increased. There is a similar but less dramatic decline in similarity for 'A' division, and the 'B' sub-division data oscillate around the 0.45 level.

There are a number of possible explanations for the differences between the data from the three test divisional areas. The causes of crime are considerably complex and the search for a simple relationship between repeat time and crime similarity may be hampered by outside factors. The

Repeat Similarity Ratios

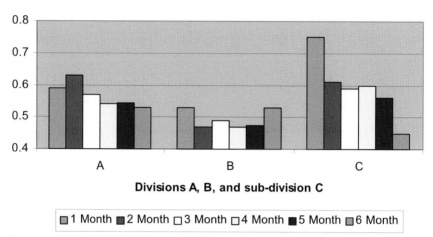

Figure 4.11 Similarity index for burglary repeats over 6 months for 'A' and 'B' divisions, and 'C' sub-division.

areas are close geographically, but are quite different socio-economically, both within divisions and between divisions. The selection of complete divisional areas as data sources is perhaps masking the relationships between repeat victimisation and other factors.

Repeat victimisation and social deprivation

The work outlined above indicated that the course of repeat victimisation was not the same in all areas, and that large area analyses could mask relationships that were seen to exist at a local level. Other variables, especially those related to socio-economic data, were thought likely to account for local variability in repeat victimisation. Research linking the distribution of crime and social conditions is common in criminology (for a starting point, see Elliott and Ellingworth 1996; Farrington 1996; Hakim 1982; Reilly and Witt 1992), as is the search for relationships between deprivation and property and violent crime (Herbert 1976; Mayhew *et al.* 1993). The use of census-based areal units and factorial ecological techniques to study the link between crime and social structure is a common theme (Hirschfield *et al.* 1995; Hirschfield and Bowers 1997).

   An earlier research study (Ratcliffe and McCullagh 1998a) determined that repeat domestic burglary victimisation locations showed a different spatial distribution from lone burglary and that the repeat times in different areas were variable. Another study (Ratcliffe and McCullagh 1999) showed a statistically significantly different social deprivation level for repeat properties, compared with houses victimised by a lone burglary event, with the location stressed rather than the number of incidents at a particular site. The existence of a relationship involved calculating an areally weighted spatial average of the Index of Local Conditions (Department of Environment 1995) derived from census data associated with enumeration district boundaries, in the vicinity of repeat and non-repeat burglary locations. The Ratcliffe and McCullagh study applied the technique to the full 'C' division of the previous example, an area with a broad rural/urban mix encompassing a wider variety of deprived and affluent areas than the sub-division studied initially. The following discussion explains and expands some sections of the analysis conducted for that study.

The calculation of a spatially weighted average of the ILC was necessary because point locations of crime were being assigned a social deprivation

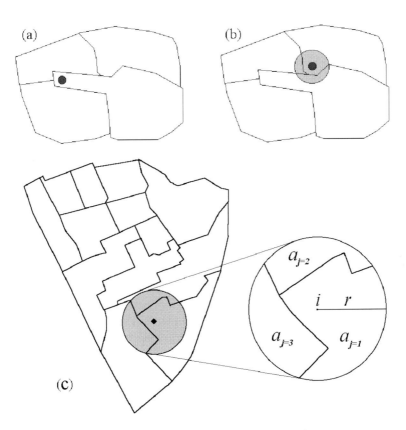

Figure 4.12 (a) Peninsula effect; (b) the possibility of error due to inaccurate geo-referencing, and (c) *vicinity*-type extraction of areally weighted variable from surrounding polygons.

index based on the census enumeration areas in which they fell. This problem, and its solution, can be seen in Figure 4.12 where in Figure 4.12a the burglary shown as a geo-referenced dot would be erroneously associated with the bottom right polygon, even though the two left polygons are close to the point. This is the peninsula effect. Geo-referencing itself is also not without error, possibly up to 100 metres if the PAF (postcode address file) is relied on rather than the Ordnance Survey address point (Gatrell 1989). This type of inaccuracy is demonstrated in Figure 4.12b where a different point (same enumeration district background) is shown within its area of error. The grey circle shows the region where the true location might lie. Any use of the deprivation index for a single enumeration district would be incorrect in either case, and a spatially weighted amalgam would be necessary from all the surrounding districts.

The final value of the deprivation variable for Figure 4.12c is called the 'vicinity' value (V) and calculated as:

$$V_i = \frac{\sum\limits_{j=1}^{j=n} x_j a_j(r)}{\sum\limits_{j=1}^{j=n} a_j(r)} \quad (1)$$

where V_i is the *Vicinity* calculation of a variable at a point i, with a number of regions (j) within radius r of i, and $a_j(r)$ represents the area of a region within r of i. When used with crime locations and the ILC, we are able to calculate a deprivation index centred on the burglary location instead of using the location's single enumeration district social deprivation value.

The local sub-divisional study

From the original burglary data 843 premises were identified as being 'unique' burglary sites and 89 locations were the sites of 'repeat' incidents. A significant question when applying an areal weighting is the radius to use. Different results could be expected for different circle radii. Three different buffer sizes were employed, 200 metre, 350 metre and 500 metre radii, to identify any significant differences in the results. Table 4.1 lists the

Table 4.1 Mean areally weighted deprivation values for six sub-divisional data-sets

	200 m buffer	350 m buffer	500 m buffer
Repeat locations	−1.869	−1.980	−2.051
Unique locations	−3.060	−3.080	−3.069

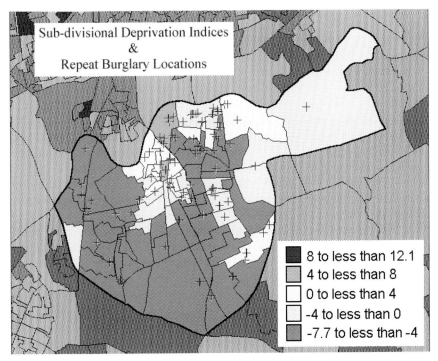

Figure 4.13 The deprivation index values across the local subdivision police area is shown as a shading, and the location of repeat burglaries as crosses.

results which show that repeat locations appear to display higher values for social deprivation (a positive value indicates greater deprivation) at all scales examined.

The study area does not demonstrate as great a heterogeneity of deprivation index values as the whole of the division, but it does show a variation in the Index of Local Condition values in its mainly affluent suburbs. In Figure 4.13 higher values of the deprivation index mark areas of higher deprivation, but 'high' should be interpreted in the light of Tower Hamlets exhibiting values three times higher than the highest here: this is a fairly affluent neighbourhood! It is visually very clear that the repeats are found in the more socially deprived enumeration districts.

A Mann–Whitney test compared deprivation values calculated for each burglary location in repeat/non-repeat victimisation groups for each areal weighting radius choice. The test results show that differences between the distribution of the vicinity deprivation values for the unique and repeat burglary locations are significantly different at least at the 0.005 level at all scales examined. Repeat burglary locations are found in significantly more deprived areas than unique burglary sites in the police sub-division.

Vicinity study at full divisional level

The results from the local study appeared to show a significant relationship between repeat victimisation and the spatially weighted deprivation index. However, conclusions based on the results of a small study such as this should be treated with caution. The research was extended both to increase the numbers in the data-sets and to use a more heterogeneous social area including affluent suburbs, council estates and rural villages. During the study time, 3,549 separate locations were identified as being the victim of a lone burglary and 519 locations were identified as having at least one repeat incident in terms of domestic burglary data for the two-year period April 1995 to April 1997. When mapped to the relevant police division boundaries, 499 enumeration districts lay within the study area. This data-set includes the area covered by the local sub-divisional study.

A difficult question is to determine how big the areally weighting circle radius should be for this type of analysis. The choice of radius for the analysis was considered relative to the average size of the enumeration districts in the study area. An upper limit could be a circle with a radius of about 750 metres as this would approximate the same area as the average enumeration district within the division. Larger size would lead to averaging too many enumeration district areas and the characteristics of each would be lost. Also there is a considerable variation in the size of enumeration districts in the division owing to its mixed rural and urban nature. A smaller radius would be essential in urban areas to reduce averaging of areally small enumeration district values, with possibly very different deprivation characteristics. It was essential that the radius chosen be sufficiently large to ensure that any misplacement of the crime location due to standard recording difficulties be adequately compensated, perhaps up to a distance of 100 metres. In addition in urban areas the radius needs to be large enough to allow for the peninsula location problem described previously. Five different radii of 0, 100, 200, 350 and 500 metres were examined to see if distance affected the outcome of the analysis of the full study. The zero metre buffer returns the exact deprivation value for the polygon in which the crime lies, and was included to test whether the radii-based Vicinity solution was generating vastly different and possibly unreasonable values. As expected the data extremes are reduced by the weighted averaging process compared with the exact values for a zero metre buffer, and are eroded steadily as radius increases. At each of the chosen radius levels there is a noticeable difference in the mean calculations for the Vicinity results, with the mean levels for the repeats appearing to be more positive (i.e. deprived) than for unique locations at all scales.

The question remains as to what radius should be chosen to represent deprivation scores at a given crime location. A Kruskal–Wallis H test of all the unique burglary locations showed no significant difference between radii choices in terms of calculated deprivation value. This indicated that the homogenising effect of the radius controlled areal weighting calculation of deprivation generated very similar data-sets for different radii, but were marginally different from the zero metre radius set. The reason for this difference lies in the spatial nature of the data which has at least as much importance as the statistical parameters of the data. The need to avoid the distribution problems of point locations mentioned earlier demands the acceptance of a spatially averaged smallest reasonable radius of 100 metres.

Separation of unique and repeat burglary distributions

The spatial distribution of the unique burglary locations, and those at which two or more burglaries have been committed within the two-year data-set across the division is shown in Figure 4.14. Figure 4.14a shows the distribution of the 3,549 unique burglaries, and Figure 4.14b shows the distribution of the 519 sites which were burgled more than once. The inset square delimits the area of magnification and provides an expanded view for the urban areas in the division. The majority of burglaries of all forms are concentrated in these urban areas, but the pattern of repeats can be seen to be much more patchy within the urban area, indicating a possible

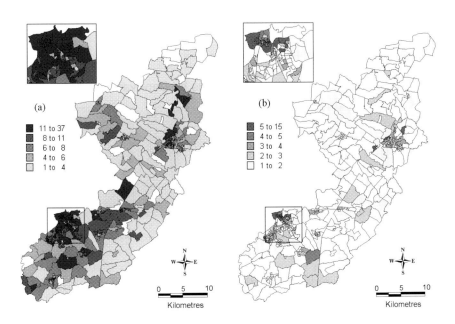

Figure 4.14 The maps show the number of (a) unique burglaries, and (b) repeat burglaries for every enumeration district in the full divisional area. Unshaded categories had no burglaries in the two-year study period.

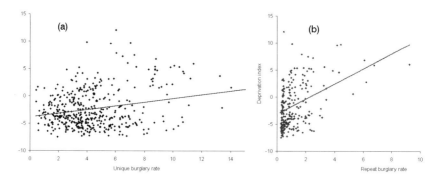

Figure 4.17 Data clouds and linear regression lines for unique (a) and repeat (b) burglary rates.

detailed discussion of the analysis is given in Ratcliffe and McCullagh (1999). A burglary rate in each ED was calculated for all unique and for all repeat data as the percentage of houses burgled during the two-year crime data-set window. The results of linear regressions between the unique and repeat burglaries and deprivation index are given in Figure 4.17.

Both regressions in Figure 4.17 were significant to at least the $p=0.01$ level, and all the regression slope coefficients were significantly different from zero. Both slopes showed a positive correlation between the number of crime events and an increase in deprivation index. In addition, the slope of the unique crime regression was significantly different and flatter than that of repeat burglary. The slope of the regression for repeat victimisation is about four times steeper than that for unique events. The slopes would indicate that there is a definite but limited relationship to increasing social deprivation for unique burglaries throughout the division. Both lines intercept the deprivation axis within less than one unit of each other for zero burglaries. This indicates more affluent (negatively deprived) EDs are those tending strongly to have low burglary rates. At a burglary rate of zero the regression lines are less than one unit apart at a value of about −3.5. Increasing numbers of repeat victimisation cases, on the other hand, are clearly indicative of rapidly increasing social deprivation. Deprivation values increase slowly with a rise in the unique event rate, but increase rapidly with rising repeat victimisation.

Spearman rank non-parametric correlations between deprivation index and unique and repeat burglary sets represented in the graphs were all significant at at least the 0.01 level. The results from these tests can be interpreted alongside the regression line, and indicate that there is a correlation between the unique and repeat rates of burglary and the deprivation index, and the slopes of the linear regressions are significantly different from each other.

Possible reasons for repeat burglary patterns

This large divisional study concentrated on location and determined that the level of social deprivation, as measured by the ILC, in the vicinity of unique burglary sites and repeat burglary sites is significantly different. The deprivation index rises slowly in relation to an increase in unique burglary, but rapidly against repeat victimisation. It is reasonable to consider why this pattern should emerge. First, perhaps the availability of crime prevention resources is one explanation (Kennedy and Veitch 1997; Spelman 1995). Deprived areas with higher crime rates may not be able to afford either privately or from the public purse to take counter measures. In more affluent areas, however, direct home-owner action (for instance, the installation of burglar alarms) may defeat many repeats.

Second, recent work on policing style (Klinger 1997) suggests that police become more tolerant to minor crime in high crime areas. This feeling of crime as inevitable can be passed on to the local population who may likewise feel that the additional cost and effort of crime prevention measures may be worthless. In more affluent areas, police officers may perceive a lower crime rate and consequently have more time to perform routine patrolling. They may even be able to target actively their patrol routes to keep an eye on recently burgled premises. One of the authors of this chapter has some personal experience of this. Prior to entering academia the author worked for ten years in both Tower Hamlets and Central London as a police officer. Central London exhibited a low burglary rate and each incident was actively pursued by the local force with follow-up visits, crime prevention advice and increased patrolling. During the late 1980s and early 1990s, Tower Hamlets was the most deprived district in the UK (Department of the Environment 1995) and the burglary rate high. The sole crime prevention officer only attended those locations where the reporting officer felt any benefit would be achieved, and the sheer volume of criminal activity in the area meant that additional patrols were usually only ever increased for violent and drug gang-related incidents. Burglary was seen as inevitable.

Summative conclusions

The intention of this chapter was to investigate areas of concern in current crime analysis and to examine where new and remodelled spatial and temporal investigation techniques could improve the analysis of high volume crime at a local community level. The recent move within British policing towards a more decentralised, proactive style has shifted the analytical focus on to analysts and intelligence officers at the police divisional level who are now expected to be the hub of the local intelligence gathering effort. For high volume crime, this has left an analytical void. Force level analysis techniques are neither appropriate nor subtle enough to elicit any meaningful information at a local level from the mass of crime data generated within the police service.

An analysis of crime must be sure data have been both correctly extracted from a database and be positioned in the correct temporal context. This led to the necessity of outlining a new method of selecting accurately temporally unspecific crimes (aoristic and probabilistic aoristic search techniques) and also of identifying distinct spatial and temporal variations. Detection of hotspots of crime is essential to recognising patterns amidst noisy data-sets, and is a growth area within crime analysis. It is seen as one of the positive ways in which spatial analysis can usefully aggregate high volume crime data. A new two-stage process using a localised surface generation algorithm followed by a Local Indicator of Spatial Association (LISA) statistic was proposed as the best method available for outlining crime hotspots within a statistically significant limit.

Once the spatial and temporal definition of crime location is certain the use of geo-referenced crime data analysed within a GIS can be employed as an improved method of identifying repeat victimisation. It can be extended, using a new vicinity aggregation method, to reveal aspects of the distribution of burglary crime with respect to local social deprivation levels. The recognition that repeat victimisation is concentrated in more deprived areas should be of benefit to crime prevention agencies to target resources more accurately.

The current changes in British policing that are being mirrored elsewhere around the world are changing the way that intelligence is gathered within the police service. This is likely to see continued development of local high volume analysis techniques as new possibilities are considered by police officers and academics. It is also likely that a revision of the place of crime mapping and analysis within the integrated crime management model (Amey *et al.* 1996) will prompt changes in focus and drive new techniques.

Note

1 Aoristic, without defined occurrence in time, from; Aorist (*SOED*); one of the past tenses of the Greek verb, which denotes a simple past occurrence, with none of the limitations of the other (past) tenses.

References

Amey, P., Hale, C. and Uglow, S. (1996) *Development and Evaluation of a Crime Management Model*, Police Research Group Police Research Series Paper 18, London: Home Office, p. 37.

Anderson, D., Chenery, S. and Pease, K. (1995) *Biting Back: Tackling Repeat Burglary and Car Crime*, Police Research Group Crime Detection and Prevention Series Paper 58, London: Home Office, p. 57.

Anselin, L. (1995) 'Local indicators of spatial association – LISA', *Geographical Analysis* 27(2): 93–115.

Bailey, T.C. and Gatrell, A.C. (1995) *Interactive Spatial Data Analysis*, London: Longman.

BCMP (1997) *Crime Awareness News*, Brent Crime Mapping Project, London.

Berkeley Police Department (1997) 'The Police Department GIS Prototype', http://www.ced.berkeley.edu/aegis/orna/orhtm.html.

Berry, W. and Jones, H. (1995) 'Investigating spatial patterns of crime through police statistics, crime surveys and census profiles – findings from Dundee housing estates', *Scottish Geographical Magazine* 111/2: 76–82.

Burquest, R., Farrell, G. and Pease, K. (1992) 'Lessons from schools', *Policing* 8: 148–55.

Campbell, G. (1992) 'GIS in the police environment', in J. Cadoux-Hudson and I. Heywood (eds) *Geographical Information 1992/3: The Yearbook of the AGI*, London: Taylor & Francis, pp. 114–18.

Clegg, M. and Robson, M. (1995) 'May the force be with you: as quickly as possible using GIS', Mapping Awareness 9: 30–3.

Department of Environment (1995) *Index of Local Conditions*, London, Department of the Environment.

Ekblom, P. (1988) *Getting the Best Out of Crime Analysis*, Police Research Group Crime Prevention Unit Series Paper 10, London: Home Office, pp. 1–42.

Ellingworth, D., Farrell, G. and Pease, K. (1995), 'A victim is a victim is a victim?', *British Journal of Criminology* 35(3): 360–5.

Elliott, C. and Ellingworth, D. (1996) 'The relationship between unemployment and crime – a cross-sectional analysis employing the British Crime Survey 1992', *International Journal of Manpower*, 17(6–7): 81.

Farrell, G. and Pease, K. (1993) *Once Bitten, Twice Bitten: Repeat Victimisation and Its Implications for Crime Prevention*, Police Research Group Crime Prevention Unit Series Paper 46, London: Home Office, p. 32.

Farrington, D. (1996) 'Quantitative criminology in the UK in the 1990s – a brief overview', *Journal of Quantitative Criminology* 12(3): 249–63.

Fox-Clinch, J. (1997) 'Crime and the digital dragnet', *Mapping Awareness* 11: 22–3.

Gatrell, A.C. (1989) 'On the spatial representation and accuracy of address-based data in the UK', *International Journal of Geographical Information Systems* 3(4): 335–48.

Gatrell, A.C., Bailey, T.C., Diggle, P.J. and Rowlingson, B.S. (1996) 'Spatial point pattern analysis and its application in geographical epidemiology', *Transactions, Institute of British Geographers* NS 21: 256–74.

Getis, A. and Ord, J.K. (1992) 'The analysis of spatial association by use of distance statistics', *Geographical Analysis* 24(3): 189–206.

—— (1996) 'Local spatial statistics: an overview', in P. Longley and M. Batty (eds) *Spatial Analysis: Modelling in a GIS Environment*, London: GeoInformation International.

Grescoe, T. (1996) 'The geography of crime', *Geographical Magazine* 9: 26–7.

Grogger, J. and Weatherford, M. (1995) 'Crime, policing and the perception of neighbourhood safety', *Political Geography* 14(6): 521–41.

Hakim, C. (1982) 'The social consequences of high unemployment', *Journal of Social Policy* 11: 433–67.

Harlequin (1997) 'Harlequin Criminal Intelligence System', http://webserver. harlequin.com/products/hcis/hcis.html.

Herbert, D.T. (1976), 'The study of delinquency areas: a social geographical approach', *Transactions, Institute of British Geographers* NS1: 472–92.

Hirschfield, A. and Bowers, K.J. (1997) 'The effect of social cohesion on levels of recorded crime in disadvantaged areas', *Urban Studies* 34(8): 1275–95.

Hirschfield, A., Bowers, K.J. and Brown, P.J.B. (1995) 'Exploring relations between crime and disadvantage on Merseyside', *European Journal on Criminal Policy and Research* 3(3): 93–112.

Hirschfield, A., Brown, P. and Todd, P. (1995a) 'GIS and the analysis of spatially referenced crime data: experiences in Merseyside, UK', *International Journal of Geographical Information Systems* 9(2): 191–210.

Hirschfield, A., Yarwood, D. and Bowers, K. (1997) 'Crime pattern analysis, spatial targeting and GIS: the development of new approaches for use in evaluating community safety initiatives', *Crime and Health Data Analysis Using GIS* Sheffield: SCGISA.

Hope, T. (1995) 'The flux of victimization', *British Journal of Criminology* 35(3): 327–42.

Hough, M. and Lewis, H. (1989) 'Counting crime and analysing risks: the British Crime Survey', in D.J. Evans and D.T. Herbert (eds) *The Geography of Crime*, London: Routledge.

i2 (1997) 'i2 crime analyst's notebook', http://www.i2ltd.demon.co.uk/.

ICJIA (1996) Illinois Criminal Justice Information Authority, *STAC User Manual*, Chicago.

ICL (1995) 'Press release: ICL take command at Nottinghamshire Police', http://www.icl.com/news/press_releases/03May95.html.

Johnson, S.D., Bowers, K. and Hirschfield, A. (1997) 'New insights into the spatial and temporal distribution of repeat victimization', *British Journal of Criminology* 37(2): 224–41.

Kennedy, L.W. and Veitch, D. (1997) 'Why are crime rates going down? A case study in Edmonton', *Canadian Journal of Criminology* 39(1): 51–69.

Klinger, D. (1997) 'Negotiating order in patrol work: an ecological theory of police response to deviance', *Criminology* 35(2): 277–306.

Knox, E.G. (1964) 'Epidemiology of childhood leukaemia in Northumberland and Durham', *British Journal of Preventive and Social Medicine* 18: 17–24.

Langran, G. (1989), 'A review of temporal database research and its use in GIS applications', *International Journal of Geographical Information Systems* 3(3): 215–32.

—— (1993) 'Issues of implementing a spatiotemporal system', *International Journal of Geographical Information Systems* 7(4): 305–14.

La Vigne, N. and Wartell, J. (1998) *Crime Mapping Case Studies: Successes in the field*, Washington, DC: Police Executive Research Forum.

Maltz, M.D., Gordon, A.C. and Friedman, W. (1991) *Mapping Crime in its Community Setting: Event Geography Analysis*, New York: Springer Verlag.

Mantel, N. (1967) 'The detection of disease clustering and a generalised regression approach', *Cancer Research* 27: 209–20.

MapInfo (1997) 'Mapplication: Crime Analysis', http://www.mapinfo.com.

Mayhew, P., Maung, N. and Mirrless-Black, C. (1993) *The 1992 British Crime Survey*, Home Office Research Study 132.

Mitchell, D. (1997) 'Crime, policing and GIS: an emerging technology?', *Association for Geographic Information Publication* 10.

Nagle, G. (1995) 'Urban crime: a geographical perspective', *Geographical Magazine* 56–7.

Northwood Geoscience (1998) *Vertical Mapper Version 2.0 Manual*, Ontario, Canada: Nepean.

Nulph, D., Burka, J. and Mudd, A. (1997) 'Technical approach to developing a Spatial Crime Analysis System with ArcView GIS', Washington, DC: US Department of Justice.

Openshaw, S. (1984) 'The modifiable areal unit problem', *Concepts and Techniques in Modern Geography*, 38: 41.

Openshaw, S. and Charlton, M. (1987) 'A mark 1 Geographical Analysis Machine for the automated analysis of point data-sets', *International Journal of Geographical Information Systems* 1(4): 335–58.

Openshaw, S., Craft, A.W., Charlton, M. and Birch, J.M. (1988) 'Investigation of leukaemia clusters by use of a geographical analysis machine', *Lancet* 1: 272–3.

Openshaw, S., Cross, A., Charlton, M. and Brunsdon, C. (1990) 'Lessons learnt from a post mortem of a failed GIS', *2nd National Conference and Exhibition of the AGI*, Brighton.

Ord, J.K. and Getis, A. (1995) 'Local spatial autocorrelation statistics: distributional issues and an application', *Geographical Analysis* 27(4): 286–306.

Page, J. (1997) 'Dial M for mapping', *Mapping Awareness* 11: 25–7.

Pease, K. (1997) 'Crime Prevention', in M. Maguire, R. Morgan and R. Reiner (eds) *The Oxford Handbook of Criminology*, Oxford: Clarendon Press, p. 1267.

Peuquet, D.J. (1994) 'Its about time – a conceptual-framework for the representation of temporal dynamics in Geographical Information Systems', *Annals of the Association of American Geographers* 84(3): 441–61.

Peuquet, D.J. and Niu, D.A. (1995) 'An event-based spatiotemporal data model (ESTDM) for temporal analysis of geographical data', *International Journal of Geographical Information Systems* 9(1): 7–24.

Polvi, N., Looman, T., Humphries, C. and Pease, K. (1990) 'Repeat break-and-enter victimization: time course and crime prevention opportunity', *Journal of Police Science and Administration* 17(1): 8–11.

Polvi, N., Looman, T., Humphries, C. and Pease, K. (1991) 'The time course of repeat burglary victimization', *British Journal of Criminology* 31(4): 411–14.

Raafat, H., Yang, Z.S. and Gauthier, D. (1994) 'Relational spatial topologies for historical geographical information', *International Journal of Geographical Information Systems*, 8(2): 163–73.

Ratcliffe, J.H. (1999) 'The genius loci of crime: revealing associations in time and space', PhD thesis, University of Nottingham, 314 pp.

Ratcliffe, J.H. and McCullagh, M.J. (1998) 'Aoristic crime analysis', *International Journal of Geographical Information Science* 12(7): 751–64.

—— (1998a) 'Identifying repeat victimisation with GIS', *British Journal of Criminology* 38(4): 651–62.

—— (1999) 'Burglary, victimisation and social deprivation', *Crime Prevention and Community Safety* 1(2): 37–46.

—— (1999) 'Hotbeds of crime and the search for spatial accuracy', *Journal of Geographical Systems* 1(4): 385–98.

Read, T. and Oldfield, D. (1995) *Local Crime Analysis*, Police Research Group Crime Detection and Prevention Series Paper 65, London: Home Office, p. 61.

Reilly, B. and Witt, R. (1992) 'Crime and unemployment in Scotland', *Scottish Journal of Political Economy* 39(2): 213–28.

Salinas Police Department (1997) 'Law enforcement use of Geographic Information Systems', http://www.salinaspd.com/gis_vb.html.

Sampson, A. and Phillips, C. (1995) *Reducing Repeat Racial Victimisation On an East London Estate*, Police Research Group Crime Detection and Prevention Series Paper 67, London: Home Office, p. 53.

Smith, P. (1997) 'High performance ambulances provide an intelligent response', *Mapping Awareness* 11: 19–21.

Spelman, W. (1995) 'Once bitten, then what – cross-sectional and time-course explanations of repeat victimization', *British Journal of Criminology* 35(3): 366–83.

Tempe Police Department (1997) 'Tempe Police Department's Crime Analysis Unit', Tempe, Arizona, http://www.tempe.gov/cau/default.htm.

Unwin, D.J. (1996) 'GIS, spatial analysis and spatial statistics', *Progress in Human Geography* 20(4): 540–1.

Weisburd, D. and McEwen, T. (1998) *Crime Mapping and Crime Prevention*, New York: Criminal Justice Press.

Wrighton, T. (1987) 'Crime pattern analysis – an application on the Police National Computer', *Journal of the Forensic Science Society* 27(5): 349.

Part II

Local authority applications

5 Combating crime through partnership

Examples of crime and disorder mapping solutions in London, UK

Spencer Chainey

The Crime and Disorder Act (1998) makes it a requirement for local organisations (such as the local authority, health authority and probation service) to work in partnership with the police for combating crime and anti-social behaviour. Essential to these partnerships is the sharing of information to help identify those areas to which crime prevention resources need to be targeted. Four of London's boroughs (Hackney, Brent, Southwark and Harrow) have been particularly active in establishing information-sharing arrangements between each community safety partner, and developing strategies to reduce crime and disorder in their local communities. Central to these partnerships for the identification of crime and disorder 'hotspots' has been the use of geographical information systems (GIS). Through the use of GIS, applications to support operational policing and crime prevention initiatives through crime pattern analysis have been developed. Each borough project has also benefited from the experiences of its London neighbours and working together have overcome many of the operational and technical issues surrounding the accessing, processing and analysis of crime and disorder data.

This chapter begins by reviewing some of the issues that other examples of GIS applications for crime pattern analysis have had difficulty in overcoming and in some cases have led to the failure of such projects. It is felt that attention to these issues by the four London boroughs has helped develop the successes that are now being achieved. Examples of applications and analyses generated by the projects will be illustrated, with emphasis placed on the importance of a partnership approach in using GIS to help combat crime. The way in which the projects are assisting local decision-making and informing the public, councillors, staff within each of the partner's respective authorities, local community groups and businesses will also be explained. The chapter will also demonstrate how the availability of these crime and disorder data is also adding value to other borough-wide initiatives, such as urban regeneration.

Introduction

The Crime and Disorder Act (1998) has made it a statutory duty for local authorities (with co-operation of other agencies such as the Probation

Service and Health Service) to work in partnership with their local police to reduce crime and disorder. Essential to these partnerships is the sharing of information to help identify those areas to which crime and disorder prevention resources need to be targeted. Four of London's boroughs (Hackney, Brent, Southwark and Harrow) have been particularly active in establishing information-sharing arrangements between each community safety partner, and developing strategies to reduce crime and disorder in their local communities. Central to these partnerships for the management of this information and the need to identify crime and disorder 'hotspots' has been the use of geographical information systems (GIS). Through the use of GIS, applications to support operational policing, crime and disorder auditing, and crime and disorder prevention initiatives through mapping and analysis have been successfully implemented.

This chapter will describe the approach that these borough partnerships have developed for information sharing, project partnership and the processing of crime and disorder data for mapping and analysis. Examples of applications and analyses generated by these borough projects will be illustrated with descriptions on how these outputs are assisting local decision-making and informing public consultation. The chapter will also demonstrate how the availability, mapping and analysis of this crime and disorder data is benefiting the preparation of funding bids for crime and disorder reduction programmes and adding value to other borough-wide initiatives, such as urban regeneration.

Project partnership and information sharing

The mapping and analysis of spatial patterns of crime is an effective tool for helping to generate a clearer picture of local criminal activity. In the United Kingdom this interest in mapping patterns of crime is no longer limited to just the police. Local Authorities in particular, acting on their new duties following the Crime and Disorder Act (1998), require access to police records on crime and disorder and see mapping these events as an effective way to help inform the process of understanding the location of crime 'hotspots' and the targeting of their community safety resources. However, whilst access to these records between local authority and police partnerships is now granted (based on a standard local Information Sharing Protocol signed by all relevant local partners) many local authorities are still having great difficulty in using police (or other partner's) data. Most problems arise from data that are not of a format that can be easily processed and prepared for mapping, that meet data protection requirements, and are accessible in a manner that is cost-effective for all concerned.

Many of the current problems in project partnership and information sharing were highlighted in a post mortem of a failed GIS (Openshaw *et al.* 1990). This failed project coincidentally applied GIS to assist in the mapping and analysis of crime data between a local police, council and university partnership. The mistakes and problems highlighted in this post mortem are becoming familiar barriers affecting many community safety partnerships across the UK. It is the awareness of such problems and barriers that the partnerships in Hackney, Brent, Southwark and Harrow have largely overcome and have helped each of these boroughs to develop their recognised successes.

In any such information-sharing and partnership arrangement, issues that need to be resolved include:

- clearly identifying requirements for data collection, data manipulation, appropriate types of analysis and outputs
- complete and consistent sets of crime (and other) data
- the availability of up-to-date information
- automated process for geocoding events
- a simple method and well structured procedure for handling information
- a high level of communication between data providers and data users
- appropriate type of GIS and supporting statistical analysis software, including ensuring the compatibility of data transfer and analytical techniques between software packages used by data providers/partners
- clearly establishing system expectations and project aims, plus the time-frame within which outputs should be expected
- consideration on who would be the most appropriate (and skilled) staff member(s) for the day-to-day operation of the project, and in which department would the project most appropriately be based for guidance, access to data, use of outputs, management reporting and impact on policy
- documenting procedures and analyses to a high standard and different readership forums
- user support by software vendors
- the availability of funding to make changes/updates to the system or training of user.

(adapted from Openshaw *et al.* 1990)

Many of the points above are linked to issues surrounding the need for a high level of communication between those partners engaged in information sharing. Issues of technology and system cost have largely been overcome by GIS software developments and reducing prices over the last ten years, but the lack of sufficient GIS expertise and knowledge still represent a barrier for those who want to develop day-to-day practical applications. For example, it is extremely rare to find in your local police station an officer who has knowledge in GIS and who could design mapping solutions that would have real value in operational policing.

Some of the more successful community safety partnerships that have implemented GIS have focused heavily on the development of a successful data-sharing and intelligence-sharing partnership between the local authority, the police and other partners. Of initial importance to many of the London partnerships was the securing of an efficient method to extract information held on the Metropolitan Police's Crime Report Information System (CRIS) and Control and Dispatch Management Information System (CADMIS), prepare the data for mapping, and sanitise those records that were to be passed over to the local authority (or other third party). The procedure of sanitising the data is required to meet compliance with the Data Protection Act (1998) and involves the deleting of any information that could in any way be traced back to identify an individual, whether he or she be the victim, offender, witness or informant.

Many of the London partnerships have also been addressing the issue of the lack of expertise in GIS within the police (and the lack of expertise in criminology within the Council) by the pooling of knowledge and in some cases, personnel within the partnership. By complementing expertise through intelligence sharing, both the council and police can develop more effective crime prevention initiatives. Working in this manner, and with guidance from a Crime and Disorder Mapping Steering Group – made up of senior management and the officers in charge of the operation of the system – has the additional benefit of establishing trust and the communication of outputs to the appropriate 'decision-makers' in the partnership's respective organisations. However, to ensure the effectiveness of any such outputs, of central importance is the accuracy of the crime and disorder data that is to be mapped.

Processing crime and disorder records for mapping and analysis

The requirement for detailed geocoding of police crime or disorder records (using the address information entered into a record) was not a requirement drawn into the original design of a CRIS or CADMIS record sheet. Geographic coordinates are added automatically to each record using the address details entered. Using the example of CRIS records, these co-ordinates are specific to a point that relates to a 250 m grid that covers the Metropolitan Police Service area. Thus any event that is recorded is assigned the coordinate (in this case the south-westernmost point) that is specific to the 250×250 m square within which the event occurred. These coordinates are sufficient for large scale analysis, but are not precise enough for more detailed identification of crime patterns. For many crime mapping applications and focused resource targeting, crime events need to be mapped to the precision of the individual property (or location they refer to) or to the relevant full postcode (represented by a centroid point that relates to approximately 14 properties).

Using the Ordnance Survey AddressPoint product as the geocoding reference database for assigning property precise coordinates to crime events, a typical hit rate for such events using a standard GIS geocoding operation is often less than 10 per cent (Chainey 1997). This poor hit rate is largely due to information on the crime being entered into the wrong CRIS field (and consequently not matching with AddressPoint's arrangement of address information), misspelt street names, address abbreviations, unrecognised addresses that are only of local reference, address information that is not property-specific (such as car parks) and are not contained in Address-Point, and property that has been constructed since the latest release of AddressPoint. Problems also lie in AddressPoint itself, where tests conducted by the Brent Crime Mapping Project revealed AddressPoint to be only about 80 per cent accurate. Inaccuracies in AddressPoint related to: (1) information pertaining to the property, such as business names being incorrect or not noted in AddressPoint, and the formatting/column entry of information such as flat or building suffix numbers being inconsistent; and (2) and the spatial accuracy of the eastings and northings coordinates for the property, where for example AddressPoints would be mapped to the wrong location.

For the volume of information that these London borough partnerships require to process each month (that include approximately 3,000 crime records per borough) a method that is quick and efficient in its geocoding, plus consistent in its output was required. In addition a process was required that would accurately sanitise each record.

Each of the four London borough partnerships use OmniData, a product designed by Infoshare Ltd, to extract Metropolitan Police crime and disorder records and geocode these events to the accuracy and precision required. OmniData uses AddressPoint as its foundation, then builds upon it by including local authority-held property information (see Figure 5.1). Many local authorities have some form of property gazetteer. For example, in the London Borough of Hackney the Council maintains a gazetteer of all properties they manage and rent to local residents. Building this locally managed and centrally updated local authority property information on top of AddressPoint creates an OmniData reference property gazetteer of greater content and often of improved accuracy. The OmniData product also allows data entry of locations that are not postal specific (e.g. recreational parks, cemeteries, playgrounds and car parks), and place names that are only of local reference. The result is a comprehensive property and location gazetteer that is richer in content and will improve geocoding hit rates.

Before batch geocoding of crime and disorder events begins, OmniData performs a data cleaning process on each event's listed address information. This crucial address cleaning process uses the property and location gazetteer to correct any spelling mistakes, re-write in full any word abbreviations (e.g. Rd to Road), and correct the formatting of information where parts of an address have been entered into the wrong field (for example, cut street numbers from the record where they appear in the

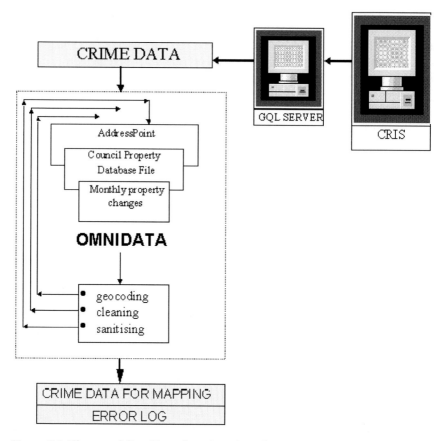

Figure 5.1 The use of OmniData for extracting, cleaning, sanitising and geocoding crime data for the purpose of mapping.

same column as the street name, and paste them to a separate street number column). The processing of 3,000 CRIS records through Omni-Data's automatic data cleaning procedures, using a standard 448 MHz Pentium II computer, with 64 Mb of RAM, running Windows NT, takes approximately one hour. The result is a clean and correctly formatted address-based event record that is written in a consistent format and that matches the address listing format of the property and location gazetteer. This cleaning process also reads the fresh address listing and writes its accurate full postcode. Once this process has finished, the geocoding of each of the 3,000 records is completed in little more than a few seconds.

Two geocoded output files are written from OmniData:

(1) A police file – that contains all information pertaining to a crime, geocoded to individual property precision; and

(2) A council file – that is sanitised to comply with the Data Protection Act, 1998. Crimes are geocoded to the precision of the full postcode (using the full address information available as displayed in the Police file to assign the accurate postcode) and do not contain any other information that relate to any individual (such as person names).

An error log is also written that tells the user of any corrections that have been made to the crime data during the cleaning and geocoding process. This error log can be used by the crime analyst to check for assumptions made by OmniData during its data cleaning process and also flags up properties or locations that were not referenced in the property and location gazetteer. The analyst is required to geocode these events manually, but is invited to enter the property/location details for this non-geocoded event so that next time a record appears with this address it will be automatically geocoded.

For certain crimes, full address information is difficult to collect. For example, if a person has been robbed on the High Street the victim will often have no idea whether the offence occurred outside number 32 High Street or number 76 High Street. This means that the address information contained in the CRIS report may only contain 'High Street, Hackney'. In these events most other procedures (either manual or those run as programmed operations) will geocode the record to the street centre point, or other common point along the street. If this happens on numerous occasions over a period of time the result creates a cluster of crime allegations at this centre point which may result in a false 'hotspot' at this location. OmniData addresses this problem using a combination of two methods:

• The CRIS record contains a field called 'Location text'. In situations when a crime has occurred and the victim does not know the street number or exact premise name of where the offence took place, text details describing the location of the crime are often written instead into the 'Location text' field. For example, a person has been mugged on the High Street, but does not know the street number outside which the offence took place, but does know that it was near the store Sainsbury's. The CRIS record would contain the address details:

Street number:
Street name: High Street
Town: Hackney
Postcode:
Location text: near Sainsbury's
OmniData will recognise 'Sainsbury's' as the business name of the address and using the up-to-date gazetteer will geocode the offence to the appropriate location. Similarly, OmniData also recognises

'Location text' that contains '. . . junction with . . .' or '. . . j/w . . .'.
Thus, a CRIS record containing the address details:

Street number:
Street name: High Street
Town: Hackney
Postcode:
Location text: High Street j/w Jones Street

will also automatically be geocoded to the point that is computed to be
the property or location reference point from the OmniData gazetteer
that is closest to the intersection of the two streets. Approximately
25 per cent of reported crime allegations do not contain full address
information in the CRIS address field (Chainey 1997). Of these 75 per
cent contain useful 'Location text' that can be used to improve mapping accuracy.

- One quarter of crime records that do not contain full address information also do not contain useful 'Location text' (in total this represents
  approximately 6 per cent of all CRIS records). Whilst all these crimes
  will be geocoded to the correct street and have a high probability of
  being mapped with the use of OmniData to within 150 m (Chainey
  1997), an additional technique is used to improve the accuracy of
  where the offence was likely to have occurred. This final OmniData
  process works by

  (a) identifying the crime type of the record that can not be precisely
      geocoded
  (b) performing an operation similar to looking up and down that
      street to identify similar crimes by type that have been geocoded
      with a high degree of confidence (i.e. full address information was
      available)
  (c) geocodes this event using a weighting calculated from the distribu-
      tion of confidently geocoded points of the same crime type. This
      weighting is based on both an element of random distribution
      along the road and a gravity pull to points representing similar
      crimes that have been geocoded confidently.

In addition, OmniData writes a 'validation code' describing the address
information that was available to geocode the event. Using this validation
code we can select those crimes where there is an element of locational
uncertainty in where they actually occurred and colour code them accordingly.

The unique way in which OmniData cleans and organises the file to be
geocoded and the advanced detail of information contained in its property
and location reference gazetteer allows us to map crime allegations both accurately and to the two levels of precision the borough partnerships require.

In an experimental study, using OmniData as a geocoding tool resulted in a 99 per cent hit rate and a final geocoding accuracy at property precision of 90 per cent and at postcode precision of 96 per cent (Chainey 1997).

Crime mapping analyses and applications

Described below are examples of how the London Boroughs of Hackney, Brent and Southwark are applying geographical information systems to assist in tackling their local crime and disorder problems.

Deploying police resources

An output of Brent's Crime Mapping Project, an innovative two-year programme that began in 1996 to help develop police and local authority partnered work in combatting local community safety problems, was the production of twice weekly patrol briefing maps. These maps were incorporated into intelligence reports to assist in identifying recent crime patterns and problem forecasting. The maps (see Plate 4) showed three elements of recent crime trends:

- an underlying trend in high volume crime hotspots based on the previous four weeks of offences
- crimes (mapped with a relevant symbol) showing those offences that had occurred over the past four days
- and crimes (using a similar symbol set) showing offences that had occurred over the eight days prior to this four-day period.

The darkness of the symbol shading represents the degree of certainty attached to the mapped location (the darker the shading the greater the confidence placed in the offence location). The maps proved effective in capturing and displaying short-term against longer-term crime trends. For example, maps of this type would highlight areas of recent activity where previously there had been very little. By combining this mapped inform-ation with other intelligence such as time of day analyses, methods of entry, goods stolen and offender profiles, briefing officers could more effectively deploy their patrolling officers to areas of recent events in an effort to help prevent crimes of similar type from re-occurring.

A three-month period of consultation with patrolling officers, crime analysts and detective inspectors was carried out to test the feasibility of different types of map design. From the day the maps first went 'live' these outputs continued to evolve and to meet requests made by end users.

The generation of these briefing maps proved to be effective in helping to target resources to areas of emerging crime concerns and was seen to act as an important tool that helped the police to reduce crime by 14.5 per cent during the course of the two-year project.

The production of this type of output also proved to both sides of the Crime Mapping Project partnership the added benefits that can come from partnership working. The close working relationship that operated between each partner's dedicated Crime Mapping Officers allowed skills in GIS, cartographic design, criminology, software engineering and user consultation to be transferred and delivered outputs that produced benefits for the local community.

Crime and disorder auditing and reduction strategies

The use of GIS has been important in helping the production of recent Crime and Disorder Audits in many community safety partnerships across the United Kingdom. This has been particularly so in the London Borough of Hackney where the use of GIS was at the heart of the process for selecting and presenting area-based crime and disorder information (see http://www.hackney.gov.uk). GIS was used in Hackney to map hotspots of crime for particular crime types, provide summary tabular information by crime type for ward areas, perform area-based time analysis (such as crime type day of the week prevalence), and area-based offender and victim profiles. The generation of these types of GIS-based outputs proved to be essential in the consultation and presentation process that followed. Information displayed as maps, graphs and clearly structured tables made it easier for the local community to understand some of the issues and to be more confident in contributing their own ideas.

The provision of this map-based information also provided the starting point for Hackney's Crime and Disorder Reduction Strategy Group to address priorities, set targets and coordinate community-based programmes for combating these local problems.

Working on from this success, the use of GIS now provides the central role in helping to inform strategic management across Hackney's community safety partnership with monthly area crime reports. These monthly reports provide the vital level of detail required to prompt discussion on recent crime and disorder events, crime trends, the results of targeted crime reduction initiatives and the definition of new priority areas. These monthly reports include hotspot maps for particular crime categories, tables describing crime counts at ward and neighbourhood levels, and graphs showing the change in crime types by neighbourhood and for the borough as a whole over the last 13 months.

Hackney's focused crime category working groups (such as those responsible for delivering strategies to reduce robbery, burglary or anti-social behaviour) receive quarterly reports, similar in structure to the monthly neighbourhood area profiles, which show the recent volume and patterns of specific crimes. These are used to inform each group of changing patterns and help prompt discussion about underlying causes and action plans. For example, Hackney's Burglary Reduction Working Group receives area reports profiling residential burglary, non-residential burglary and burglary artifice (i.e. burglary allegations that result from bogus callers). Additional information supplied by Hackney's GIS team help show possible links to offender behaviour, housing type and other socio-economic causes. These area reports also provide a quick method for measuring the impact of recent targeted crime and disorder reduction programmes, and prompt discussion for their improvement or direction to other areas of similar need.

GIS crime mapping solutions for closed circuit television

Closed circuit television (CCTV) has become one of the main tools for preventing, detecting and deterring street crime and disorder in many town centres in the United Kingdom. As the demand for CCTV has grown, there has also been an increased need to target areas which stand to benefit most from this particular form of crime prevention more effectively and to provide cost-effective means for measuring their effect. GIS has again been seen as one of the best tools to assist this process particularly for prioritising sites for CCTV installation, optimising camera locations, mapping their coverage, and monitoring how their use impacts upon local crime patterns (Chainey 1999; Hough and Tilley 1998).

The London Borough of Hackney is using the crime hotspot outputs it can produce from its GIS to identify priority areas for CCTV installation. By deciding on priority areas, the borough can prepare more competitive bids to the Home Office for funds to invest in CCTV installation. The maps Hackney produce show the general distribution of crime across each hotspot area from which a crime profile describing the type and nature of each hotspot can be generated. From this, optimal sites for CCTV camera locations can also be decided. This optimising process does not require a large amount of sophistication, where often local crime hotspot maps and knowledge of the area provide the level of detail required to help optimise camera views. These site proposals then present the CCTV site engineers and planners with options for camera location and potential coverage. Where GIS does provide an additional role is in measuring the area camera coverage of these site options to help plan for the minimum number of cameras for the maximum required view. For example, if ten cameras in more optimal locations instead of eleven can cover the area required, immediate savings of one camera (approximately £12,000) can be made.

Hackney's CCTV surveillance officers and local police officers also require detailed maps that show individual CCTV camera locations and the areas they cover. These are important reference materials for relating local crime and disorder events to potentially captured incriminating evidence. Figure 5.2 shows an example of a mapped CCTV camera coverage. The map shows the location of the camera and three different coverage descriptions that relate to the on-screen image height of the

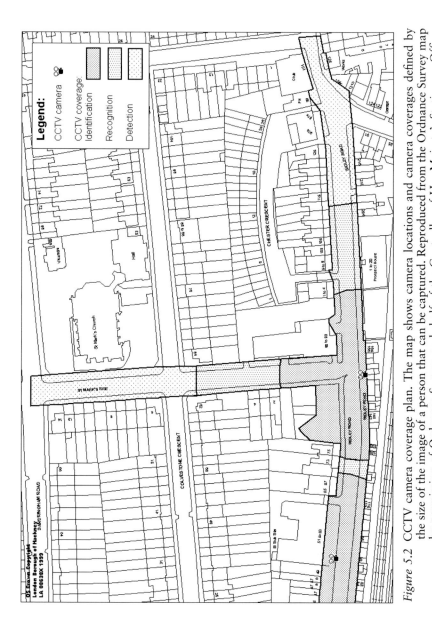

Figure 5.2 CCTV camera coverage plan. The map shows camera locations and camera coverages defined by the size of the image of a person that can be captured. Reproduced from the Ordnance Survey map by permission of Ordnance Survey on behalf of the Controller of Her Majesty's Stationery Office, © Crown Copyright ED 275514.

person captured in the camera's view (see Chainey 1999 for further details on calculating and defining coverage descriptions). These mapped camera coverages also act as the source areas from which to monitor changing crime counts and the drawing of local and neighbourhood buffer zones for monitoring potential crime displacement.

The mapping of these camera coverages has enabled the London Borough of Hackney to measure accurately and cost effectively, reductions in street robbery within areas covered by CCTV in Dalston Town Centre (a reduction of 31.6 per cent), and in Hackney Town Centre (11.2 per cent reduction). GIS-based analysis also revealed there to be no apparent local displacement. Instead street robbery in the area immediately neighbouring CCTV coverage also significantly reduced.

Spatial and temporal patterns of repeat burglary

The ability to be able to identify areas of repeat burglary continues to be a popular method for attempting to target the limited resources that are often only available in a manner that will have the highest impact on reducing the overall local burglary rate. Repeat burglary alone typically accounts for approximately 15 to 20 per cent of all burglaries in any one area (Ratcliffe and McCullagh 1998; Johnson *et al.* 1997; Farrell and Pease 1993). Both Hackney and Brent have conducted repeat burglary analyses where results have contributed to helping to form strategies that aim to reduce local burglary problems.

In studies that followed a similar methodology to Johnson *et al.* (1997), Hackney and Brent identified hotspots of repeat burglary and charted the time delays that existed between repeat events. Both analyses were conducted at local borough police stations due to the restrictions imposed on sharing information that is property-specific for the purposes of strategic analysis. Outputs listing particularly vulnerable properties can though be shared across the partnership to aid resource targeting.

The use of the OmniData data cleaning and geocoding product was seen by both boroughs to be essential in helping to overcome the many problems that Johnson *et al.* (1997) experienced in recognising repeated addresses in a crime database. For example, if a burglary was reported at 'Flat 10a, St Martins Road', the address can be entered into a database in a number of different ways. Examples could include:

- 10a St Martin's Rd
- Ground Floor Flat, 10 Saint Martins Road
- Flat 10a St. Martyns Rd
- Flat A, 10 St Martin's Road.

If we were then to perform a selection from the database where all burglary records that were listed more than once were grouped and assigned a count representing the number of times they appeared, the results would not provide a comprehensive picture of the repeat burglary problem. Many police forces and local authorities wishing to identify properties across their borough that have been repeatedly burgled are still experiencing many of these address recording difficulties when it comes to performing selections. Several police forces have attempted, but with little success, to use a flag in the burglary crime record that can be filled in when the victim is questioned about the incident and any previous events. Problems in this method are usually linked to the inconsistent filling in of this field on the crime record or the use of the flag to identify that the victim had previously been a victim of crime, but of a crime of a different type.

Through the use of OmniData in Hackney and Brent, archived crime record databases containing consistent address output and consistent easting and northing coordinates are written for each address record. If the address Flat 10a, St Martin's Road and all its variations were held in CRIS and passed through OmniData, OmniData would clean the address to a consistent single format and geocode it to its singular easting and northing coordinate. At the user's disposal would be a database upon which selection commands could be made to identify all those properties where there had been multiple burglaries more easily and more comprehensively.

The London Borough of Hackney has recently introduced a more advanced method that is making the selection of repeat burglary even easier to perform. Selecting and grouping repeat burglaries by their easting and northing coordinates is slightly prone to error due to the exactness and full consistency that must be required in each record's coordinate reference. Hackney has adapted Ordnance Survey Landline cartographic data from a line and arc set of vectors to one that is made up of polygons. Therefore, cartographic features such as building outlines exist as individual building polygons rather than as a selection of inconsistently connected lines and arcs. These building polygons act as the denominator to which crime points can be aggregated. To validate this information and add other records of burglary repeats, a query that selects repeats based on the cleaned address text can be performed. For example, where burglaries have been mapped precisely to the outline of the building to which the record relates, a query can be structured where the result returns a count value of the number of burglary points contained within each building polygon. This is validated with a text search on the address listing, after which a further selection based on the number of times a record appears can identify properties repeatedly burgled. The building polygon object can also act as the area that is thematically mapped, where the burglary count is the value used to display ranges in the number of repeats. This method is immediately visually appealing and can help to identify physical features that may link the building to its vulnerability (see Figure 5.3).

Brent's repeat burglary analysis identified that repeats alone accounted for 16 per cent of the total number of residential burglaries. Furthermore,

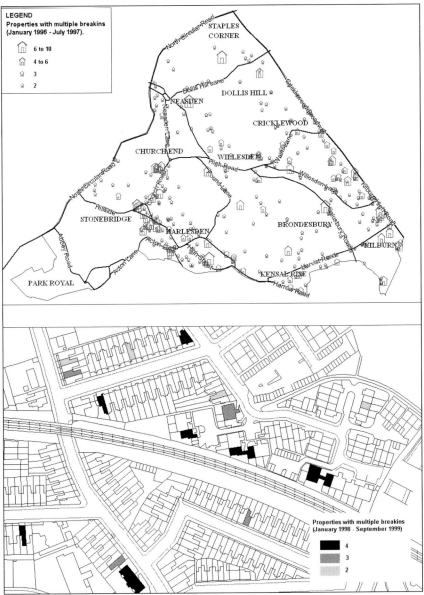

Figure 5.3 Mapping patterns of burglary repeats: (a) Symbol sizes that relate to the number of repeats provide an immediate general impression of burglary repeat incidence across a study area; (b) At smaller scales, thematic shading of building polygons describing burglary repeat incidence is a visually appealing method and can help to identify surrounding physical features, such as railway lines and end of terraces, that may expose reasons to the property's vulnerability. Reproduced from the Ordnance Survey map by permission of Ordnance Survey on behalf of the Controller of Her Majesty's Stationery Office, © Crown Copyright ED 275514.

almost 28 per cent of all burglaries for the time period queried were concentrated in less than 0.5 per cent of all properties. Analysis of the number of days between the first and repeat events revealed that:

- Thirteen per cent of all repeats over the 80-week period queried took place in the first week immediately following the initial event.
- Twenty-seven per cent of all burglary repeats took place within the four weeks of the initial incident.

Similar results were also generated in the London Borough of Hackney. Armed with these results both the council and police have been able to make more informed and structured decisions on where to target burglary prevention resources and how quickly they must respond to prevent the possible recurrence of similar events.

Residential burglary hotspots and their relationship with deprivation, social class, housing tenure and population age

As part of Brent's Crime Mapping Project, the innovative cross partner sharing of geographic information enabled the exploration of links between crime patterns and information describing the physical, social and economic characteristics of small areas. The Brent Project was particularly innovative as it began at a time prior to the Crime and Disorder Act (1998) after which it became a statutory duty for local authorities to work in partnership with the police to reduce crime and disorder.

One such analysis at Brent investigated links between residential burglary and factors such as deprivation, social class, housing tenure and population age structure. The aim of this was to help further inform the process of understanding spatial patterns in burglary and to provide useful guidance in targeting residential burglary prevention resources.

One of the most important results of the analysis identified that the distribution of residential burglary is not driven purely by one contributing socio-economic factor. The associations between crime and sociodemographic conditions which were uncovered proved to be useful in assisting the spatial targeting of resources. The analysis of crime patterns with these other geographic data types also exposed the potential of using underlying demographic data to assist future area based project work, such as exploring links between youth offending and the environments in which these offenders lived.

The most interesting result to emerge from the analysis was that of the correlation between levels of deprivation and residential burglary. Following methodology performed by Johnson *et al.* (1997), enumeration districts (EDs) were separated into ten different sub-divisions (or deciles) of the Index of Local Conditions (The Index of Local Conditions (ILC) is used to measure relative levels of deprivation. The Index combines a number of indicators – chosen to cover a range of economic, social, housing and environmental issues – into a single deprivation score for each area.) Each decile contained 10 per cent of the total number of EDs, grouped according to their levels of deprivation. The sum of residential burglaries grouped into these 10 deciles was calculated.

A chi-square calculation was used to indicate whether the level of residential burglary in an area was below or above that of the expected figure. Table 5.1 shows the chi-square value for each decile. The expected number of residential burglaries was calculated by dividing the total number of residential burglary by ten (the number of deciles). A negative chi-square value would show that the number of residential burglaries in the decile was less than expected. A positive chi-square would identify that a greater number of residential burglaries was observed than was expected.

The 10 per cent of EDs that were the most deprived (decile group 10) had the highest chi-square value. Thus, it appeared that the most deprived areas suffered more from residential burglary than any other area. In decile group 1 (the least deprived/most affluent collection of EDs) the chi-square value was negative, indicating that if one lived within one of these EDs there would be a lower probability of one's house being burgled than that of the average for the whole study area. The distribution of chi-square values across the deciles was not linear. Calculated chi-square values increased and stabilised between decile groups 1 to 3, but then fell for deciles 4, 5 and 6. Chi-square values increased to between 6.74 and 4.22 for deciles 7, 8 and 9, but then increased dramatically for decile 10. These calculations were then repeated using burglary rate figures for each decile and revealed an identical trend.

Table 5.1 Index of local conditions decile and chi-square value for expected residential burglaries in the London Borough of Brent

ILC decile (1 =least deprived 10 =most deprived)	Residential burglaries between (Dec 1995– June 1997) per decile	Expected residential burglaries (Dec 1995– June 1997) per decile	Chi-square value
1	278	342	−11.98
2	341	342	0.00
3	347	342	0.07
4	269	342	−15.58
5	285	342	−9.50
6	246	342	−26.95
7	390	342	6.74
8	384	342	5.16
9	380	342	4.22
10	503	342	75.79

Notes: Formula for calculating chi-square: $\Sigma\ [((Oi-Ei)(Oi-Ei))/Ei]$ for $i=1$ to k; O=observed value; E=expected value.

Subsequent analyses in these lower than expected residential burglary rates in areas representing deciles 4, 5 and 6 revealed a link to the targeting of local burglary prevention initiatives and the responsiveness of certain sectors of the community to burglary prevention funds. It had previously been assumed that an area's level of deprivation was closely linked to its residential burglary problem – the higher the deprivation level, the higher the burglary rate. This linear correlation has been demonstrated in many other similar studies (e.g. Johnson *et al.* 1997). However, in the years for which residential burglary data were analysed, many areas in Brent had been recipients of crime prevention initiatives from Brent Council, Kilburn Police and Harlesden City Challenge. Further work revealed that people who lived in the EDs represented by deciles 4, 5 and 6 had been the most receptive to the funding opportunities that were being provided by the borough's community safety partnership. These were most commonly people who lived in a terraced or semi-detached property, were concerned about their general well-being and aspired to improve their quality of life. They were likely to be on low to average incomes, in a skilled/partly skilled occupation, or retired, and either rented privately or owned their home. The type of burglary prevention initiatives that had been introduced over the period for which data were available included Neighbourhood Watch schemes and funding to fit home security systems (e.g. window locks) on privately rented or privately owned properties. Additional criteria included that recipients were to be in receipt of some form of income, housing or council tax support. These types of properties were particularly dominant in deciles 4, 5 and 6. EDs representing decile 10 tended to be made up of multiple-occupancy low-rise and high-rise blocks, housing residents who rented their property from Brent Council or from a local housing association. For these types of dwelling, security improvements usually needed to be more comprehensive to help reduce burglary. This would often require the installation of a more effective and more personal intercom system, the installation of CCTV on an estate, the co-ordination of services to maintain areas of public space, or the total redesign and redevelopment of the block or whole housing estate. These types of initiatives are more expensive and often cannot be met by funding of the type available through borough community safety burglary prevention strategies. In the case of those EDs represented by deciles 4, 5 and 6, the properties and the residents who lived in them were most commonly in the best position to meet the criteria to receive these low-cost burglary prevention funding schemes and that evidence of these initiatives successes were shown in the lower than expected burglaries in these decile groups.

It was then proposed that results from this analysis could help to target the use of the borough's burglary prevention funding in future years. Other areas of vulnerability could be exposed that house residents who would be in a position to be able to meet the criteria set by the funding schemes available (i.e. residents in deciles 3 and 7). The results also revealed the vulnerability to residential burglary of those residents who live in the most deprived areas. This information could then be used to assist in further informing larger-scale regeneration programmes such as the Single Regeneration Budget, citing the need to consider physical design aspects for areas, particularly social housing, that are vulnerable to crime and disorder.

Presenting the case for attracting crime prevention funding

The London Boroughs of Brent and Hackney have recently been successful in being awarded Home Office funding to help tackle local residential burglary problems. Central to both boroughs' preparations in their bids submitted was the use of GIS to identify and explain that the criteria set for funding were adequately met.

In Hackney's case the first need was to identify areas that had experienced a residential burglary rate that for three years was consistently twice the national average (i.e. a rate of fifty-four burglaries per 1,000 households). This required selecting mapped CRIS records of residential burglary, grouping counts by enumeration district for each of the three years and calculating annual burglary rates using enumeration district household counts obtained from the 1991 Census. The mapped results helped to prompt the initial discussions for identifying areas of priority and directly led to three areas being chosen for further work. This included detailed statistics describing burglary patterns in these areas and supporting information on deprivation, housing type, housing density, and other regeneration opportunities being explored. The Home Office then visited each area with local community safety representatives. From these visits the De Beauvoir area was chosen for priority and consultation began with local community representatives and council officers including the housing estate managers. GIS again proved crucial at this stage by providing detailed cartographic plans of the area, by revealing the nature of the local burglary problem, and by describing other physical and socio-economic conditions. The bid for this area was recently selected by the Home Office as one of three example model funding applications, and the De Beauvoir area has been awarded £60,000 to help tackle its residential burglary problem.

In late 1998, the London Borough of Brent prepared a similar bid to the Home Office for funding to help combat residential burglary. This first round of funding opportunities was once again to be allocated on a competitive basis to sixty areas that could meet the criteria, namely, that:

- the area had to comprise between 3,000 and 5,000 properties
- the area had to have a burglary rate of fifty-four burglaries per 1,000 properties per annum for each of the past three years.

The first task Brent performed was to create a residential burglary hot-spot surface that could reveal several peaks in the data where burglary rates were higher than two burglaries per hectare per year. This surface was contoured, enabling the peak areas to be selected and the number of properties within each area determined using the Council's Property Gazetteer. This then yielded a ratio of burglaries to properties. Once a contour had been established which contained the required number of properties and the appropriate number of burglaries, study areas were identified and submitted to the Home Office for review. Brent is fortunate in that it maintains a BS7666 compliant property database, wherein each property in the borough is given a unique property reference number (UPRN). This data-set is invaluable in linking property-based crime data to other information, such as the type, tenure and number of houses in any given area in the borough.

The method that Brent adopted meant that its application for funding was greatly enhanced, as it was much easier to explore the data in the relevant areas of high residential burglary. In this instance, the GIS proved to be a vital tool in building the case for central government investment and for extracting spatial and temporal burglary data. By using the GIS to identify concentrations of high residential burglary, the process of identifying where burglary had actually occurred in the previous three years became manageable and, importantly, was accessible and malleable in terms of decision support and case building. By using GIS effectively within its bid, Brent gave itself an edge over competing boroughs. The tangible benefit was to obtain £60,000 in funding to tackle burglary in a proven problem area. Without GIS at the core, it was felt that there was little doubt that the bid would have been less likely to stand up to Home Office scrutiny (Doyle *et al.* 1999).

Mapping noise nuisance in the London Borough of Southwark

The use of mapped police crime and disorder data is being advanced in the London Borough of Southwark by adding council-recorded noise nuisance complaints to its existing community safety database. These noise nuisance events are processed in a similar way to that of the Metropolitan Police's CRIS records and CADMIS disorder calls for service are prepared for partnership sharing and mapping. In this case it is the council who retain the property precision version of the data file that is mapped and the police (or other external partner) who are granted access to a sanitised version of these events. The mapping of these noise nuisance events is helping Southwark to determine and provide a clearer picture of disorder and anti-social behaviour patterns, beyond what was previously available from the police records.

The need to have access and integrate noise nuisance events with other anti-social behaviour and disorder records collected by the police was a key aim set out in Southwark's Crime and Disorder Reduction Strategy. Anti-social behaviour can include a range of activities such as noise victimisation and public disorder and its effect has a serious impact on the quality of life in Southwark. Noise nuisance complaints have been a key indicator in determining the levels and patterns of anti-social behaviour across the borough. Using the address reference of the noise nuisance complaint as the denominator to integrate with police recorded mapped data on anti-social behaviour is helping to better inform and target strategies for dealing with disorder.

Southwark used GIS and the mapped datasets of noise nuisance to identify in their 1998 Crime and Disorder Audit that complaints were concentrated in certain areas of the borough. Of the calls made to the council noise service, 40 per cent were from people reporting repeat or persistent victimisation. Through GIS-based analysis of these and other types of borough-wide patterns of noise nuisance complaints a more pro-active and problem-solving approach to tackling these problems has been introduced. Hotspots of noise nuisance were particularly centred on housing estates. The identification of these problems has led to the setting up of a multi-agency task group to look at the wider issues of crime and disorder in these areas, and to explore whether or not the pattern of noise nuisance complaints is an effective indicator of current or emerging crime and disorder events.

Holistic approaches to crime and disorder reduction strategies

The applications described above have shown how the mapping of crime and disorder data are helping to better inform the targeting, allocation and monitoring of community safety resources. Several examples have also shown how GIS can be used as the common platform to which information from disparate sources can be integrated to assist clearer decision-making and in some cases to identify possible causal factors underpinning crime and disorder. An example of how GIS can be used as this common platform to help bring together information is being demonstrated by the London Borough of Harrow in its attempts to help tackle local drug problems.

The Harrow DAT (drugs action team) Information Group was initially established in February 1998. The group's aim was to address the development of a local substance misuse database, a requirement of the White Paper, 'Tackling Drugs Together', with the objective of assessing the nature and scale of local drug problems in Harrow. This remit was then extended to encompass the Crime and Disorder Act, 1998. Information that the group wanted to bring together included:

- Metropolitan Police reported incidents of crime
- Police 999 calls for service
- London Ambulance Service call-outs
- Clients in drug and alcohol treatment programmes

- Young people in the criminal justice system
- School exclusions
- 1991 Census data
- Department of Environment, Transport and Regions deprivation data.

Referencing this information by its location proved to be the common denominator that would enable the integration of these data. This would then allow the group to identify more clearly, the nature of the local drugs problem and generate outputs in a format that could be easily understood by all members of the partnership. This process and use of GIS has allowed the Harrow DAT Information Group to identify where the main drug-related crime and substance misuse problems are, enable problems and solutions to be defined more easily, and aid the targeting and allocation of resources for substance misuse programmes. Importantly, the group recognised that a GIS in itself is not the solution or answer to any particular crime problem, but a powerful tool that can greatly aid in the corporate sharing, management and understanding of information.

This use of GIS in helping to bring information together from a variety of sources and in different formats to provide a more holistic approach to tackling an area's crime, disorder and associated problems is also being demonstrated in the London Borough of Hackney. Spatial patterns of crime and disorder are increasingly being used to assist Hackney's other corporate initiatives such as urban regeneration and combating social exclusion. The availability of these data helps to provide a more informed picture of some of the problems that have led to an area's conditions of deprivation and is helping Hackney to put together more holistic strategies that tackle these connected problems. A further example of this is a developing application at Hackney where data on crime incidents, demography, youth offending, housing, deprivation, and urban regeneration is providing a fresh approach to how the council tackles school exclusions and poor educational attainment.

Informing the public

An important component in crime and disorder prevention is informing and liaising with the public over proposed council and police initiatives. Many of the borough partnerships are attempting to do this through public consultation and presentations where mapped output can help identify the problems that need tackling. The Brent Crime Mapping Project was particularly innovative in its approach in informing local residents and businesses about local community safety issues. One of the most successful formats that the Brent Project used was its quarterly 'Crime Awareness Newsletter' (distributed externally to councillors, community groups, local businesses, and made available at libraries and council one-stop shops).

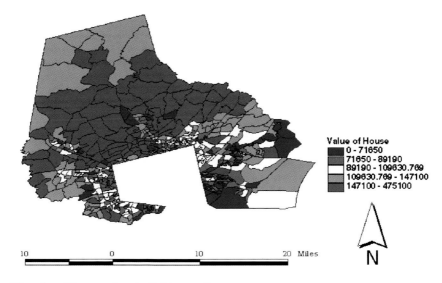

Plate 1   House values in Baltimore County.

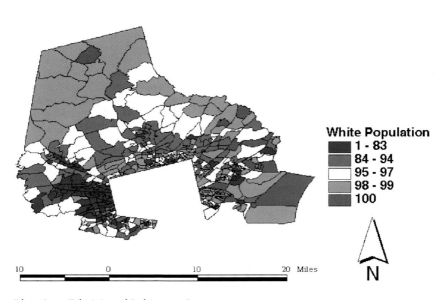

Plate 2   Ethnicity of Baltimore County.

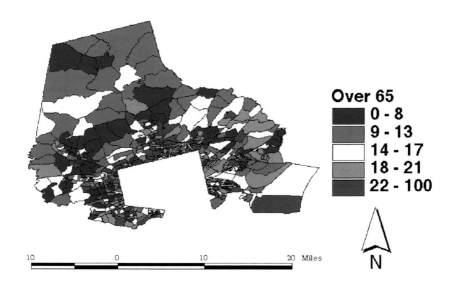

Plate 3   Elderly residents, Baltimore County.

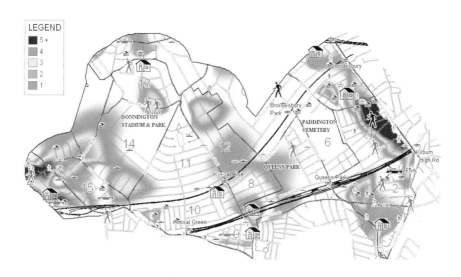

Plate 4   Police patrol briefing map.

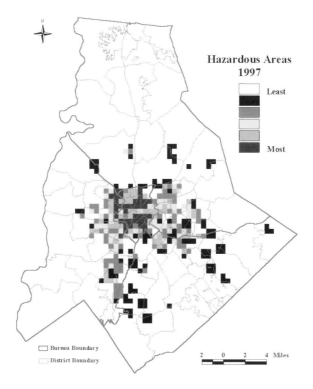

Plate 5 The geographic distribution of hazardous areas in Charlotte-Mecklenberg.

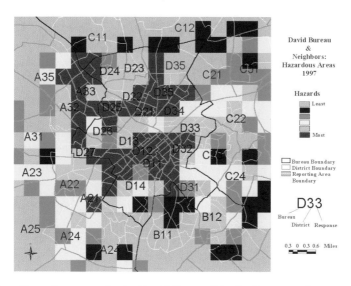

Plate 6 Hazardous areas in the David Bureau District Response Area.

Number of criminal damage incidents reported at Wirral Bus Stops (1/2/99 - 30/9/99)

Number of incidents reported over period
- 1
- 2 - 3
- 4 - 5
- 6 - 8
- 9 - 13
Wirral Bus Stops
Wirral Roads

Plate 7   Criminal damage to bus stops on the Wirral, Merseyside.

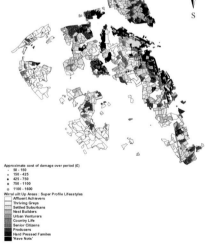

Super Profile Lifesytle Characteristics for Wirral Built Up Areas Compared to the Approximate Cost of Damage of Criminal Incidents Reported at Wirral Bus Stops (1/2/9-30/9/99)

Approximate cost of damage over period (£)
- 50 - 150
- 150 - 425
- 425 - 750
- 750 - 1100
- 1100 - 1600

Wirral Built Up Areas : Super Profile Lifesstyles
Affluent Achievers
Thriving Greys
Settled Suburbans
Nest Builders
Urban Venturers
Country Life
Senior Citizens
Producers
Hard Pressed Families
'Have Nots'

Plate 8   Cost of criminal damage to bus stops on the Wirral, Merseyside.

This newsletter described recent crime trends, provided a platform to promote good news stories about crime and disorder reduction, and gave details of new grant opportunities that residents could apply for to help improve the security of their own property. The newsletter also acted as a useful press release that could prompt local newspaper and television coverage of the project and bring into discussion, through community groups, issues or fears which local residents wanted highlighting. By involving the public and informing them about the proactive crime and disorder prevention initiatives in which the Council and Police were involved, the effect was to raise community satisfaction in policing and community safety services.

There is, though, a thin line between, on the one hand, being cautious about the amount of detailed information that is published but, on the other hand, releasing a sufficient amount of detail to enable the public and local communities to have an informed debate and to be proactive in their thinking about crime prevention. Crime and disorder maps that are released to the public by many of the London borough partnerships show crime trends over a period of months rather than days in order to divert attention from any single offences. Additionally, categories of crime are usually aggregated together in order to divert attention from any particular type of offence. Issues of sensitivity over the release of crime and disorder data were explored with community groups in the London Borough of Brent. Feedback gathered showed that people in Brent knew that certain areas had a crime problem. Previous surveys had also shown that the fear of crime was a major concern to local people and that public spending to tackle community safety was placed higher than education, traffic congestion, housing and care for the elderly as the top priority to which more resources should be directed. Residents acknowledged that the Brent Crime Mapping Project identified, in detail, those areas where people suffer most from being the victims of crime, but was important in demonstrating how the council and police were working in partnership to tackle those areas in most need, rather than directing resources to areas where people 'shouted the loudest'.

Conclusion

The crime and disorder reduction partnerships in the London Boroughs of Hackney, Brent, Southwark and Harrow have been developing many innovative and pragmatic solutions that are helping to combat local problems of crime and disorder. At the heart of many of these solutions has been the use of GIS to map incidents of crime and disorder and analyse spatial and temporal patterns. The use of GIS has played an important role in integrating data from their many disparate sources across the partnerships, presenting information in a way that can better involve the local community, provide outputs that assist strategic decision-making and the monitoring of targeted reduction initiatives, plus help build the case and support bids for investment.

Each borough has paid particular attention to efficient and accurate geocoding of crime and disorder records whilst ensuring that full compliance of the Data Protection Act (1998) is met. The benefits of having accurate crime data and the appropriate resources in place to deliver outputs have been the keys that have made many of the applications described possible, and have led to several of them being used as best practice examples by the Home Office, the Audit Commission and the United States Department of Justice. Particular efforts have been made by these London borough partnerships to adopt effective procedures for gaining access to information, for data management and for the use of the most suitable methods available for analysis.

All four of the London borough crime and disorder mapping partnerships continue to develop. Through their close working, the exchange of ideas are active between the boroughs, especially as new data (such as health service data) become available that can be integrated into analyses and help further inform strategies for, and that support, crime and disorder reduction. The use of GIS continues to be at the core of many of these processes, providing the link between presenting the information collected, and directing efforts that sustain the targeted reductions in crime and disorder.

Acknowledgements

The author would like thank those officers from Hackney Police and Hackney Council who have continued to support crime and disorder mapping efforts in the London Borough of Hackney, Simon Doyle (London Borough of Brent), Romy Conroy (London Borough of Southwark) and Felicity Holland (London Borough of Harrow), for their contributions, and Des O'Grady, Michael Read, Simon White (all London Borough of Brent), and Paul Green (Brent Police) for their vision and guidance during the period the author worked on the Brent Crime Mapping Project. The author would particularly like to thank Mark Patrick (previously Brent Police, now Scotland Yard) for his enthusiasm and commitment that made many of the early Brent applications effective, and his valued comments that continue to support the development of crime and disorder mapping applications across London.

References

Chainey, S.P. (1997) 'Accessing police crime data for the purpose of mapping: a re-evaluation of OmniData', *Brent Crime Mapping Project Report OD/2*, London Borough of Brent.

—— (1999) 'GIS crime mapping solutions for street closed circuit television', in *Crime Mapping Case Studies: Successes in the Field, Volume 2*, United States Police Executive Research Forum and the National Institute of Justice.

Doyle, S., Morris, C., and MacLean, A. (1999) 'Using geographical information systems for crime auditing and analysis', *Proceedings of the 1999 AGI Conference*, Section 5.8.

Farrell, G. and Pease, K. (1993) *Once Bitten, Twice Bitten: Repeat Victimisation and Its Implications for Crime Prevention*, Police Research Group Crime Prevention Unit Series Paper 46, London: Home Office.

Hough, M. and Tilley, N. (1998) *Getting the Grease to the Squeak: Research Lessons for Crime Prevention*, Police Research Group Crime Prevention Unit Series Paper 85, London: Home Office.

Johnson, S.D., Bowers, K., and Hirschfield, A. (1997) 'New insights into the spatial and temporal distribution of repeat victimisation', *British Journal of Criminology* 37(2): 224–1.

Openshaw, S., Cross, A., Charlton, M., Brunsdon, C., and Lillie, J. (1990) 'Lessons learnt from a post-mortem of a failed GIS', *Proceedings of the 1990 AGI Conference*, Section 2.3.

Ratcliffe, J.H. and McCullagh, M.J. (1998) 'Identifying repeat victimisation with GIS', *British Journal of Criminology* 38(4): 651–61.

6 A GIS-linked database for monitoring repeat domestic burglary

Kate Bowers, Martin Newton and Richard Nutter

One important consideration for practitioners in crime prevention is the identification of suitable targets for assistance through a particular initiative. In order for an initiative to maximise its impact, it is important to target those that are most vulnerable. All too often, practitioners will attempt to implement a scheme without adequate or up-to-date information, or without a systematic framework for making decisions on who, where and when to target. In the context of domestic burglary, it is particularly important to be in a position to respond quickly to data on recent incidents, since research has found that victims are most at risk of a repeat burglary immediately following an initial incident (Pease 1993). This chapter describes the development of a GIS-based database application which has been set up to assist in the identification of vulnerable targets for a domestic dwelling target hardening scheme run by the Safer Merseyside Partnership (SMP) in the Merseyside area. This system uses defined criteria to prioritise recent victims of burglary. Since it would be impossible to assist every victim of burglary on Merseyside, certain victims are given priority on the basis of their age and sex, their geographical location, their history of victimisation and the type of burglary they suffered. This prioritisation system is unique in that, it is operated from Merseyside Police Headquarters and, therefore, can produce targeting information on a daily basis. This ensures that vulnerable victims are contacted and assisted in a very short timescale.

Introduction

A central concern in the implementation of a crime prevention scheme is ensuring that the resources available have the greatest possible impact. One of the mechanisms which can be used to help achieve this aim is the selective targeting of particular areas, properties or individuals. The targets of a particular initiative are often outlined in original proposals for funding. For example, a crime prevention scheme might focus on a solid area of two streets, particular types of individual, such as young people or residential dwellings within a certain boundary.

Where there are resources available for every property or every possible recipient in an area to be assisted, the targeting task is fairly straight-forward. However, where there are numerous potential recipients and limited resources, the targeting process is likely to be more complicated. In this latter case it is important to ensure that the most vulnerable properties or individuals receive assistance.

Unfortunately, without adequate information, achieving this is virtually impossible. Information on the geographical location of neighbourhoods, properties and individuals that suffer from excessive levels of crime is a good starting point for identifying where efforts might be concentrated. In order to do this effectively, not only does appropriate information about crimes affecting areas, properties and individuals need to be available, but also the knowledge, skills and tools for processing that information to generate the right type of intelligence for resource allocation.

Geographical Information Systems (GIS) are central to the production of such intelligence. The targeting of crime prevention strategies can be facilit-ated greatly by information systems capable of handling spatially referenced crime and incident data and cross-referencing them with contextual information on land use, infrastructure and demographic and social conditions (Ekblom 1988). This is where GIS-linked applications have the most to offer. Good intelligence in this area is also essential for evaluating the impact of crime prevention programmes, as well as being an effective aid in the planning of police operations against crime.

The facilities of a GIS enable, at the most basic level, the spatial mapping of grid-referenced crime data. This gives the user an immediate visual impression of the distribution of particular offences, victims of crime and offender addresses and some indication of the clustering of crimes in space. Potential problem areas can be identified visually and hence focused upon. Further facilities allow the superimposition of different layers of inform-ation. For example, information about land use and populations of different areas can be related, both visually and through databases, to data describing individual crimes.

A clear advantage of GIS is that they enable links to be established and spatial relationships to be explored between data derived from different sources (e.g. calls to the police, crime reports, census variables, transport information and land use), and where appropriate data are available (e.g. grid-referenced individual level crime records), analyses can be undertaken which overcome the confounding effects inherent in the use of spatially aggregated data for pre-determined geographical boundaries (e.g. police beats). The types of analyses involved would include systematic searches for non-random clusters in point distributions through the derivation of standard deviational ellipses (e.g. delineation of crime 'hotspots'), by means of nearest neighbour analyses and through the application of other techniques (e.g. Ebdon 1988). GIS also enables the user to impose a specific geographical framework on crime data. For instance, one technique involves the aggregation of crime data to regular grid squares, and the cross-referencing of population data with this enables the identification of areas with particularly high crime rates, at a level of resolution specified by the user. This technique will be described further in this chapter. More general discussions about crime pattern analysis techniques can be found elsewhere (Hirschfield *et al.* 1997).

A further concern in the targeting of crime reduction initiatives is the scale at which target selection and sifting is conducted. Targets of crime and disorder which need protecting may be individuals, households and family units, social, ethnic or client groups, properties, organisations and institutions or public places. In a similar way, crime prevention measures aimed at reducing the vulnerability of potential targets may be directed at different scales. For instance, personal attack alarms, mediation programmes, racial harassment units, target hardening and CCTV are examples of crime prevention that work at different scales.

There is also the question of when to target. In proactive crime prevention strategies, for instance, there will be a need to reach vulnerable targets before they become victimised. Alternatively, the programme might seek to protect victims of crime from further victimisation. The targeting decision in this case may be influenced by data on recorded crime and the location of past 'hotspots'.

In some cases screening criteria for resource allocation are defined which utilise several scales or entities. For example, an initiative designed to impact upon repeat victimisation might offer assistance only to those individuals that have suffered more than one incident of a certain type of crime in the last year. There may be a further criterion which restricts assistance to victims who reside in a particular area. Furthermore, if available resources are particularly scarce, the targeting could be further refined by aiding individuals with certain characteristics (e.g. lone parents or vulnerable pensioners). Thus three scales or levels of targeting would be applied simultaneously: the property (i.e. whether it has suffered a repeat crime), the area and the social or demographic group (i.e. whether or not they are in a vulnerable client group).

The logistics of identifying the set of vulnerable targets to be assisted is therefore, by no means straightforward. The rest of this chapter will describe a software application that was produced to assist in the monitoring and target selection of properties suffering from domestic burglary.

The Safer Merseyside Partnership

For several years, the University of Liverpool in collaboration with the Safer Merseyside Partnership[1] (SMP) and Merseyside Information Service[2] (MIS) has been developing information systems to inform the targeting of initiatives to reduce repeat domestic burglary, business crime, arsons and hoax calls to the fire brigade, assaults and criminal damage on public transport and juvenile disturbances. The role of the information systems has been to produce effective procedures which assist in the targeting, monitoring and evaluation of crime prevention schemes.

An example of an SMP initiative which experienced initial problems with targeting was the Small Business Strategy (SBS). This scheme aimed to identify vulnerable small businesses within the partnership's operational areas (Pathway areas: European priority areas for the lowest income households) for potential financial assistance with security measures. In the absence of any victimisation information on businesses, the partnership implemented an 'open door' application procedure, where interested businesses were invited to apply to the partnership. The outcome of this was that businesses that were fairly well-off and were not struggling to survive were more likely to see and have the time to respond to the publicity. The partnership was inundated with requests for assistance and was finding it hard to make decisions on which businesses were in greatest need.

After a review of this procedure, a second phase of the Small Business Strategy was implemented. In this case, a targeting system was imposed. This started with a Merseyside-wide database of businesses. Those businesses that were small, and located within a residential part of a Pathway area were then selected. These businesses were then surveyed and information was obtained on the level of victimisation they had experienced and the number of crime prevention measures they had already installed at their premises. This information was then used to prioritise businesses. This meant that in the second phase of the SBS, businesses were assisted on the basis of need. The SBS demonstrated that an intelligence-led grant allocation system greatly facilitated the targeting, monitoring and evaluation of the scheme.

The vulnerable domestic dwellings scheme

Burglary of domestic dwellings has been a major focus of many crime prevention initiatives in the past. There have been many success stories to date concerning the effectiveness of burglary prevention schemes. For instance, a large-scale evaluation of the Safer Cities Programme was conducted (see Ekblom *et al.* 1996). The programme was nationwide and the evaluation of its domestic burglary element utilised information collected from 300 different properties. The evaluation used 'before' and 'after' surveys and local police crime statistics. Control areas were set up so it was possible to measure the extent to which any changes in the action areas reflected changes elsewhere. The overall results were encouraging, in that both victimisation surveys and the crime figures identified reductions in levels of burglary.

A further residential burglary intervention, the 'Biting Back' initiative, was implemented in an area of Huddersfield and concentrated efforts on victims of repeat burglary. An in-depth evaluation of that scheme demon-strated that it had been successful in reducing both overall levels of burglary and levels of repeat burglary against domestic dwellings over its period of operation (Chenery *et al.* 1997).

The SMP was keen to combat domestic dwelling burglary throughout Merseyside by implementing a scheme that offered financial assistance with target hardening to the most vulnerable households, in a similar way to the Huddersfield initiative.

As in the case of the Small Business Strategy, the target hardening scheme for domestic dwellings experienced problems in an initial phase of implementation. This first phase was very complex and operated differ-ently in the various districts of Merseyside. Essentially, in three of the five districts, the process involved faxed information from Merseyside Police's recorded crime system (the Integrated Criminal Justice System or 'ICJS') being received by Victim Support offices. In the remaining two districts, ICJS information was accessed directly by crime prevention officers.

The SMP had devised scoring criteria by which the vulnerability of different residential properties could be compared. The criteria gave the most weight to repeat victims of burglary, who had certain characteristics and only considered properties located within deprived regions of Merseyside (Pathway areas) for possible assistance. Therefore, after receiving the burglary information, all of the districts did an initial sift of this information to identify those likely to qualify for SMP assistance. The different districts had various individuals who then went out to visit and to elicit further information from the identified victims. In some areas, a crime prevention officer carried out this task, in other areas, it was a Victim Support volunteer and one of the districts had a dedicated surveyor in post for this task. The form used to make the final assessment, 'Form 52x' was completed in all cases. These were then scored. If the victim reached the threshold score specified by the partnership they were offered target hardening assistance. If they accepted this, the details were faxed directly to the contractor who carried out the work and then invoiced the SMP.

The SMP requested a management information audit of this system, in order to automate the system following the pilot phase. This was carried out by MIS and identified some problems with this manual paper-based system of target hardening:

- There was no central database that recorded information concerning the properties that were selected for target hardening. Neither were there any accessible records of those that had not qualified for assistance. This made it impossible to monitor and evaluate the scheme effectively and therefore, very difficult to assess its impact.
- Due to the fact that there were different systems of operation across the districts, it is likely that the initial sift and the scoring of Form 52x

was approached differently in each district. Although there were objective criteria for those qualifying, there were differences in the way that individuals interpreted these criteria or gathered the required information from the victim. This means there were problems with the comparability of the system across districts.

- Decisions regarding those to be offered assistance were taken by different organisations in the various districts. There was concern that since the SMP was not involved in this decision-making process; it would have less control over the dispensing of the budget. For instance, in a particular month, many people could be offered assistance and accept. This might lead to over-expenditure of the SMP budget for that time period. Furthermore, the system could be subject to the bias of those involved in offering grants.

These concerns indicated that the best way to progress the system was to substantially overhaul the way it was administered and to have a central mechanism for grant allocation.

Grant allocation application

The SMP grant allocation application is a modular application that deals with all aspects of the grant allocation process. The application was developed by MIS and an overview of the application is shown in Figure 6.1.

Application overview

The application is written in Visual Basic, Access Basic and is built on a Microsoft Access database. The application runs on a PC within Merseyside Police HQ, has a network connection to the police mainframe and is designed to take the operator through the grant allocation assessment procedure step-by-step. A dedicated member of staff, working for the SMP but employed by the police, operates the grant allocation application.

New burglary records from the Police Integrated Criminal Justice System (ICJS) are downloaded via the network link on a daily basis and the initial task of the operator is to process the downloaded ICJS data. Approximately 1,000 burglaries are recorded by the ICJS each month. This amounts to a weekly figure of approximately 250, which in turn translates into between thirty and fifty records per day.

A system with the ability to respond to burglaries which occurred as recently as the previous twenty-four hours is still relatively uncommon. It is possible in this case due to the location of the system within police headquarters. A great advantage of the immediacy of the procedure is that it enables assistance to be given to vulnerable victims in a very short timescale. This is often of vital importance, since research has consistently

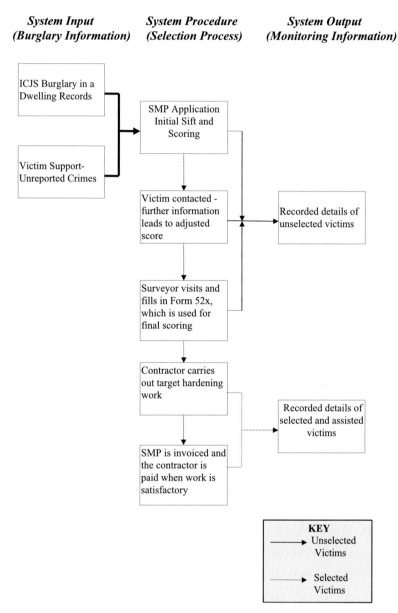

Figure 6.1 Grant allocation procedure.

found that the victims of burglary are at a heightened risk of re-victimisation immediately following an initial incident (e.g. Johnson *et al.* 1997; Bowers *et al.* 1998).

The daily download of burglary data is then analysed and cross-referenced with other information to:

- establish whether or not the burgled property is located within the deprived target (Pathway) areas
- establish whether or not the incident is a repeat
- establish whether the occupants of the property fall into defined vulnerable groups
- establish whether the burglary occurred in an area of high criminal activity (a 'hotspot').

This analysis determines whether or not a particular burglary qualifies for grant assistance and then gives all eligible properties an initial 'vulnerability score' on the basis of the information available from the ICJS. However, some of the ICJS data fields (i.e. gender or age of victim) may not be completed on the burglary record. Therefore to avoid vulnerable properties or victims being excluded due to lack of information, a weighted score is also produced. To obtain this weighted score the application adds the maximum score for any missing data to the initial score. For example, if the age of the victim has not been entered on to the ICJS record, then the maximum score that can be assigned to the victim's age (in this case that associated with an elderly victim) is added to the initial score. The scoring criteria are considered in greater detail below.

These initial and weighted scores are calculated for each of the downloaded burglary records. The operator then selects those with the highest vulnerability scores and moves them to a 'daily list' which details all those that will be involved in further intervention on that day. Remaining records, which may still indicate a certain level of vulnerability are then either assigned to a future listing or can be dropped from the system and archived. The operator is forced to enter a reason for any records that are dropped at this stage.

Having compiled a daily list the next stage is for the operator to get in touch with the victims concerned. This is a quicker process if telephone contact is possible but where this is not possible, victims are contacted by letter. The application contains a telephone contact module which is completed for each victim on the daily list for whom there is a telephone number. This module collects information on the operator's attempts to contact the victim, including the dates and times on which contact was attempted and an outcome of each contact attempt. For instance, there may be no reply nor answerphone on the first contact and it may take three or four attempts before the victim can be contacted. After five unsuccessful attempts at telephone contact, or after two weeks have elapsed since contact was first attempted, the record can either be moved to the mail monitoring module (and an attempt made to contact the victim by post) or archived. Victims responding to the mailing are asked to supply a telephone contact number, and their burglary records are then included in the records to be processed on that day.

This contact made by the operator serves a number of purposes. First, the operator verifies the information held on the ICJS record and completes any missing data fields. Second, the contact is used to obtain additional information from the victim on:

- Whether or not they live in student accommodation
- Whether or not they recall being burgled in the last 12 months
- Whether or not they live alone
- Whether they are single parents
- Whether or not they receive benefits and, if they do, what type they receive.

Third, the pilot phase of the initiative identified that often the most vulnerable individuals were the persons hardest to contact after a burglary. Consequently, the procedure emphasises the need to manage the efforts made to contact these individuals who are often elderly and staying with relatives after a burglary incident.

This additional information is then used to adjust the initial score given to the victim to produce a final vulnerability score. A decision as to whether or not to offer grant assistance is taken on the basis of this final score. The SMP set a threshold score for grant assistance and the application informs the operator whether or not the threshold score has been reached. If it has, then the operator explains the potential grant to the victim and asks whether or not the victim would agree to a visit from a surveyor to assess the scale of target hardening that might be required. Providing the victim agrees the application flags the record for a surveyor's visit. There is a facility for the operator to make notes concerning the appointment that might be of use to the surveyor (e.g. times and dates a visit would be convenient).

Information relating to any victims who fail to qualify for assistance at the contact stage is archived. There will also be a percentage of those qualifying who refuse a visit by the surveyor. Information on these victims is also archived.

Details of the victims that qualify and agree to a visit are sent to the surveyor on a daily basis. The surveyor visits the victim and completes Form 52x which details the crime prevention measures suitable for the particular property. Options include;

- Front door mortice locks, chains or viewers
- Window snap locks or screw locks
- Rear door mortice locks, bolts and key or hinged bolts
- A new front or rear door.

The surveyor obtains the agreement of the victim to contribute to the costs of this work and then sends details of the required work to the appointed contractor who carries out the recommended work. The SMP representative then liaises with the victim to ensure that they are satisfied with the work done. The contractor is then paid by the SMP.

In addition to streamlining the grant allocation process the application has had a number of other beneficial impacts. In particular, information is now retained on properties or victims that do and do not qualify at all stages of sifting. This ensures that any subsequent evaluation can trace any further victimisation of both those that did and those that did not qualify for assistance. In addition, the criteria used to produce a vulnerability score for each victim are objectively scored by the application itself, thus removing the possibility of bias and ensuring that the most vulnerable people in the most vulnerable properties are targeted for assistance. Computerisation of the grant allocation process also adds major new element to the scoring system, namely the geographical location of victims in relation to crime 'hotspots'. It is this part of the application that is linked to output from a GIS.

The remaining sections of this chapter examine some of the application modules in more detail, concentrating on the scoring criteria, geographical sifting and the identification of repeats.

Vulnerability scoring criteria for domestic dwellings

Table 6.1 shows the score given to the criteria that are used to define vulnerability. The mechanism does not include a score for whether or not a victimised property is within a Pathway area, because only properties within these relatively deprived areas qualify for grant assistance.

The Table shows that several different scales of targeting are used to produce a final vulnerability score. At the level of the property, any previous burglaries are taken into account. The type of burglary is also a key factor – if the burglary was unsuccessful then less weight is given to it. Certain vulnerable groups are also targeted – greater weighing is given to women, those living alone and the elderly. Lastly, there is an area level weighting – properties that are located within particular problem areas or 'hotspots' of burglary are given a higher score.

Address matching and repeat victimisation

The processes of geographical referencing and address matching lie at the heart of the grant allocation application. The ICJS burglary records need to be matched against a database of Pathway area properties to ascertain whether or not the victim qualifies for grant assistance. In order to identify any victims of repeat burglary, the daily ICJS data download is matched, using the address, to a Table within the application that stores the addresses of all burglaries within Pathway areas for the preceding 12 months. This Table is automatically updated by the application on a daily basis, so that the 12 months' pool of data is changing day after day, to ensure that exactly one year of previous data is used to check for the daily repeats.

If the address matching routines are to work, it is important that the address information on the burglary records is entered in a structured and

Table 6.1 Vulnerability scoring

Criterion	Score
Repeat victimisation	
Once in last 12 months	3
Two or more in last 12 months	5
Age	
Age 65–80	2
Age 80+	5
Gender	
Male	0
Female	1
Crime hotspot	3
Burglary type	
Burglary with intent	0
Burglary	2
Aggravated burglary with intent	2
Aggravated burglary	5
Student accommodation	1
Living alone	1
Single parent	1
In receipt of benefits	1

consistent format, ideally to the national address standard, BS7666. Without such a structured address it is difficult, if not impossible, to automatically match the current burglary records against the historical information.

Unfortunately, the ICJS records do not contain a structured address. In the existing ICJS addresses are entered into a single free-text field. While the different parts of the address can be separated by a comma or another specified character, there are no data entry rules to enforce this procedure on the ICJS system, so that errors inevitably occur. This means that before the ICJS record address information can be matched, the address has to be decomposed into its individual components (to isolate house number, street name, etc.) and then structured. The application contains an algorithm that undertakes this decomposition and which then attempts to reconstruct the address in a semi-structured format.

This semi-structured address is then matched against an extract from the Merseyside Address Reference System (MARS) database. MARS is a land and property database for Merseyside, maintained by MIS, which holds detailed information (including grid reference) for roughly 590,000 residential properties on Merseyside. If the semi-structured address fully matches the MARS address then an automatic match is made and the application saves the ICJS data containing the structured address fields from MARS along with a unique property reference number (UPRN).

Addresses that do not match automatically are processed further using a 'fuzzy matching' algorithm which uses partial matches (a match on a multiple street name, but no postcode to verify the correct street, for example) and soundex matching to identify possible matches in the MARS database. These possible matches are displayed on screen and the operator manually selects the correct match. The ICJS data are then stored along with the structured address and a UPRN. ICJS records for which no match can be found can be stored for later retrieval and checking.

The structured address on the ICJS record now allows the record to be easily matched to identify whether or not the burglary occurred inside a Pathway area and whether or not the property had been burgled during the last 12 months.

Geographical filters

Information on burglary 'hotspots' is also included in the application. Introducing hotspots into the scoring criteria ensures that grant assistance is targeted towards properties in areas where there is a higher than average risk of crime. The rationale behind targeting hotspots is that it is likely that individual properties in these areas have a higher risk of victimisation per se. Targeting vulnerable properties, especially repeatedly burgled properties, in these areas means that assistance is given to those individuals with a particularly high risk of experiencing crime.

The hotspots used in the application are produced by calculating burglary rates for 100 m grid squares using burglary command and control calls (calls for police assistance from the public) and residential property denominators from the MARS system. A grid square is classified as a hotspot when it experiences a burglary rate that is twice the Merseyside average. Using GIS, the hotspot coverage is intersected with the MARS extract used in the grant allocation procedure, to flag those properties within Pathway areas that are also in burglary hotspots. This information is added to the ICJS data when a successful match is made with the MARS database and burgled properties within hotspots are scored accordingly. Figure 6.2 demonstrates the technique of mapping grid square burglary 'hotspots' in relation to several of Merseyside's Pathway areas.

Unreported crime

The application has the functionality to process details of burglaries that have not been reported to the police. In addition to ICJS data, information on un-reported burglaries is also collected by Victim Support. There is a facility in the administration system which allows information from Victim Support to be manually entered, so that victimisation information from

Table 6.2 Subsequent burglaries of scheme beneficiaries

	Number of domestic dwellings target hardened	Properties re-victimised after security measures fitted	% of properties re-victimised after security measures fitted	Properties receiving further burglary after enhanced package
Initial phase (1/4/95– 31/3/98)	3,332 (21.3 per week average)	20	0.60	0
MIS grant allocation system (1/4/98–18/10/99)	2,024 (26.6 per week average)	7	0.35	0

The Table demonstrates that in both phases of the target hardening scheme, less than one per cent of victims that had received assistance suffered from a re-victimisation. This repeat burglary rate is far below the average for Merseyside, calculated using recorded crime information, which was found to be 6.2 per cent over a one year period (Johnson *et al.* 1997). The target hardening scheme is, therefore, proving to be effective at preventing further victimisation. Table 6.2 also shows that the tiny percentage that were re-victimised has fallen by half from 0.6 per cent to 0.3 per cent following implementation of the grant allocation system, which may well reflect an even more effective strategy. A reason for this may be that the new system is able to target-harden vulnerable properties within a very short timescale following an initial incident, due to the fact that it is able to process burglaries that occurred on the previous day.

The efficiency of the scheme also seems to have increased following implementation of the MIS system, with a greater average number of domestic dwellings being target-hardened per week. The initial phase handled approximately twenty-one cases per week, whereas, the grant allocation system handles approximately twenty-seven. This 29 per cent increase in productivity has increased efficiency without over-stretching the available resources.

Table 6.2 also shows that there were no further re-victimisations following the administration of an enhanced package. These enhanced packages were provided to all twenty-seven victims that had experienced further burglary since target hardening. The enhanced package involves a further survey which is carried out by a crime prevention officer, who assesses whether or not additional security measures are required. These measures include a basic alarm package and security lights. This two-tier approach, which gives extra assistance to those experiencing burglary after initial target hardening, reflects systems that have been used in other successful schemes (e.g. the Kirkholt scheme, Forrester *et al.* 1990). Table 6.2 shows that the enhanced package for those that have been re-victimised has been 100 per cent effective to date, with no incidents of further victimisation of beneficiaries.

Conclusion

This chapter has described the development of a grant allocation system for the target hardening of domestic dwellings throughout the Pathway areas of Merseyside. An initial phase of the scheme used a variable procedure in each of the five districts of Merseyside, which caused problems with the consistency of target selection and the availability of a central source of information concerning those assisted by the scheme.

A comprehensive review of the system recommended that a GIS-linked database, which helped with the resource allocation procedure, would make the scheme easier to manage and help to increase its efficiency. The database, which was developed by MIS, computerised the selection of the most vulnerable victims of domestic burglary using geographical sifting and information on the individual characteristics of victims from recorded crime data. Further information was then received from the victims which was taken into consideration in the final scoring procedure. Victims that were most at risk were then given financial assistance towards recommended crime prevention measures.

It was found that the new grant allocation system was effective. There were only a minimal number of assisted victims that suffered from any further victimisations. In fact, a smaller proportion have suffered further victimisation since the new system commenced than did so in the initial phase of the scheme.

Recently, a project has been funded to expand the remit of the resource allocation database. To date, the scheme has concentrated on assisting victims of domestic burglary. However, a further concern is burglary to non-domestic properties such as schools, small businesses or community facilities. MIS are currently undertaking a feasibility study which will outline the steps involved in producing a similar system for such properties.

Notes

1 A nine-year Single Regeneration Budget funded initiative which aims to reduce victimisation and the fear of victimisation throughout Merseyside.
2 A local government-funded information and intelligence agency.
3 Thanks to Mike Lloyd of MIS for providing this Figure

References

Bowers, K.J., Hirschfield, A. and Johnson, S.D. (1998) 'Victimisation revisited: a case study of non-residential repeat burglary on Merseyside', *British Journal of Criminology* 38(3): 429–52.

Chenery, S., Holt, J. and Pease, K. (1997) *Biting Back II: Reducing Repeat Victimisation in Huddersfield,* PRG Crime Detection and Prevention Series Paper 82, London: Home Office.

Ebdon, D. (1988) *Statistics in Geography*, Oxford: Blackwell.

Ekblom, P. (1988) *Getting the Best Out of Crime Analysis*, PRG Crime Prevention Unit Paper 10, London: Home Office.

Ekblom, P., Law, H. and Sutton, M. (1996) 'Domestic burglary schemes in the safer cities programme', *Research Findings 42*, Home Office Research and Statistics Directorate, London: Home Office.

Forrester, D., Frenz, S. , O'Connell, M and Pease, K. (1990) *The Kirkholt Burglary Prevention Project: Phase II*, PRG Crime Prevention Unit Paper 23, London: Home Office.

Hirschfield, A.F.G., Yarwood, D. and Bowers, K. (1997) 'Crime pattern analysis, spatial targeting and GIS: the development of new approaches for use in evaluating community safety initiatives', *Crime and Health Data Analysis Using GIS: Workshop Proceedings*, Sheffield: SCGISA.

Johnson, S.D., Bowers, K.J. and Hirschfield, A.F.G. (1997) 'New insights into the spatial and temporal distribution of repeat victimisation', *British Journal of Criminology* 37(2): 224–41.

Pease, K. (1993) 'Individual and community influences on victimisation and their implications for crime prevention', in D.P. Farrington, R.J. Sampson and P.-O. H. Wikstrom (eds) *Integrating Individual and Ecological Aspects of Crime*, Stockholm: National Council for Crime Prevention.

Part III

GIS in the police and emergency services

7   Mapping out hazardous space for police work[1,2]

James L. LeBeau[3]

Geographic information systems are becoming valuable tools for law enforcement agencies. Their use, however, has been mainly restricted to crime analysis. Using information from the Charlotte-Mecklenburg, North Carolina Police Department, this research discusses using GIS for assessing and visualising hazardous space for police work.

Five different type of incidents and calls for police services are considered hazardous: calls for service requiring an emergency response; gun assaults and armed robbery calls for service; incidents involving officer use of force; incidents resulting in injuries to officers; and incidents where officers require immediate help.

Density grids are constructed for each type of hazardous incident and threshold values indicating an extremely high density are selected. Selecting out all the grid cells equal to and greater than the threshold levels creates integer maps. The integer maps are added together to yield the hazardous space map with cells yielding a score of five as being most hazardous. Less than 8 per cent of the grid cells covering Charlotte-Mecklenburg had any type of hazard, in general, while less than 1 per cent of the cells were the most hazardous, in particular.

Introduction

Geographic information systems, automated mapping and spatial analysis are becoming valuable tools for policing. These tools have been mainly employed in crime analysis and are functionally linked with police computer-aided dispatch and records management systems. These systems routinely capture a wealth of data about the specifics of crimes and calls for service including precise information about location. This mass of data contains useful information for crime analysis, but from this information we can also find out about the details and locations of incidents or calls where police officers are injured, use force, request immediate help, and are dispatched to potentially dangerous situations. The commonality among these different types of incident is that they are all some type of dangerous or hazardous situation. Combining these hazardous incidents and mapping out their geographic attributes allows one to visualise the spatial variation of hazardous incidents. This following is a discussion on using GIS for delineating and visualising hazardous spaces for police work

The research site

The data for this research emanate from the Charlotte-Mecklenburg, North Carolina, Police Department for the year 1997. During 1995, the police departments of the city of Charlotte and the county of Mecklenburg consolidated into one police department. During 1997, the CMPD dispatched 416,584 calls for service.

Figure 7.1 depicts the spatial organisation of Charlotte Mecklenburg Patrol Operations. The largest geographic unit for delivering patrol service is the Service Bureau for which there are four (Adam, Baker, Charlie and David). Each bureau is subdivided into three service districts (nine districts), each district is further subdivided into response areas (ninety-three in total). Finally, the response areas are subdivided in reporting areas of which there are 892 across the entire jurisdiction.

Data

Table 7.1 lists the types of calls or incidents and their frequencies during 1997 that are used for delineating hazardous space. Emergency calls are considered hazardous for two reasons: first, the emergency designation implies a situation which is life-threatening or in immediate danger of escalation; and second, this type of call requires that multiple patrol units proceed to the call as fast as possible, hence increasing the probability of traffic accidents or other calamities. The 21,592 emergency calls constitute 5.18 per cent of the 416,584 dispatched calls for service during 1997.

Armed robberies and gun assaults are the next most frequent type of hazardous call. Obviously, weapon use merits the inclusion of this type of call into the scheme.

Uses of force incidents are included in this scheme, because obviously, officers became involved in situations where force is necessary. These are officer-reported use of force incidents (Table 7.1). It is standard policy for an officer to report when he/she has to use any type of force with a suspect. These data are not differentiated by severity, but range from pushing to wounding a suspect. Furthermore, these data did not emanate from an automated information system, but had to be retrieved from paper reports.

Injuries to officers are another type of hazardous incident or call that had to be retrieved from paper reports. These data include all injuries to sworn police officers in the field. Eliminated from these data are injuries received during training and injuries to civilians and officers in an office setting. Like the use of force, the injury data are not differentiated by severity and were retrieved from paper reports.

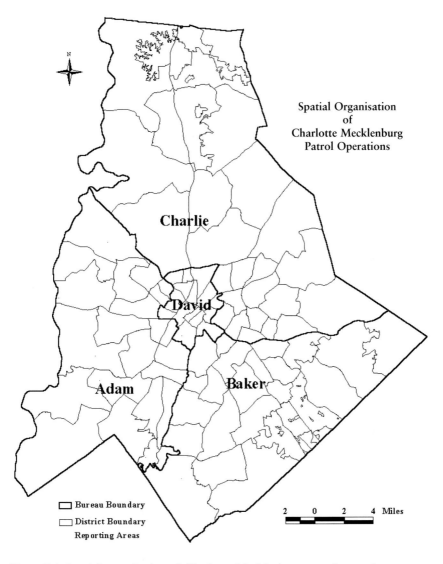

Figure 7.1 Spatial organisation of Charlotte-Mecklenburg patrol operations.

Table 7.1 Hazardous incidents and calls

Calls incident types	Number
Emergency calls for service	21,592
Armed robberies and gun assaults	3,523
Use of force incidents	410
Injuries to officers	245
Help me quick calls	44

The last type of call is the least frequent, but in many respects is the most hazardous. The 'Help me quick call' is one where an officer is in the field and becomes involved in a situation where he or she requires immediate assistance or backup. As revealed in Table 7.1, there were forty-four such incidents during 1997. This type of call generates a rapid response from numerous patrol units. During 1997, a total of 245 patrol units responded to the forty-four calls. This is an average of 5.5 units per call while the maximum number of patrol units responding to one of these calls is 35.

Procedures

Three interrelated pieces of software are used for this analysis. ESRI's ArcView GIS software and its Spatial Analyst extension are used for managing, and analysing data and producing maps.[4] The Crimestat's nearest neighbour analysis routine is the third piece of software (Levine 1999).

The rationales and justifications will be discussed later, but there are seven basic steps in the analysis: (1) the point coordinates for the street block addresses of the incidents/calls are acquired through address matching; (2) using Spatial Analyst a $\frac{1}{2}$ mile grid coverage is constructed for Charlotte-Mecklenburg; (3) five grids are constructed measuring the density of the specific types of calls or incidents per square mile; (4) frequency histograms of the grid densities are constructed for each incident/call; (5) extreme significant thresholds levels for each density grid are selected from inspecting the histograms and descriptive statistics; (6) new threshold integer maps are constructed with grids meeting or exceeding the thresholds determined in step 5 receiving a score of one while other grids set to 0; and (7) the five threshold maps are added together with grids recording a score of five being the most hazardous.

The rationale and justification for the $\frac{1}{2}$ mile grids is rather involved. There are numerous rationales or rules of thumbs for selecting the grid size and a search radius for smoothing the data if one were to use kernel methods (see Williamson *et al.* 1999). However, the purpose of this analysis is to show the spatial co-variation of five phenomena, but the spatial properties for each vary greatly. This conclusion was reached after examining the nearest neighbour statistics for each incident or call types (see Bailey and Gatrell 1995: 88–90; Levine 1999: 137–42). The mean nearest neighbour distances were too dissimilar, so as an alternative a _ mile grid cell size and search radius are used because a $\frac{1}{2}$ mile is the average first order nearest neighbour distance between and among the centroids of the 892 reporting areas. This procedure produced a grid of 4,118 cells.

Most researchers have found crime density grid data rarely conform to a normal distribution, so in order to identify thresholds for each type of incident or call it was necessary to inspect descriptive statistics and histograms of the grid cell density distributions (see Olligschlaeger 1997). Initially, three standard deviations above the mean served as a rough guideline for a threshold, the histograms revealed values that were close to three standard deviations, but the proportion of the total grid cells containing threshold values ranged from 2.9 per cent (help me quick) to 4.6 per cent (emergency calls) (Table 7.2). Therefore, the selected thresholds for each call constitute less than 5.0 per cent of the total grid cells (Table 7.2).

Two judgement calls are made for this analysis. The first is that all grid cells recording a 'help me quick' call density greater than zero are included. The low frequency of this call, but its extreme severity requires that all incidents are included in delineating hazardous areas. The second pertains to the issue of the intercorrelation between and among the different incidents and calls. The fact of the matter is that there is significant intercorrelation, but including the redundant information weights the grid cell. A 'help quick me call' is an emergency; it can involve an armed robbery or gun assault; it can involve injuries to officers; and it can involve the use of force.

Finally, another caveat that needs to be mentioned is that this analysis is focused on defining hazardous space by identifying the spatial co-occurrence of high densities of the five incident-call types. Thus, risk rates are not assessed or produced in this analysis.

Results

Figure 7.2 shows the emergency calls per square mile during 1997. The highest emergency call densities are mainly confined to the central portion of the map within the David patrol bureau (compare Figures 7.1 and 7.2). This patrol bureau has the greatest opportunities for generating large volumes of emergency calls because the central business district is a majority of the bureau. This area is the focus or hub of a majority of the daily commuting activity for work, business and entertainment. Moreover, this patrol bureau contains a mixture of different land uses (e.g. commercial, industrial, and residential) which present additional opportunities for emergency calls. Finally, many of the residential neighbourhoods within this bureau are lower income, public housing settings. These are settings that are

Table 7.2 Thresholds for hazardous incidents and calls

Incident and call types	Threshold/ sq miles	No. grid cells	% of total cells
Emergency calls for service	>145.89	193	4.60
Armed robberies and gun assaults	>27.82	189	4.58
Use of force incidents	>3.77	162	3.93
Injuries to officers	>2.34	159	3.86
Help me quick calls	>0.00	123	2.90

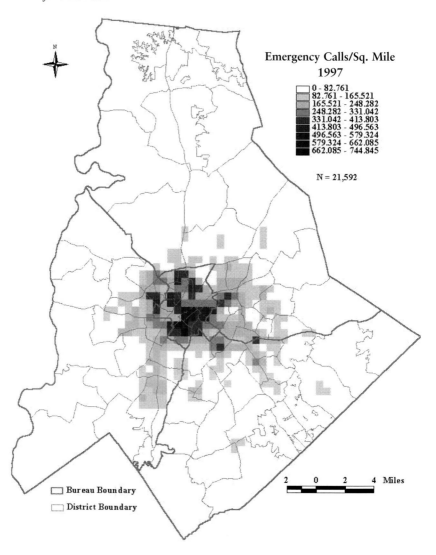

Figure 7.2 Emergency calls per square mile.

both attractors and generators of crime, in general, and presumably emergency calls, in particular (see Brantingham and Brantingham 1995).

Figure 7.3 depicts the grids which exceed the threshold value. The majority of the grids in the David bureau exceed the threshold limit.

Figure 7.4 is Armed robberies and gun assaults per squre mile in 1997. The spatial pattern of these incidents is similar to the emergency calls (compare Figures 7.2 and 7.4). The David bureau has a majority of high density grids, but other high density grids in other bureaux are adjacent to

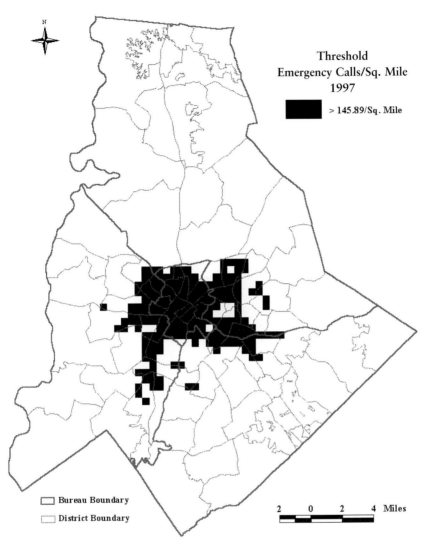

Threshold
Emergency Calls/Sq. Mile
1997

▮ > 145.89/Sq. Mile

☐ Bureau Boundary
☐ District Boundary

2   0   2   4   Miles

Figure 7.3 Threshold emergency calls per square mile.

the David bureau boundaries. The threshold map confirms the contiguity of high density armed robbery and gun assault grids to the David boundary, but also reveals an areal extension of the grids to the east and west of the David bureau and a linear extension of the high density grids in the southwest and the southeast (Figure 7.5).

The use of force per square mile in 1997 is shown in Figure 7.6. The areal extent of the use of force is much less than the emergency or armed robbery calls (compare Figures 7.2, 7.4, 7.6). Still the highest density grids

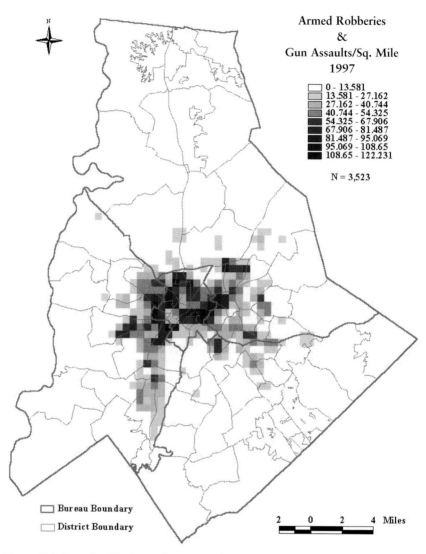

Figure 7.4 Armed robberies and gun assaults per square mile in 1997.

are within the David bureau in the central city. However, within the David bureau there are two distinct regions. First in the central portion of the David bureau, there are four high-density grids which are connected by a corridor of high density grids extending to the eastern boundary of the bureau. The second lies in the west and northwest portions of the David bureau adjacent to high density use of force grids in the Adam bureau. The former region encompasses the heart of the downtown and to its east are lower income public housing residential areas. The latter region incorpor-

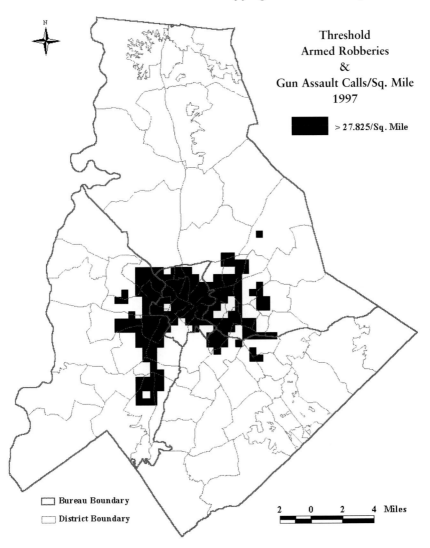

Figure 7.5 Threshold armed robberies and gun assault calls per square mile in 1997.

ates similar residential neighbourhoods, but also has a large mix of commercial and industrial land use. The threshold map (Figure 7.7) indicates the threshold use of force grids are mainly contiguous. However, there is not the contiguous linear extension of grids in the southwest and the southeast. There are, however, isolated small clusters of grids or islands of the use of force in the outlying areas.

Figure 7.8 depicts injuries per square mile in 1997. The frequency of this type of incident is lower than the previously discussed incidents; hence

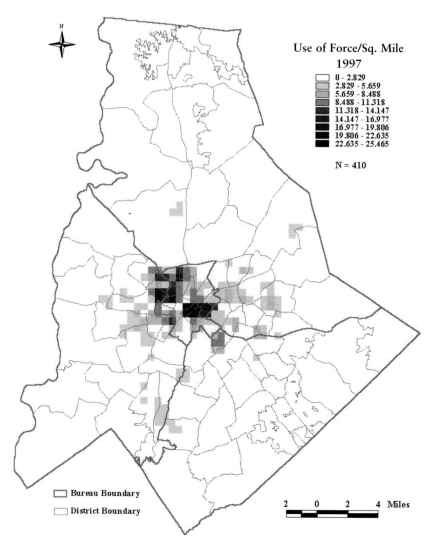

Figure 7.6 The use of force per square mile in 1997.

the areal extent is less. Nevertheless, the David bureau contains the highest densities of officers' injuries. The injury patterns within the David bureau are similar to the use of force patterns. The threshold map (Figure 7.9) indicates that the David bureau has the largest concentration of high density injury grids. While there are isolated clusters or islands in the outlying areas one can clearly discern three corridors or linear patterns of high injuries. The first is due east of the David bureau in the Charlie bureau. The second is due south of the first lying on the boundary between

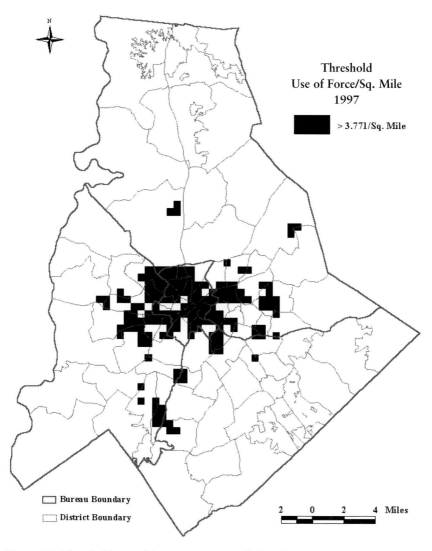

Figure 7.7 Threshold use of force per square mile in 1997.

the Charlie and the Baker bureaux. The third lies southwest of the David bureau in the Adam bureau.

Figure 7.10 is 'help me quick (10–33)' calls per square mile in 1997. This map also serves as the threshold map since all of the 'help me quick' calls are used in this analysis. Like the other calls and incidents these have their highest concentrations in the central part of the city in the David bureau. This would be expected, however, as there are numerous grids or islands outside the central concentration recording a high density of calls.

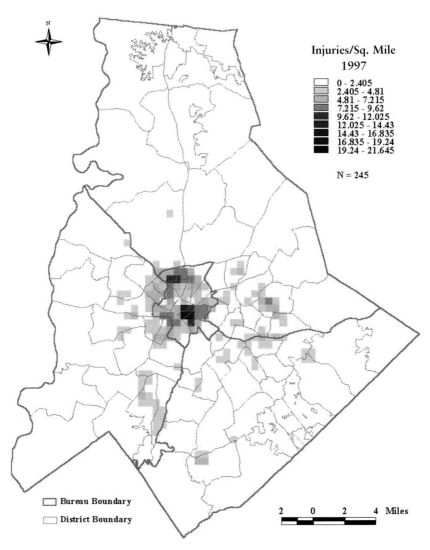

Figure 7.8 Injuries per square mile in 1997.

The paucity of 'help me quick' calls would make any generalisations about their spatial persistence short-lived if one mapped out similar calls for other years. For example, during other years there would still be the central concentration of calls, but the locations of the outlying calls might vary from year-to-year – they may be spatially random. Nevertheless, as previously stated, the severity of these calls requires that they all are included in the delineation of hazardous space.

The sum of the five threshold maps is presented in Plate 5. Grids

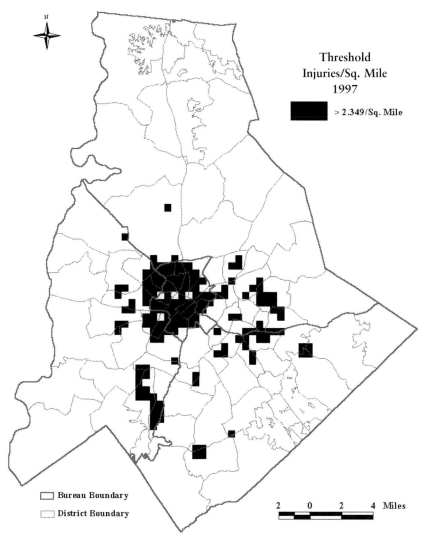

Figure 7.9 Threshold injuries per square mile in 1997.

receiving a score of five are presented in red, thus having the highest density of all five hazardous calls or incidents. Only 39 grids or 0.95 per cent of the total 4,118 grids record the highest hazard level (Table 7.3). Viewed another way, less than 8 per cent of the grids constituting Charlotte-Mecklenburg contain any level of hazard whatsoever.

The spatial pattern of the hazardous areas should not be a surprise given the review of the five threshold maps (Plate 5). The general impression of the geographic distribution of hazardous areas throughout

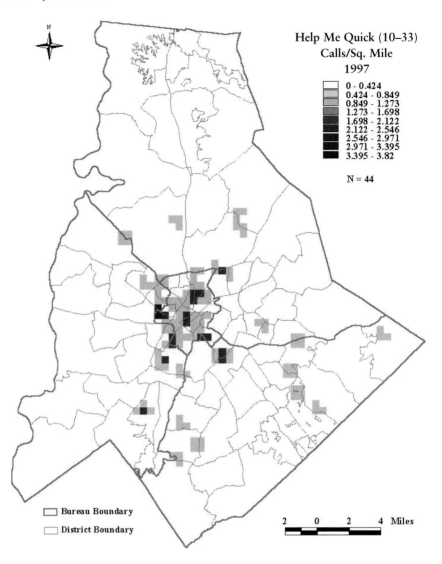

Figure 7.10 'Help me quick (10–33)' calls per square mile in 1997.

Charlotte-Mecklenburg is that there is a distance decay effect. The greater the distance from the central part of the city and the David bureau, the lower the hazardousness. This effect is not uniform in all directions, or there is directional bias. For example, east and southeast of the David bureau there is a large contiguous mass of hazardous grids of varying levels. A similar pattern appears in the west and southwest. Conspicuously inactive or missing are hazardous grids immediately north and south of the

Table 7.3 Areal extent of hazard levels

Hazard level	No. grids	% of total
0	3,793	92.11
1	109	2.65
2	69	1.68
3	54	1.31
4	54	1.31
5	39	0.95

David bureau. An important question to be answered through examining similar data from several time periods is: are the outlying lower level hazardous areas likely to increase through time?

Plate 6 focuses on the bureau–district–response areas in the David bureau and the immediate neighbours in other bureau–district–response areas. While the David bureau has a majority of the most hazardous areas, the Adam bureau in the west has some as well. The most hazardous areas are laid out in two distinct regions. There is a southern region containing grids in D27, A22, A21, D14, D13, D12, D11, D31, D33 and B11. The northern region has grids in A35, A33, A32, D24, D25, D26, D22, D21, D34, D35. The southern region contains the central business district, light and heavy commercial land use and different types of residential neighbourhoods, including many lower income public housing projects. The northern region corresponds to lower income residential areas situated among light and heavy industrial land uses with some light commercial and institutional land uses. The bridge between the regions is the most hazardous area in D27, otherwise there is a clear buffer or transition zone of less hazardous areas between the two regions. Another important feature revealed in Plate 6 is how different bureaux, districts and response areas share a common hazard level on their common boundaries (e.g. D27 and A32). This is a graphic display of how problems are not confined to one geographical or, in this context, organisational unit.

Conclusions

This has been a discussion about how GIS can be used for delineating hazardous spaces for police work by analysing the densities of incidents and calls that are conceptually linked to danger and hazard. It must be restated that density of hazards is the focus and not the probability or risk of hazards. The problem with addressing the latter is finding the proper denominator or denominators for calculating rates. For example, many of the 'help me quick' emanated from police officers who were working off-duty. Thus, a valid rate would include a denominator measuring the average or number of police officers working off-duty. Another example pertains to injuries. One of the common injuries experienced by police officers is being sprayed in the eyes with pepper spray during a scuffle with a suspect. The source of the spray is not the suspect, but other police officers that accidentally spray an officer. Thus, a proper denominator for this type of injury should be the number incidents involving pepper spray. The point is that more research needs to be pursued searching for valid and reliable denominators.

There has been little discussion about the geography of the hazardous spaces. Namely, isolating the spatial processes, interactions and the contents of places that generate the hazardous circumstances. Sparingly, I have alluded to possible independent variables and circumstances, but this is another matter for additional research. However, altering any ecological or demographic variables causally related to hazards would involve a long-term process, but changing these conditions may significantly and positively change a range of societal ills.

Traditionally, for the short-term, reducing hazards and ensuring safety for police officers has emanated from training and enacting policy. The short-term approach could be greatly enhanced by employing geographic information systems and examining important variables related to hazards that could be modified by policy intervention. For example, officer fatigue has long been a positive correlate of accidents and injuries. Recent research suggests there are policy means for reducing the probability of officer fatigue through work shift design and compressed scheduling (Vila 1999). Using GIS, it would be possible to delineate and visualise fatigue and hazardous spaces and assess the relationships between the two.

Geographic information systems are being used for a variety of purposes and functions which focus on enhancing the quality of life. This discussion suggests that GIS should take an occupational safety focus. Therefore, there needs to be more research and investigation into using GIS for improving safety and enhancing the quality of the work environment.

Notes

1 This study was conducted using funding from the US Department of Justice's National Institute of Justice under grant number 97–LB-VX-K010. Points of view expressed here are those of the author and do not necessarily represent the official position of the US Department of Justice.
2 Points of view or opinions expressed in this research are those of the author and do not necessarily represent the official position of Charlotte-Mecklenburg, North Carolina Police Department.
3 Professor, Center for the Study of Crime, Delinquency, and Corrections and The Department of Geography. Southern Illinois University at Carbondale, Carbondale, Illinois 62901–4504.
4 Environmental Systems Research Incorporated (ESRI) is based in Redlands, California, and developed ArcView and its Spatial Analyst extension.

References

Bailey, T.C. and Gatrell, A.C. (1995) *Interactive Spatial Data Analysis*, Harlow, England: Longman Group Limited.

Brantingham, P.L. and Brantingham, P.J. (1995) 'Criminality of place: crime generators and crime attractors', *European Journal on Criminal Policy and Research: Crime Environments and Situational Prevention* 3(3): 5–26.

Levine, N. (1999) *CrimeStat: A Spatial Statistics Program for the Analysis of Crime Incident Locations*, Washington, DC: National Institute of Justice.

Olligschlaeger, A.M. (1997) 'Artificial neural networks and crime mapping', in D. Weisburd and T. McEwen (eds) *Crime Mapping and Crime Prevention*, Monsey, NY: Criminal Justice Press, pp. 313–47.

Vila, B. (1999) 'Tired cops: the prevalence of fatigue among patrol officers, and some indications of its effects on performance, health, and safety', paper presented at the Annual Meeting of the American Society of Criminology, Toronto, November.

Williamson, D., McLafferty, S., McGuire, P., Goldsmith, V. and Mollenkopf, J. (1999) 'A better method to smooth crime incidence data', *ArcUser*, Redlands, CA: ESRI.

8 GIS for spatial analysis of fire incidence

Identification of social, economic and environmental risk indicators

Steven Merrall

The urban fire problem is clearly not a random phenomenon and can be shown to be disproportionately concentrated within specific geographical areas and at varying scales. Spatial and temporal pattern identification of fire incidence provides a basis for research into the social, economic and environmental risk factors. Once areas of high fire incidence have been identified, work can be undertaken to establish the similarities and differences between those areas and the common risk factors. Profiling the characteristics of areas that have similar fire incidence counts or rates provides a context within which community fire safety planning can be more effectively managed.

The vast majority (86.5 per cent) of all residential dwelling fires in Greater Manchester for the financial year 1998–99 can be attributed to human behaviour. Analysis at electoral ward level reports that 50 per cent of these incidents occur within wards containing 23 per cent of households in the Greater Manchester area. Within continuing budgetary strictures, information of this type will enable justification, monitoring and evaluation of geographically targeted fire reduction/safety initiatives. The use of the area profile classifications derived will contribute to the targeting, content and delivery strategies of community fire safety packages.

This chapter will provide comment on and case study example of the utility of GIS and statistical analysis of fire incidence, in terms of brigade management and community fire safety service delivery.

'It is not the thunderbolts forged by Vulcan on Mount Etna for Jove (whose statue was one of the seven wonders of the world and was ironically destroyed by fire in Constantinople AD 475) that contribute to the prevalence of fire in our society. Rather the cause may be attributed to the revenge of Jove on Prometheus who through Vulcan fashioned Pandora from clay and gave her the fabled box from which all the evils that flesh is heir to flew forth, and have ever since continued to afflict the world. The last thing that flew from the box was hope.'

Introduction

The social, the economic and the environmental form a trinity within which it is the individual who is the primary player in the incidence of fire.

It is within these three arenas that geography plays a unifying role in the potential to describe and explain the variation in the distribution and concentration of fire incidence over both space and time. Two primary tools that have great potential to exploit the geographical nature of the wealth of data captured and stored by the fire service are GIS and statistics. Fire is not a random phenomenon and can be shown to be disproportionately concentrated in areas exhibiting similarities in social, economic and environmental composition. Spatial and temporal pattern identification of fire incidence provides a basis for research into where, when and why fires occur. The classification of areas by levels and type of fire incidence and the outcomes enables work to be undertaken to establish the similarities and differences between those areas and the common risk indicators. Profiling the characteristics of areas that have similar fire incidence counts and rates provides a context within which both community fire safety planning and response options are better informed and can therefore be more effectively managed.

There are few events that wield such destructive power in terms of injury, trauma and economic loss, for the individual and family than a fire. The overall cost of fire to the UK economy is some £5 billion a year (Audit Commission 1995). The human costs are devastating with an estimated 643 deaths from fires and 18,170 non-fatal casualties in 1998 (Home Office 1998). The Home Office brigade-level and national statistics show that fire is selective in terms of those who are most vulnerable (e.g. elderly households and young families) and the areas affected. However there is surprisingly little literature in the field of risk factor identification and incidence pattern analysis with respect to fire. The research conducted to date (e.g. Sutton 1994; Runyan *et al.* 1993; Chandler *et al.* 1984; Gunther 1981) highlights the need for further research into the social, economic and environmental risk factors which underpin the incidence of different types of fires and their geographical distribution. Almost all of the limited research conducted has, however, been outside the UK or is based upon data that are now relatively old and have limited applied potential within the fire service in the UK.

The fire service: an overview

The fire service in England and Wales falls under the responsibilities to Parliament of the head of the Home Office, the Home Secretary. This responsibility is devolved to local authority level, more specifically to a committee of elected representatives forming a fire authority. It is the responsibility under the Fire Services Act 1947 (as amended) of the local authority through the election of a fire authority to provide a fire service. The primary responsibilities of the fire service/brigades are to safeguard people's lives and minimise damage caused by fire to property. Historically the fire service has not been afforded the same high level of political interest that has been very evident in terms of law and order and the drive to reduce levels of crime. However, with an increasing focus on public expenditure and the drive to achieve 'best value' in all the public services, the fire service has come under increasing scrutiny. The 1995 Audit Commission report *In the Line of Fire* considered the need for, and proposed an 'agenda for change', recommending that research should be conducted to inform a future policy framework for the provision of fire cover based upon empirical evidence. They also stated that whilst maintaining the current high standards of response options that priority should be given to the development and implementation of effective fire prevention measures. Following this the Home Office commissioned and then published a report *Elaboration of a Risk Assessment Toolkit for the UK Fire Service* (ENTEC 1996), this report addressed the feasibility and applicability of a risk-based 'toolkit' for the production of national standards for the provision of local fire cover. It considered and proposed the use of classifying areas based upon the levels of fire incidence experienced, the rate of casualties and fatalities per a given number of incidents, and examining these rates in relation to discrete demographic groups and building types. The report then considered the use of the derived area classification and vulnerable demographic groups for the purpose of targeting and delivering fire safety initiatives and fire cover. A subsequent report by ENTEC, in part, concluded: 'the variation in fire incidence and fire casualty rates could be measured directly for the purpose of assessing fire cover needs, with assessment of local social-economic and demographic factors completed for the purpose of targeting fire safety education and prevention work on the highest risk households' (ENTEC 1998: 26).

If we are to consider the primary aim of the fire service 'to safeguard people's lives' then the main focus of our efforts should be directed at the identification of those groups of the population most at risk and their location. Fire Statistics United Kingdom 1998 reports that around three-quarters of all fatalities and casualties result from residential dwelling fires (Home Office Statistical Bulletin 1998: 15/99). The report of the Community Fire Safety Task Force, *Safe as Houses*, published in 1997, was produced by appointment of the Home Secretary with the following terms of reference: 'To propose a community fire safety strategy and supporting action plans which will significantly reduce the numbers of fires and fire-related casualties in dwellings' (Community Fire Safety Task Force (CFSTF) 1997: 1). The Task Force stated that 'we believe that the majority of domestic fires are preventable. They are mostly the result of a lack of care or inappropriate behaviour' (CFSTF 1997: 4). The report stated that there was a need to ensure that brigades adopted a new culture of prevention as their primary aim. Organisational changes were required to accommodate a new strategy and vision involving the inception of a National Community Fire Safety Centre to provide a national framework within which CFS would develop. The report also expressed surprise in that 'the Government currently has no targets on fire or casualty reduction nor forecasts for the future' (para 4.2), along with a lack of quantifiable performance indicators in this area. There was also a lack of planning both locally and nationally and little or no monitoring and evaluation of CFS work. Great emphasis was placed upon the need for empirical evidence derived from data analysis and targeting of resources based upon this analysis at the local level to identify and reach risk groups.

The current structure of the fire service is inherently spatial in terms of both administrative and service delivery organisation. To a great extent the fire service is defined by a hierarchy of spatial boundaries nesting within national boundaries and falling under the overall responsibilities of the Home Office for England and Wales. The individual brigades are often subdivided into divisional areas or commands and then into smaller station areas. National fire statistics are compiled and published by the Home Office Research, Development and Statistics Directorate on an annual basis and report aggregate data at brigade level. Any reporting or analysis of fire service incidents below this level has historically been left to individual brigades to undertake. This has resulted in the fire service, for various reasons, failing to develop any meaningful structure and methodology for the collection, manipulation, analysis and dissemination of fire-related data and information below the brigade level. This is not to say that individual brigades and individuals within brigades have not conducted research and implemented initiatives based upon the results. It does, however, mean that there has been a lack of communication, collaboration and focus upon the possible benefits to be derived from a greater use of evidence-based risk analysis within the fire service as a whole.

The challenge for the fire service is to reduce the incidence of fire and casualties through a new focus on prevention through community fire safety whilst maintaining the current high level of response options. The drive is for a more effective, more efficient and more proactive force that is informed by empirical evidence derived from data analysis and research. The role of GIS will be central to the success of this process. Caution should, however, be exercised in the adoption of GIS and statistics as guiding lights within the fire service and this chapter looks at some of the benefits of informed use of these techniques and highlights dangers of blind dependence upon GIS, maps and numbers.

The national picture: a survey of fire brigades

During April and May 1999, the author carried out a national survey of the fire service examining 'the use of information technology and statistics in community fire safety planning'. The survey was conducted at brigade level and was sent out to fifty-eight brigades in England, Wales, Scotland and Northern Ireland. The Channel Islands and the Isle of Mann services were not included (due to data recording procedures incompatible with the structure of the survey). Fifty-two of the fifty-eight brigades responded to the survey and there were no significant variations between the characteristics of the respondent and the non-respondent groups of brigades. The survey was designed to provide a national position statement in terms of data, software, skills, priorities and current practice with reference to community fire safety planning within the fire services of the UK.

Fire incident data reporting procedures

Fire incident data, for primary fire incidents, are recorded on a Home Office form known as the 'FDR1'. The purpose of one section of the form, the 'geocoding of incidents' section, is to 'collect information on the address, or geographical location, of the fire. . . . Where buildings are involved, it is particularly important to complete the postcode. . . . OS grid references should be provided from Command and Control systems where possible. If available give the full eight-digit Ordnance Survey (OS) national grid reference. Alternatively give the six-figure number by omitting the last digit of both four-figure references. . . . If the grid reference is not available, leave the box blank' (FDR1(94) guidance notes, section 2). The FDR1 address field is not structured in any way and as such does not provide prompts to fire fighters to provide the address information in a standardised format with discrete fields for each individual component of the address. Although software for address matching does exist, the complexities arising from the variations in the way addresses are recorded are time consuming and often difficult to overcome.

It is acknowledged that for fire incidents other than in buildings, which can be identified via a postal address, that there are practical limitations to the accuracy of a grid reference that can be obtained.

Results from the survey

In terms of practicality of access to the wealth of data recorded for each incident by a brigade on the form FDR1, the brigades were asked if they stored this data in computer files. Of the fifty-three respondents, thirty-nine brigades representing 73 per cent of the sample stated that they kept computerised incident records, with only twenty-nine brigades capturing 100 per cent of those incident records. Although not questioned directly, experience and communication with brigades reveals that amongst those who do record FDR1 data in a digital format, there is great variation in what data are captured and the quality and structure of the records. Table 8.1 shows the variation reported in the recording of a geocode for FDR1 incidents.

The explanations for choice of geocode recorded showed that 60 per cent of brigades stated that their choice reflected a recognition of the utility

Table 8.1 The variation in the geocode scale recorded for FDR1 incidents

FDR1 geocode scale	Frequency
None	8
1 km	5
500 m	9
100 m	6
50 m	1
10 m	1
1 m	13
Post code	9
Other	1

of a geocode whilst the remainder stated their method was a reflection of historical precedent or Home Office requirements. The reported level of variation in terms of the geocode scale is indicative of a lack of clear guidance and understanding of the importance of the content and structure of the data collected as well as the potential applied uses of that data.

In terms of the use of these data, thirty-one brigades reported having a statistics department while only nineteen brigades had a GIS department and seventeen brigades stated that they did not use any GIS for fire data analysis. A 1997 survey of United States law enforcement agencies reported that only 14 per cent and 35 per cent of agencies employing over 100 sworn officers were undertaking crime mapping (Mamalian and La Vigne 1998). Although there is no up-to-date comparable data for the UK police, 77 per cent of brigades stated that they made some use of GIS and computer mapping. GIS departments were also found to be predominately under the command of Operations with little or no use made of GIS for community fire safety purposes. This was not a universal finding and there are examples of brigades making increasingly effective use of GIS within the field of CFS.

The use of supplementary data sources to provide a context within which the fire incident data may be analysed was questioned. The results are shown in Table 8.2.

The survey reports only 40 per cent of brigades were using any additional source of data to provide a context for the fire incident data. Yet as part of the local government, the fire brigades have access to a wide range of contextual data sources under numerous service level agreements and licences.

The use of data within brigades was questioned in terms of resource allocation and setting quantifiable performance related targets. The results are shown in Table 8.3.

Although there were no targets set by the Home Office for the reduction of fire incidents, casualties and fatalities (CFSTF 1997: 4.2), three-quarters of brigades used data to set some form of targets for the reduction of fire

Table 8.2 The use of contextual data for fire incident analysis

Other data sources	Number of brigades producing this report	Percentage of brigades
Other data sources used? Yes	21	40
Census data	14	26
Unemployment data	4	8
Housing benefits data	1	2
Index of local conditions	2	4
Index of local deprivation	6	11
Property gazetteers	3	6
Area classifications	4	8
Insurance claim records	2	4
OS digital data products	6	11
Other digital map products	1	2
Other social economic or environmental data-sets	4	8

Table 8.3 The use of information derived from analysis of fire incident data

Data used for	Number of brigades
Data used for resource targeting	33
Data used for target setting	40
Targets set for brigade	34
Targets set for command areas	9
Targets set for station grounds	18
Targets set for other areas	2

incidents. While this is encouraging, brigade level targets are of limited applied use, only one-third of brigades set targets at station ground level and only two brigades at finer levels of geography.

In terms of how the data analysis reported in the survey was used to inform resource targeting, brigades were asked to provide details of initiatives undertaken resulting from some form of data analysis. The results are shown in Table 8.4 and are accompanied by comparative figures showing the percentage of all incidents reported in 1998 attributable to the incident type targeted by the individual initiatives.

The results highlight major disparities between the targets of the initiatives and the respective proportions of workload share and the rates and absolute numbers of casualties and fatalities for those specific incident types.

Dwelling fires were responsible for about three-quarters of the total number of non-fatal casualties. A similar proportion of fatalities also resulted from dwelling fires (Research and Statistics Directorate, *Fire Statistics United Kingdom 1998*: 23, para 2.14). The report of the Community Fire Safety Task Force, *Safe as Houses*, states that in terms of

Table 8.4 Data and geographical analysis for resource targeting purposes

Initiative	Number of brigades reporting initiatives	% of all incidents 1998 (based upon fire stats UK 1998)	% of initiatives	Cumulative % initiatives
Malicious calls	26	9.68	40.00	40.00
False alarm due to apparatus	10	26.99	15.38	55.38
Community fire safety	6		9.23	64.62
Arson	4	3.71	6.15	70.77
Chimney fires	3	2.18	4.62	75.38
Vehicle arson	3	5.78	4.62	80.00
Residential fires	3	8.17	4.62	84.62
Hotspot analysis	3		4.62	89.23
Rubbish fires	2	15.18	3.08	92.31
Chip pan fires	2	1.42	3.08	95.38
Station trends	1		1.54	96.92
Fire cover model	1		1.54	98.46
Smoke alarms	1		1.54	100.00

dwelling fire numbers 'We believe that significant in-roads can be made and estimate reductions of 8 per cent a year should be possible, delivering a reduction of 33 per cent over a five year period' (CFSTF 1997: 26). Yet only three brigades reported a targeted campaign aimed at the specific reduction of residential fires.

Only two brigades reported targeted initiatives for the reduction of the incidence of chip pan fires, yet the majority of injuries were caused by chip/fat pan fires which accounted for over one-third of all non-fatal casualties in accidental dwelling fires in 1998 (Research and Statistics Directorate, *Fire Statistics United Kingdom 1998*: 23, para 2.15).

No brigade reported targeted initiatives aimed at reducing the number of dwelling fires caused by smokers' materials. 'Smoking-related materials and matches were the most frequent source of ignition causing accidental dwelling fire deaths' (ibid.: 23, para 2.10).

'Both ministers who set overall policy for the fire service and the fire authorities who run it need to make the reduction of the number of fires and fire casualties the principal targets which drive fire service activity' (CFSTF 1997: 7, para 1.8). Over 55 per cent of the targeted initiatives reported do not directly involve fire or casualties/fatalities. In terms of current thinking and policy initiatives within the government and the fire service, these figures appear to represent a focus upon targets outside the primary aim to reduce casualties and fatalities through community fire safety fire prevention initiatives. However, individual brigades should have regard to the proportion of their response workload that malicious false alarms and false alarms due to apparatus account for. The national figures for 1998 report that malicious false alarms and false alarms due to apparatus accounted for 37 per cent of all incidents responded to (a rise of 2 per cent on figures from 1997). Rubbish fires accounted for 15.18 per cent of all incidents attended by the fire service in 1998, yet only 3.08 per cent of initiatives reported focused on this area. There are conflicts between resource allocation in terms of reducing the numbers of casualties and fatalities through driving down incidents of dwelling fires (dwelling fires accounted for 8.17 per cent of all incidents 1998 and 82 per cent of all non-fatal casualties and 76.05 per cent of fatalities), and the disproportionate demand for resources by incidents involving a very low casualty/fatality rate. The financial strictures within which fire authorities and brigades must work, and the CFSTF's assertion that 'The fire service's re-focused role need not increase the total budget of individual brigades. . . . We believe that most of the budget for these teams (CFS) can come from a reallocation of resources' (CFSTF 1997: 17, para 5.11 and 5.12) mean that the fire service will require an informed, balanced and dynamic approach to resource allocation. The achievement of such a level of informed and enabled management and service delivery is to a great extent dependent on the ability of the fire service to provide high quality, timely and relevant information to its managers. The survey asked the brigades to consider their skill levels in five different areas; a summary of the results is shown in Table 8.5.

Statistics was the only skill area in which the majority of brigades considered themselves either skilled or very skilled. A previous question established that analysis was reported only at the brigade level for the majority of brigades. This severely limits the utility of the information in terms of brigade management, providing only an overview of incidents. Effective use of the wealth of information available within brigade records would require at a minimum that 'each brigade should look to provide the station with the impetus necessary to drive the process (i.e. CFS planning) across their brigades, together with monthly statistics on the number of fires and casualties in their area' (CFSTF 1997: 18, para 5.23).

Table 8.5 Skill levels within brigades

Skill level	Not at all skilled	Not skilled	Skilled	Very skilled	Priority Yes	Priority No
Statistics	3	15	20	15	49	3
Mapping and GIS	19	15	10	9	46	7
Delineation of priority areas	26	15	7	5	31	22
Risk factor identification	17	16	12	8	36	17
Monitoring and evaluation	23	14	9	7	45	8

The ability to 'map' incidents and make use of even the most elementary functions of a geographical information system, linking incident data with other data-sets through geographical location, enables the incidents to be aggregated by a specified spatial unit and contextual attribute data to be appended to incident records. 'Special targeting . . . is needed. . . . However, many brigades are still attempting to develop their own approaches upon no harder evidence than a gut feeling' (CFSTF 1997: 10, para 2.19). Mapping and GIS use is able to produce data from which information can be extracted. However, whilst 77 per cent of brigades stated that they made use of mapping and GIS, 65 per cent of brigades consider themselves either not skilled or not at all skilled in these areas.

The use of the data produced via statistics and GIS would enable historical analysis of the spatial and temporal distribution of incidents at an appropriate level of geography and interval of time. The ability to produce this level of information provides baseline statistics, the use of which (in conjunction with other factors) enables the expectation of the community fire safety team to '. . . identify and target special local campaigns' (CFSTF 1997: 15, para 4.9), to be based upon 'harder evidence than a gut feeling'. The skills needed to produce baseline statistics via the use of GIS returned the lowest levels of self-assessed skill base within the brigades, with 79 per cent not skilled in this area. This lack of skill is reflected and to a greater or lesser degree may be in some part responsible for only 34 per cent of brigades producing reports below brigade level.

The identification of risk factors directly from analysis of fire incident data captured from the FDR1 form requires the combination of the previous three skill areas (i.e. statistics, mapping and GIS and delineation of priority areas) to provide the base data for further analysis. 'Brigades would tailor local activity to their own area to reach those 'at risk' groups as this is where local input can have the most effect' (CFSTF 1997: 21, para 5.44). In order to achieve these levels of discrimination a higher level and wider range of data manipulation, analytical skills and understanding of spatial and statistical analysis is required. 'Evaluation is crucial to demonstrate the value of CFS activity in an environment of budgetary constraint. We recommend that all future CFS work must be evaluated so that resources can be effectively deployed and continuous improvements achieved' (CFSTF 1997: 15, para 4.14). With only 29 per cent of brigades considering themselves skilled in this area and the validity of any monitoring and evaluation to a great extent being dependent upon the other skill areas to produce the information required, there appears to be a pressing and wide ranging need for the acquisition of these skills within brigades.

Further questions established whether or not each of the skill areas was considered a priority. The two areas which are perhaps the most complex in terms of the whole process were 'Delineation of priority areas' and 'Risk factor identification', and were least commonly considered priorities with

39 per cent and 33 per cent respectively of respondents stating that these areas were not current priorities within their brigades.

Community fire safety staff '. . . have often worked on the margins of brigade activity, yet the results of their work is central to how a brigade's performance ought to be considered' (CFSTF 1997: 8, para 2.2). If brigades are to rise to the challenge of the increasing focus on CFS then it is through the development and implementation of the systems and skills to capture, analyse, interpret, develop, implement, monitor and evaluate both the differential demand for fire service educational programmes and response options along with the effectiveness of any CFS initiative undertaken.

Basic data requirements for effective and informed management

'Timely and relevant statistics should be a key source of information in analysing the causes of fires, establishing priorities and evaluating campaigns' (CFSTF 1997: 8). Within individual brigades, structures for the capture, storage manipulation and analysis of such data need to be put in place.

The Home Office forms FDR1 and FDR3 already provide a template for the capture of data on fire service incidents. The author is aware that these forms are already under review and that consultation is ongoing with brigades over the structure of the forms and their content. The FDR forms do, however, already capture a large quantity of valuable information and discussion of the possibility of the re-drafting of the forms will not be pursued in this chapter. The major advantage of adopting the FDR forms as the basis for data capture and storage is that it is compulsory for one of these forms to be completed and that fire fighters are already familiar with these forms. The fact that the forms are used by all brigades and form the basis of the Home Office's fire data records enables direct comparisons to be made between brigades' incident data and centrally produced national fire incidence statistics. The FDR forms provide a core data collection template, upon which individual brigades may choose to build, capturing and storing additional information for their own purposes (e.g. greater detail about casualties). However, as was reported in the results of the national survey, one major inconsistency within the data captured via the FDR forms is that of the geo-reference. The Home Office statistics are reported at the national level and at the brigade level. Brigades producing internal reports at the brigade level and for individual station ground areas, has meant historically that any failures by brigades to capture a meaningful geo-reference below the scale of the station area in a consistent format has not been addressed. In order to maximise the utility of the large volume of valuable data produced and recorded by brigades it is essential that a geocode be captured for every incident at the most precise and accurate scale practicable (ideally the methodology of producing the geocodes should be subject to a recommended standard across all brigades). In terms of residential dwelling fire incidents, on which this chapter will concentrate, software products already exist which may be considered to provide an acceptable level of accuracy and precision. The ability to employ the software to generate a geo-reference for residential and commercial properties relies upon the satisfactory capture of the address of the incident. The failure of the FDR forms to impose a clearly defined structure for the capture of the address (e.g. the use of British Standard 7666) has resulted in brigades recording the incident address data in an unstructured and inconsistent fashion. The failure to conform to any standardised address structure both within and across brigades can severely restrict the use of the address data captured.

For practicality of access to any data captured, it is essential that the data be held in any one of a wide range of computer file formats. The precise format used for storage by individual brigades is not of great significance, rather it is the ability of the storage systems to utilise common standards for the export and import of data that is crucial. The incident data itself should be stored as individual cases, each with a unique incident identification number, and the data captured for each incident should be stored as individual variables. No aggregation of the primary data should be made as this may limit its analysis output potential.

Fire service incident data are inherently geographical in nature. Every incident occurs at a location which can be designated a geographical reference, if these location data are recorded then, in theory, the data can be imported and manipulated within a GIS environment. The key factor is the ability to attribute a given incident to a precise and accurate location via a consistent methodology of geocoding the data recorded. Ideally the incident data will be given a national grid reference and stored in a digital database format. Again the choice of the GIS and statistical analysis software is not a crucial factor, it is the ability for brigades to import and export data in an accepted common format that is the key functionality of the software.

There is significant precedent for the use of GIS in evidence-based analysis and management of fire. Fire incidents have always been mapped and decisions have always to greater and lesser degrees been based upon some level of spatial and statistical analysis. Brigades have used paper maps and coloured pins and individual officers have developed local knowledge and mental maps of that knowledge. A simple anecdotal example of this is that a fire fighter will often know roughly where he or she is going to when a call is received before they are told, depending upon the time of day and or day of the week and or season of the year. Equally they will often know perhaps with even greater confidence to where they are not going. The use of GIS and statistical analysis enhances the capacity and sophistication of the fire services information resources, enabling management decisions to be informed by quantifiable empirical evidence.

Spatially referenced data-sets for fire analysis

With the basic data structure in place, the manipulation and analysis of the fire incident data become a practical possibility. Questions previously beyond the abilities of brigades, which should be fundamental to informed fire service management and delivery become answerable. We are able to report the What? Where? and When? of fire incidents at a level of geography that enables the further consideration of Why? With the use of GIS we are able to calculate rates of fire incidents at the small area level and provide contextual data for those incidents, bringing together what were previously disparate data-sets via the common link of geography. The following three subsections outline some of the data-sets that can be brought together to help inform fire service strategic planning.

Census of population

The census of population provides the most comprehensive and consistent source of demographic and social data available at the small area level. The smallest geographical unit for which census data are made available is the enumeration district (ED). An ED typically contains between 300 and 600 residents. The adoption of census geography as the unit of analysis for the fire incident data provides a consistent and comprehensive national set of boundaries for the analysis. These boundaries are both recognised and utilised by a wide range of people and organisations and are the areas for which both census data and other data-sets are available.

As we have seen from the survey results, brigades have often limited their statistical analysis of fire incident data to reporting at the level of the entire brigade or the individual station grounds/areas. The data analysis cited in this chapter is drawn from work conducted in the Greater Manchester area. The county is composed of 5,182 of these administrative ED areas. The EDs nest within the larger areas of the ward, of which there are 214 in Greater Manchester with an average population of around 11,500 residents. In terms of the GMCFS brigade area there are approximately 2.5 million residents, equating to an average population of around 61,000 served by each of the forty-one stations within the GMCFS area. The analysis previously conducted was often restricted to basic sums of incident types within the brigade area and then converted to an incident rate per 1,000 or 10,000 of the resident population. A lack of data and skills often inhibits analysis and production of rates for incident types below the brigade level. As station area boundaries often do not conform to ward or ED boundaries, brigades do not have easy access to a methodology for calculating the resident population numbers for station grounds. The use of GIS enables the calculation of station area populations through the aggregation of ED population figures that fall within the station ground boundaries. For those EDs that are split by a station ground boundary, the population can be attributed to the appropriate station either as a function of the percentage area of the ED in each station ground or as a function of the percentage of the ED's residential dwellings located within each station ground. Digital boundaries for the brigade area, station grounds, wards and EDs were obtained and imported into the GIS and used to map the incident data and variables obtained from the 1991 Census.

Fire incident data

The primary data used for the examples given in this chapter have been obtained from Greater Manchester County Fire Service. The data consisted of computer files of full FDR1 incident records supplied with an Ordnance Survey national grid reference. The fact that the records had been stored in a digital format and that the records had a grid reference attached enabled the data to be imported into a GIS software package, with little need for further processing or manipulation. In terms of the numbers of incidents attended by the GMCFS and used in the following discussion and examples, there are on average 5,000 residential dwelling fire incidents per annum. The data used for the purposes of this chapter are drawn from the data for the financial year 1998–9.

Index of local deprivation

A further source of information used in the analysis of the incident data was the Department of the Environment, Transport and the Regions' (1998) Index of Local Deprivation. At ward level the index is based upon the following six indicators from the 1991 Census:

- unemployment
- children in low earning households
- households with no car
- households lacking basic amenities
- overcrowded households
- Seventeen-year-olds no longer in full time education.

Statistical steps were then taken to produce an index score. Only those indicators that were above the national average at ED level within the ward were summed to give the overall index score for the wards. This step was taken to make the index an index of deprivation, rather than one where good conditions in terms of some of the indicators would counteract the poor conditions in terms of the overall index score. A full explanation of the derivation of the ILD can be obtained from the DETR.

Methodology

The first task to be undertaken was to use the GIS to identify the electoral ward in which each of the residential dwelling fire incidents occurred. This was achieved by plotting the Ordnance Survey grid references of the incidents and overlaying the ward boundary data using a point in polygon procedure. The GIS was used to link the attribute tables of both data-sets and the resulting incident record with the appended ward identification code was saved. Once the ward code had been attached to the incident record it becomes a relatively simple task to append any of the census variables and the ILD score, which is reported at ward level, to the incident data via the common link of the ward code.

Having decided to use the ward as the spatial unit for the preliminary investigation of the distribution of residential dwelling fire incidents, it was important to map the association between the station grounds and the ward boundaries. This was again achieved via the use of the GIS, although this time a polygon overlay was conducted that reported the proportion of the total area of a given polygon that falls within the boundary of any other given polygon or polygons. In this case the procedure was used to report the proportion of the area of the ward that was contained within the boundary of the station areas. The resulting output was produced in tabular and map format enabling each of the command areas and stations to identify which wards fell wholly within their boundary and which they shared with another station/stations. The proportion of the area of each ward within a station ground was also reported.

In order to describe the distribution of the incidents three methodologies were chosen to provide a range of useful information to the fire service:

1   An absolute count of the number of incidents reported in each ward
2   The ward count expressed as a rate per 1,000 resident population
3   A location quotient index value comparing the incident rate of the ward with the mean or average for the GMCFS area, with the latter set at 100 (e.g. a ward with an incident rate of four per 1,000 resident population compared with the GMCFS mean of two per 1,000 would have a location quotient index score of 200 which is twice the GMCFS mean).

The incident data were then aggregated at the ward and station ground levels. This produced a count of incidents for each of the 214 wards and forty-one station grounds in the GMCFS area. From these counts the rates per 1,000 resident population were calculated. The choice of resident population rather than the number of households as the denominator was made due to the assertion that it is the people in the households that are the main cause of the incidents rather that the dwelling and its fixtures and fittings. This choice is supported by examination of the incident data that shows that 86.5 per cent of all residential dwelling fires in Greater Manchester for the financial year 1998–9 can be attributed in some way to human behaviour. The significance of calculating the rate per 1,000 population for the incident types is that there is variation in the populations of the wards and significant variation between the population numbers within station grounds. The calculation of the rate controls for the variation in population observed when reporting the distribution of incidents.

The third method of describing the distribution of incidents, as a location quotient index score, is calculated from the rates per 1,000 population. It enables the data to be displayed in a format that allows the user to see at a glance the percentage variation above or below the mean/average rate for the brigade area as a whole.

The resulting data were then processed to produce tables ranking the stations and wards in terms of the absolute count of incidents and the rate of incidents. Further calculations were then made which reported the relative concentration of incidents in terms of the cumulative percentage of incidents against the cumulative percentage of population living within the wards.

In order to consider the use of the DETR's Index of Local Deprivation as a possible indicator for fire incidence levels, correlation analysis was conducted at the ward level. The use of correlation analysis explores the direction and strength of the relationship between different incident types and the ILD.

In terms of the numbers of casualties resulting from residential dwelling fire incidents, the individual wards were aggregated into groups based upon their ILD scores. Those wards that are classed as not being deprived, those with a score of zero, were thirty-nine in number and formed one group. The remaining wards, those classed as having some deprivation, were split into quintiles of equal numbers of wards ranging from those least deprived to those classed as most deprived. The numbers of casualties for each group were then calculated. In order to control for the variation in the aggregate populations of the groups the following calculations were made:

1   The total number of casualties recorded within GMCFS were divided by the total population of the GMCFS area.

2   The resulting figure was then used as an average casualty rate per head of population. This figure multiplied by the ILD group's population produced a measure of the expected number of casualties for each ILD group. This method assumes that all other factors with the exception of the total population were equal across the groups.

3   The observed number of casualties was then divided by the expected number of casualties for the group. The resulting figures were then plotted on a graph where a value of one indicates that the expected and observed numbers of casualties were equal. A value above one indicates that a disproportionate number of casualties occurred in that group, with the percentage above the expected rate read from the unit and decimal places above the value of one (e.g. a value of 1.25 would show a 25 per cent above the mean of the GMCFS area rate).

In order to examine the relationship between the incidence of residential dwelling fire and the outcome of those events in terms of the reported number of casualties, the ILD groups were again used. The number of recorded casualties, within each ILD grouping of wards, was divided by the number of residential dwelling fire incidents within the group. The resulting figures were then transformed as previously discussed to show the variation above or below the mean rate of casualties for the whole population, where the mean is equal to one. This procedure will allow the variation in the rate of casualties per incident to be examined across the six ILD groups.

Using the same ILD groupings, the distribution of incidents involving fatalities was also examined. Due to the relatively small number of incidents resulting in fatalities, and a lack of social, economic and environmental data relating specifically to those households, only a basic descriptive analysis of the distribution was undertaken.

Results

The ability to identify variation in the distribution of incident types and the relative concentrations within discrete spatial areas is essential for the effective targeting, monitoring and evaluation of fire service resources. The ward level analysis and the resulting targeting tables (Table 8.6) have been anonymised but illustrate the level of spatial concentration for:

1   Residential dwelling fire incidents
2   Malicious ignition residential dwelling fire incidents
3   False alarm malicious call incidents
4   Malicious ignition vehicle fire incidents
5   Residential Dwelling Fire Incidents resulting in recorded casualties.

From Table 8.6 it can be seen that specific categories of fire incidence and the incidence of casualties have been shown to be highly spatially concentrated when analysed at the aerial unit of the electoral ward. The concentration of residential dwelling fires shows that 30 per cent of all incidents occurred within twenty-three of Greater Manchester's wards that contain only 10 per cent of the county's population. Details of the concentration of a selection of other incident categories that require reporting under the Crime and Disorder Act are also shown. These malicious ignition incidents show even higher levels of spatial concentration with 50 per cent of all Malicious Ignition Dwelling Fire incidents occurring within wards that contain a total of only 10 per cent of the population of Greater Manchester. The incidence of casualties resulting from residential dwelling fires also shows a high level of spatial concentration, with wards again containing 10 per cent of the county's population accounting for 27 per cent of all recorded casualties for the financial year 1998–9.

Table 8.6 A ranked cumulative frequency ward-level analysis of the concentration of fire service incidents within the population of Greater Manchester

Residential dwelling fire incidents		Malicious ignition dwelling fires		False alarm malicious calls		Malicious ignition vehicle fires		Casualties from residential dwelling fires	
Culm % incidents	Culm % pop	Culm % incidents	Culm % pop	Culm % incidents	Culm % pop	Culm % incidents	Culm % pop	Culm % incidents	Culm % pop
2	>1	4	>1	4	>1	4	>1	2	>1
4	1	7	1	7	1	6	1	3	>1
5	1	10	1	9	2	8	1	5	1
7	2	14	2	11	2	11	2	6	2
8	2	17	3	12	3	13	2	8	2
10	3	20	3	14	3	15	3	9	3
11	3	22	4	16	3	17	3	10	3
13	4	25	4	17	4	18	4	11	4
14	4	28	4	18	4	20	4	13	4
16	5	30	5	20	4	21	5	14	5
17	5	32	5	21	5	23	5	15	5
18	6	34	6	22	5	24	6	16	6
19	6	36	6	24	6	25	6	18	6
21	7	37	7	25	6	27	7	19	6
22	7	39	7	26	7	28	7	20	7
23	8	41	7	27	7	29	8	21	7
24	8	42	8	28	8	30	8	22	8
25	8	44	8	29	8	31	8	23	9
26	9	45	9	30	9	33	9	24	9
27	9	47	9	32	9	34	9	25	9
28	9	48	9	33	10	35	10	26	10
29	10	50	10	34	10	35	10	27	10
30	10								

The use of the rate of specific incidents calculated as a function of population, controls for the variation observed in the relative populations contained within wards. The largest population contained within a single ward in the county is around 17,000 which is almost three times the smallest ward population of under 7,000 residents. Although wards, with high incident numbers are often high incident rate wards there are significant variations observed. Each statistic describes a different measure of the distribution of fire incidents and is equally valid and valuable in gaining a greater understanding of the nature of the problem being considered.

Once the distribution of fire incidents had been demonstrated to be highly spatially concentrated, work was undertaken to explore the possible links between the incidence of fire and various social, economic and environmental variables. The DETR's Index of Local Deprivation was used in a bivariate correlation test with selected incident categories. Table 8.7 lists the resulting correlation coefficients. All the categories of fire incidence resulted in relatively high levels of correlation with the ILD. Residential Dwelling Fire incidents show the highest level of correlation with the ILD indicating a strong link between levels of deprivation and the incidence of different categories of fire incidence. The indication of the possibility of a link between these two factors, as described by the correlation coefficient, should in no way be considered as casual. However, there does appear to be a positive relationship between the two independent variables.

In order to consider the relationship between deprivation and fire incidence at the ward level further, the wards were split into six groups as described earlier. One group of wards was classified by the ILD as not deprived and the remaining wards were split into five groups containing equal numbers of wards. The analysis resulted in all of the incident types examined indicating that the rate of incidents within each ILD group increased significantly as the levels of deprivation increased. The most marked variation between the groups was shown by the analysis of the Malicious Ignition Residential Dwelling Fire incidents, with the most deprived group rate being around fourteen times that of the group described as not deprived.

The variation in the incidence of casualties resulting from residential dwelling fire incidents was also analysed using the ILD ward groups and the results are shown in Figure 8.1. Again a strong relationship between increasing numbers of casualties can be observed with increasing levels of deprivation. This result is roughly in line with the distribution of residential dwelling fires within the six ILD groups and is in fact predominately a result of higher numbers of fires resulting in higher numbers of casualties. A more interesting question was that of the outcome of residential fire incidents in terms of casualty rates per incident. The resulting rates are plotted in Figure 8.2.

Table 8.8 shows the numbers relating to the graph shown as Figure 8.2. It can be seen that the wards classified as most deprived by the ILD have the lowest rate of casualties per residential dwelling fire incident. The wards described by the ILD as not being deprived have a casualty rate per

Table 8.7 Fire incident category correlation coefficients

Incident category	Correlation coefficient
Residential dwelling fire	0.712
False alarm malicious	0.655
Malicious ignition residential dwelling fire	0.594
Malicious ignition vehicle fire	0.583
Residential dwelling fire resulting in casualty	0.548

Note: Produced via SPSS, Pearson correlation, significance level 0.000.

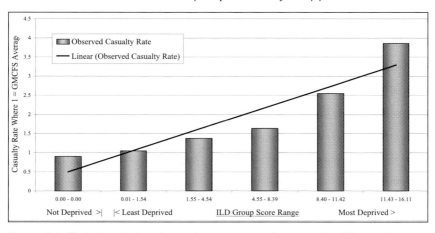

Figure 8.1 Variation in the observed casualty rate between the ILD ward groups 1998/1999.

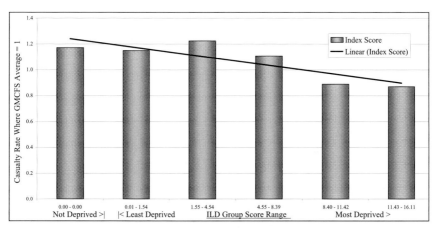

Figure 8.2 Variation in the observed casualty rate per residential dwelling fire incident between the ILD ward groups 1998/1999.

incident that is 35 per cent higher than that of the most deprived 20 per cent of the wards within the county. The highest level of casualties per incident, 0.44, is found within the group of wards with ILD scores between 1.55 and 4.54. This rate is 40 per cent higher than the rate of the most deprived group of wards.

Levels of preventable fatalities resulting from fire incidents are relatively small in number. Within the county of Greater Manchester the fatalities were plotted on a choropleth map which simply shows those wards classed as deprived and those wards classed as not deprived. The map, Figure 8.3, shows that for the year 1998 all but one of the incidents resulting in a fatality occurred within wards that are classed as deprived.

Table 8.8 Variation in the observed casualty rate per residential dwelling fire incident by ILD ward groups

	ILD score ward groups	Residential dwelling fires	Number of casualties	Casualty rate per residential fire incident	Index score
Not deprived	0.00–0.00	456	192	0.42	117.19
Least deprived	0.01–1.54	431	178	0.41	114.95
	1.55–4.54	484	213	0.44	122.49
	4.55–8.39	674	268	0.40	110.67
	8.40–11.42	1,024	327	0.32	88.88
Most deprived	11.43–16.11	1,607	502	0.31	86.95

Even accounting for the predominance of wards classed as deprived within the county (80 per cent) there is disproportionate concentration of fatalities within those wards classed as deprived. However as with the casualties when we consider the number of fatalities in relation to the number of residential dwelling fire incidents, the disproportionate concentration within the wards classified by the ILD as deprived, is explained by the greater number of incidents within those wards.

Figure 8.3 The spatial distribution of incidents resulting in preventable fatalities and deprivation at ward level within Greater Manchester 1998.

Data quality and potential community fire safety applications

The concept of and the need for community fire safety is not new. The United States of America has since 1973 published statistical justification for and opinion about the need for increased efforts in these areas. 'Because so many fires are due to human carelessness . . . the Commission has placed great emphasis on education as a means of reducing the Nation's fire losses' (National Commission on Fire Prevention and Control 1973: 134). To this end they identified the need maintain 'continuous and complete data collection and analysis to identify fire protection problems and solutions as top priorities' (FEMA 1990: 102). Research conducted in the UK by Goodman and Mason (1985) examined fire incident data for Gateshead January 1981 to December 1982: 600 fires; and for Tameside October 1980 to September 1982: 500 fires. The research found that 'thirty-six of the 492 EDs in Gateshead accounted for 127 of the 415 fires (thus 7 per cent of the EDs accounted for 31 per cent of the fires. . . . Local knowledge confirmed that these EDs tended to occur in the more deprived areas of the borough' (Goodman and Mason 1985: 5).

With the high levels of geographic concentration of incidents demonstrated in the analysis conducted and the apparent relationship exhibited between high levels of incidence and high levels of deprivation, the case for the use of GIS and statistics is strong.

The ability to make use of GIS as an effective analysis tool is highly dependent upon the precision and accuracy of the geographic reference recorded for each incident. The term precision refers to the minimum distance that can be recorded, while accuracy describes how close the measurement is to its true location. Both factors are crucial to the ability to justify the validity of any spatial attribution and analysis undertaken. Interim guidance from the Home Office with reference to the fire cover review and community fire safety initiatives recommends the capture of a twelve figure, Ordnance Survey National Grid reference for each incident. This one metre grid reference is stated as the ideal and that grid references should be as accurate as possible but have a maximum error of ten metres. The requirement for such a high level of spatial precision and accuracy is explained by the situation illustrated in Figure 8.4.

Those brigades recording the 500 m risk category grid square in which an incident occurs cannot attribute the wealth of contextual data available at the small area level (the Enumeration District) to their incident data. Figure 8.4 shows that an incident within the 500 m grid square shown could have occurred within any one of the fourteen EDs highlighted. However the ability to meet the requirements recommended by the Home Office of one metre precision accurate within ten metres has practical limitations. For addressable locations, the use of existing address matching and geo-referencing software is possible and will produce a grid reference precise to 0.1 metre. The accuracy of these references does not however

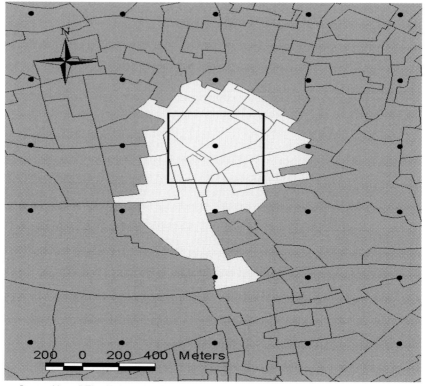

Steven Merrall The University of Liverpool

Figure 8.4 The need for accurate and precise spatial referencing: possible ED
location of a 500 m grid ref.

always meet the recommended levels of the Home Office. For non-
addressable locations, location proximity information is often recorded
and used to derive a geo-reference for fire service incidents. Again this
practice will not meet the recommended levels of accuracy and as such
would require an improved methodology to be applied.

In order to ensure that all future data captured retains its maximum
potential utility, meeting the requirements of the fire cover review and
beyond, a full review of data capture and recording procedures would often
be required. It is essential that the highest standards are set and adhered to
at the level of the control room, the scene of the incident, and in post-
incident data processing. The following recommendations are made:

Control room

1   The data recorded in the address field should be subject to a clearly
    stated and strictly adhered to set of rules and conventions.

2   The address field should be exclusively reserved for address details with the use of a separate field for location proximity information.
3   Adequate training and explanation should be provided to the control room staff to ensure adherence to the address recording conventions.

At the incident

1   It should be the responsibility of the officer in charge (OiC) at the incident to ensure that the correct location information is recorded. In terms of addressable locations, the record must include:
    (i) The property number and/or name if applicable
    (ii) The full street name and suffix (e.g. Street, Road, Avenue)
    (iii) The district name.
2   If the incident occurs at a non-addressable location (e.g. a skip fire or a grass fire) the nearest addressable location details should be recorded in accordance with pre-specified criteria, and location proximity information recorded.
3   Alternatively for non-addressable locations especially for those which are geographically remote from addressable locations, a hand-held Global Positioning System (now relatively inexpensive and increasingly accurate) could be employed.

Post incident

1   The OiC should be responsible for the confirmation, validation and updating of the incident location record. His record will be the final validated location record for the incident taking precedence over the Command and Control recorded data (often vague, incomplete or incorrect).
2   For non-addressable locations, the OiC should be responsible for producing an accurate and precise grid reference for the incident location from a standard map base used by the brigade.
3   For addressable locations full address details captured and stored in accordance with the stated convention would allow an address match to be made and a geo-reference to be generated via software and databases currently available.

Once the basic data standards have been satisfied the distribution of fire incidents can be analysed at varying spatial levels. The identification of high incident number areas along with the ability to link demographic data and produce rates for incident types informs the management of the fire service beyond what was previously possible. Access to the wealth of contextual social, economic and environmental data available at the small area level enables the links between fire and contextual variables to be explored. The use of the ILD as a correlate of fire incidence has demonstrated a link between the incidence of fire and the incidence of relative deprivation. Further research is being conducted to give a much finer level of risk factor identification. Individual variables often prove inert in terms of a given hypothesis, but when they occur in combination with one or more variables may prove highly significant. Research in the area of natural disaster vulnerability at the household level (Hearn Morrow 1999), shows that far from being mutually exclusive, risk factors tend to occur in combinations (or may arise from combinations) and intensify risk exponentially. It is the identification of the combinations of individual variables that coincide with high levels of fire incidence categories that may prove useful as risk indicators within communities and specific groups within those communities.

Often the much vaunted benefits and possibilities for improvement from technological advances within organisations come to nought. This is often due to over optimistic and unrealistic expectations of current and future computer hardware and software capabilities. The human factor can also be underestimated in terms of the knowledge required not only to operate the systems but more importantly to understand the data, the methodologies employed and the analytic utility and integrity of the information produced. For these reasons the author presents a limited overview of what is possible today, sitting at his desk, with his own ageing PC, working with relatively inexpensive retail software packages and using data generated within the brigade or available to many brigades through existing local authority service level agreements. The human factor is more difficult to quantify and to a great extent would depend upon the level of analytical sophistication a brigade would wish to achieve. Even at a basic level of data manipulation and analysis a failure to understand the principles of spatial, temporal and statistical analysis can result in well presented, convincing, but erroneous information being produced. Failure to ensure that appropriately skilled personnel are employed in this field of work would severely restrict the potential benefits of any investment in this area and may result in costly mistakes being made.

With an effective and adhered to data capture and storage system in place and access to a GIS and statistical analysis software brigades have the potential to:

- Map and quantify the distribution of fire incidents within varying geographies and by incident types.
- Consider the distribution of incidents in terms of rates as well as basic counts, through linking the incident data with basic demographic information.
- Overlay the incident data on to a meaningful map base or digital aerial photography creating risk maps of areas at any given scale and for any specific incident category.
- Link a wide range of contextual data sets with the incident data at the small area level.

- Conduct cluster analysis to identify hotspots of incidents removing the restrictions of the use of pre-existing administrative and delivery boundaries.
- Conduct analysis into the relationships between individual and multiple social economic and environmental variables and any given set of fire incidents.
- Identify high-risk areas and vulnerable demographic groups within those areas.

The results of these functions and analyses may enable the production of a series of predictive models relating to specific demographic groups, ethnic groups, area types, building types, and fire incident categories. These models and the information used to derive the models can be incorporated into the strategic management of the brigade, from the county level right down to sub-groups within small areas. The ability to perform these sorts of procedures is facilitated by the use of GIS, enabling a high degree of sophistication to be applied to the production of empirical evidence to inform the management and service delivery of the fire service.

The incidence of fire and the complexities of the interaction of people with their environment have shown the importance of considering the incidence of fire in different ways to contribute to the understanding of different questions. Basic counts of incidents can provide a measure of demand for resources, rates provide a comparative measure of the prevalence of a given incident type or outcome within an area or population. Table 8.8 illustrates the value of considering two ways of assessing the levels of casualties experienced within wards grouped by ILD scores. High levels of casualties are experienced within the most deprived wards of the county, yet when the rate of casualty per residential dwelling fire incident is calculated it is the most deprived areas that have the lowest casualty rate of all the groups. Efforts to reduce the incidence of residential dwelling fire within the most deprived areas may be needed, while in the more affluent areas it may prove more effective to provide education about what to do in the event of a fire to avoid becoming a casualty.

Conclusions

It is not that the explanation of the causes of fire incidents is thought to be primarily spatial in nature, rather that spatial analysis provides a consistent and comprehensive framework within which analysis may be conducted. While only 4 per cent of the public consider that they are likely to have a fire in the home, the respective figures for burglary and road accidents are 44 per cent and 35 per cent (CFSTF 1997: 11, para 3.3). One major difference between crime, road traffic accidents and fire is that you are often not a victim of fire but a contributory causal factor. The individual's behaviour within their own household is often the principal reason resulting in the ignition and contributing to the outcome of the fire in terms of casualties and fatalities. Historically, in Japan, 'a destructive fire disgraces the person who allows it to happen: once upon a time, it was sufficient cause for crucifixion' (National Commission on Fire Prevention and Control (1) 1973). It is perhaps in this area that the greatest challenge lies with the need to influence and maintain long-term changes in the public attitude towards fire safety behaviour. 'The single most critical factor to be considered is that public attitudes, behaviour and values contribute significantly to our high fire losses' (FEMA 1990: 101). The role of GIS and statistical analysis in this area is in its infancy, but even at this early stage they can be used to identify at risk groups and areas and to inform, target, monitor and evaluate community fire safety initiatives and resource allocation.

Within the changing nature of the political and organisational priorities of the fire service the flexibility of GIS as a spatial analysis tool along with the underlying ability to link what had previously been, for practical purposes, disparate data-sets, means that they will prove to be an important tool. We need to identify and demonstrate our knowledge of the root of the fire problem and accept that we are not seeking a solution but striving for a methodology of maximising the effectiveness of the utilisation of limited resources. GIS analysis outputs should be used to inform the decision process rather than the decision-making process relying upon GIS. There are practical limits to the levels of information that can be produced within and from GIS analysis. The identification of any limitations should always be vigorously pursued and supplementary evidence whether supportive or conflicting should always be considered. It is important to recognise that it is not blind dependence upon GIS and statistics but the ability to harness the functionality and the analytical power of these systems and methodologies which will enable the management of the fire service to move towards a best value service provision. The ability to move forward is not dependent upon some futuristic speculation about what will be possible, but rather it is a current reality that is capable of producing truly immense advances well within today's capabilities.

References

Audit Commission (1995) *In the Line of Fire, Value for Money in the Fire Service – the National Picture*, London: HMSO.

Chandler, S.E., Chapman, A. and Hallington, S.J. (1984) 'Fire incidence, housing, and social conditions – the urban situation in Britain', *Fire Prevention Journal* 172.

Community Fire Safety Task Force (1997) *Safe as Houses*, London: Home Office, HMSO.

DETR (1998) *1998 Index of Local Deprivation Summary Notes*, London: DETR.

ENTEC (1996) *Elaboration of a Risk Assessment Toolkit for the UK Fire Service*, London: Home Office, HMSO.

—— (1998) *Development and Trial of a Risk Assessment Toolkit for the UK Fire Service*, London: Home Office Fire Research and Development Group 5/98.

Federal Emergency Management Agency, United States Fire Administration (1987) *America Burning Revisited*. USGPO 1990.

Goodsman, R.W. and Mason, F. (1985) 'Housing factors and fires in two metropolitan boroughs', *Building Research Establishment Note 48/85*, Borehamwood: Building Research Establishment.

Gunther, P. (1981) 'Fire cause patterns for different socio-economic neighbourhoods in Toledo, Ohio', *Fire Journal 75*.

Hearn Morrow, B. (1999) 'Identifying and mapping community vulnerability', *The Journal of Disaster Studies, Policy and Management 23(1)*.

Home Office Fire Statistics and Research Section (1998) *Fire Statistics, a User Guide for Research*, Fire Statistics Research Section 1/98, Watford: Home Office Building Research Establishment.

Home Office Fire Statistics Section (1994) *FDR1(94) Guidance Notes*, London: Home Office, Fire Statistics Section.

Mamalian, C. and La Vigne, N.G. (1998) *The Use of Computerised Crime Mapping by Law Enforcement: Survey Results*, Washington, DC: National Institute of Justice.

National Commission on Fire Prevention and Control (1973) *America Burning: The Report of the National Commission on Fire Prevention and Control*, USGPO.

Research and Statistics Directorate (1997) *Fires in the Home in 1995, Results from the British Crime Survey*, Home Office Statistical Bulletin Issue 9/97, London: IPG.

—— (1998) *Fire Statistics United Kingdom 1998*, Home Office Research, Development and Statistics Directorate 15/99, London: IPG.

Runyan, C.W., Bangdiwala, S.I., Linzer, M.A., Sacks, J.J. and Butts, J. (1993) 'Risk factors for fatal residential fires', *Fire Technology Journal*.

Sutton, F. (1994) *Community Characteristics of Residential Fire Risk*, Wellington, New Zealand: New Zealand Fire Service.

Part IV
International perspectives

9 Tools in the spatial analysis of crime

Doug Williamson, Sara McLafferty, Philip McGuire, Timothy Ross, John Mollenkopf, Victor Goldsmith and Steve Quinn

This chapter examines four statistical/mapping techniques that are useful for the spatial analysis of crime: block aggregation, Voronoi diagrams, kernel smoothing and animation. Each technique is discussed in terms of its application to crime analysis, its utility for displaying crime patterns, and its ability to monitor changes in crime patterns over time. Using examples from a software package developed in collaboration with analysts at the New York City Police Department (NYPD), we illustrate the application of the methods in a GIS environment and the strengths and limitations of the methods when linked with broader crime reduction policies.

Introduction

Spatial analysis and spatial clustering methods are important tools for mapping, analysing, and visualising crime data. Researchers are adapting and refining such methods as point pattern analysis, nearest neighbour analysis, and spatial clustering analysis to support crime analysis and decision-making. Advances in GIS and spatial analysis make it possible to visualise and analyse real-time, geo-coded crime information in ways unimaginable decades before. Law enforcement agencies are beginning to use these methods to examine the associations between crime and environmental features, to pinpoint concentrations of criminal activity and to allocate resources for crime prevention to areas where they are most needed (Block *et al.* 1995). This chapter discusses several spatial analytic tools that are useful for crime analysis and describes a GIS-based application that integrates the tools in an easy-to-use system. The tools – block aggregation, kernel smoothing, Voronoi diagrams and animation – provide a powerful means of exploring, analysing and visualising crime patterns through space and time.

Two general classes of methods exist for identifying spatial concentrations of crime: area-based methods and point-based methods. In area-based methods, crime data are aggregated into geographical areas such as blocks, precincts or census tracts. For each area, the analyst computes a measure of crime intensity such as the total number of crimes or the incidence of crime in relation to land area, population or opportunities. Using standard choropleth mapping methods, levels of crime intensity can be displayed to show geographical variation. Other more robust methods, such as local indicators of spatial autocorrelation (Anselin 1995), explore the spatial association among crime rates for neighbouring areas to determine geographical concentrations of high- or low-crime areas.

Rather than aggregating crime data to areas, point-based methods work with a series of points that identify incident locations, the sites where crimes occur. Traditionally crime analysts would prepare 'pin maps' to examine geographical concentrations of crime incidents. Computerised point-based methods begin with digital pin maps and compute statistical measures of spatial clustering. One of the most widely used point-based methods for crime analysis is the Spatial and Temporal Analysis of Crime (STAC) system. STAC works by counting the numbers of crimes that occur in overlapping circles spread evenly across the study area (Block 1995). 'Hot circles' are circles that contain the largest numbers of crime incidents and 'hot ellipses' identify the areas of densest crime activity. Many law enforcement agencies currently use STAC to summarise, visualise and analyse the large quantities of spatial crime data that they handle on an ongoing basis (Block 1997). Although STAC is one of the most well-known point-based methods, analysts have recently examined other spatial clustering methods, including the Geographical Analysis Machine (Hirschfield *et al.* 1997), kernel smoothing (McLafferty *et al.* 1999) and Knox's test of space-time clustering (Canter 1997). The CrimeStat system, developed by Levine (1999) includes a suite of point- and area-based methods for exploring crime patterns.

This chapter describes a Crime Mapping and Analysis Application (CMAA) that incorporates both area- and point-based methods in a user-friendly tool for mapping and analysing crime patterns. The application allows users to query crime data and perform four different types of mapping and spatial analysis. Specifically, the application: (1) performs 'block aggregation' to generate choropleth maps of incidents aggregated to several types of geographic units (census blocks, police sectors, police precincts, etc.); (2) creates smoothed density maps of crime incidence using kernel estimation; (3) prepares Voronoi diagrams (Theissen polygons) of individual crimes and performs a coverage analysis based on the areas of Voronoi regions; and (4) creates map animations to show changes in crime patterns over time. Although the CMAA incorporates several complex methods, the goal was to create tools for rigorous display of distribution and change in crime patterns within an easy-to-use system aimed at non-specialists. Wherever possible, technical details were hidden from the user, parameters were 'hard-coded', and options were presented as clearly as possible. The application utilises MapInfo, a widely available GIS system; however, due to the complexity of the methods, we also relied on related software including MapX, Vertical Mapper and Visual Basic. This chapter begins with a brief overview of the CMAA. We then discuss the four spatial analytic tools that were incorporated in the CMAA and review issues and challenges associated with application of the tools.

Overview of the Crime Mapping and Analysis Application

The CMAA was designed to facilitate the querying, mapping and exploration of spatial and temporal crime data. In its simplest form, the application consists of four Visual Basic forms or windows: the main parent window, the selection/query window, the map window and the tool window. The *main parent* window is the window where all other smaller windows reside. The primary function of this window, apart from acting as a parent to all the 'child' windows, is to give the user some basic functionality common to most Windows programs (Figure 9.1). For example, from the File pull-down menu, users can exit the application, print maps, export maps and save layers. From the Select pull-down menu, users can open the query builder window, or run existing queries that have been saved from an earlier session. The final pull-down menu, the Window pull-down, allows users to open or bring to the front any of the windows that are present.

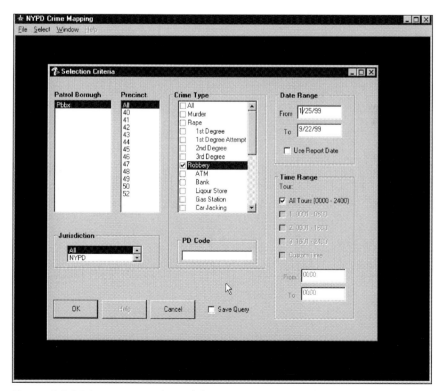

Figure 9.1 Main parent window of the crime mapping and analysis application.

The *selection/query* window allows the user to create a subset of the crime data by performing a query based on SQL (Structured Query Language). From this window the user can query the data. These may be based on patrol borough, precinct, jurisdiction, type of crime, date of incident (or report) and time of incident, as well as combinations of these attributes (Figure 9.1). The window also allows the user to save a query so that it can be used a number of times. The specifications for this window came from extensive discussions with crime analysts. They wanted the application to include a flexible environment for the creation of queries. A key element was the ability to search for patterns in the large volumes of crime information collected on a routine basis. The selection/query window facilitates the search for patterns based on type of crime, time and location of incident, and detailed attributes of the crime.

The *map window* is the heart of the application. It is here that the maps are displayed and more importantly, where the users can specify which type of map they would like to generate and which of the four spatial analysis tools they would like to use (Figure 9.2). The mapping 'engine' utilised is MapX SDK version 3.5.2 by MapInfo. In general, MapX SDK allows programmers to deploy mapping applications utilising technology from the

Figure 9.2 Map window of the CMAA.

GIS, MapInfo Professional. MapX does not have all the functionality of MapInfo Pro. Instead, it incorporates the most common attributes, such as creating dot maps and thematic maps, for example.

The limits imposed by MapX's functionality are important for two reasons. First, since functions and commands are limited, users do not have to spend a lot of time familiarising themselves with the software. Therefore, the learning curve is not nearly as steep as it is with a fully-fledged GIS, so scarce resources do not need to be devoted to training. On the other hand, since MapX lacks functionality, it is not nearly as powerful as a full-blown GIS. Because of this, many of the tasks and tools that one would normally expect from a GIS are not present. For example, in the version of MapX used by the application, users cannot directly query native MapInfo tables (.tab files). Instead, the programmer must use a different query environment such as Open Database Connectivity (ODBC), or in this case, MapBasic scripts to perform the query in MapInfo.

In addition to the four spatial analysis tools, the map window includes several additional features. From the map window, the user can call dialogues to change the appearance of map layers, set layers to visible or invisible, or change the drawing order of layers. The user can also exit the application, or reset the map to its initial state. Also on the map window are a status bar, which relays messages to the user, and a progress bar, which shows the amount of time left for a process.

The final window, the tool window, contains the basic tools and functionality required for navigating in a map window. It includes tools for zooming in, zooming out and panning. It also contains a tool for labelling features and adding text, as well as standard tools for selecting features.

Tools for the spatial analysis of crime patterns

The CMAA incorporates four spatial analysis tools that are useful for visualising, exploring and analysing crime patterns. All of the tools are relatively easy for non-specialists to use and comprehend. Linked into the CMAA with mechanisms for querying crime data, the tools provide a powerful means of looking at where various types of crimes occur in space, examining how the locations change over time and exploring the geographical associations of crime patterns with social and environmental characteristics.

Block aggregation

The first method, block aggregation, involves aggregating crime incidents into geographical areas and generating a choropleth map in which those areal units are shaded based on the number of incidents within them. The name, block aggregation, is a misnomer of sorts because any geographic unit can be used, not just blocks, but census tracts, police sectors, police precincts, or any other polygon layer in the application (see Figure 9.3). In short, block aggregation is a simple point-in-polygon analysis. This type of analysis enables the user to determine quickly which areas have a high incidence of crime and allows them to 'zero in' on those areas and perform further analysis. It is also useful for creating tables that show counts of crime by area and changes in crime incidence over time.

The block aggregation technique has several advantages. First, it is easy to calculate. Other than the acquisition of a digital census block map, there is no additional cost to employing the method. In addition, the output is easy to explain. Whether the audience is executive staff, beat cops, or community groups, block aggregation maps are easily understood, and do not require technical expertise to interpret. The technique is precise yet flexible. While many cluster identification techniques incorporate non-hotspot areas into their hotspots, the block aggregation technique precisely identifies which blocks have large amounts of crime and which do not. One can easily see situations where a crime-free block sits next to a crime-ridden one. However, two blocks with the same overall levels of crime may be significantly different in the way in which crime is distributed within them. Notwithstanding this limitation, analysis at block level can still be

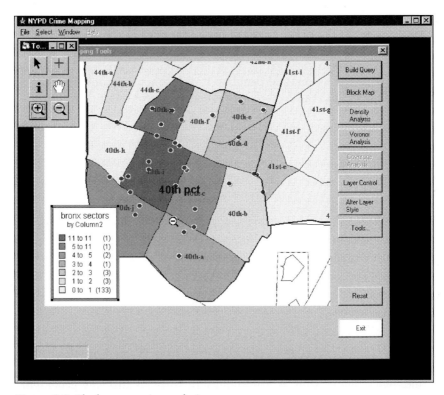

Figure 9.3 Block aggregation technique.

very useful. By ranking the blocks based on numbers of crimes, it is possible to create graphs showing the percentage of blocks that would need to be patrolled to cover a given percentage of crime incidents.

Finally, census block maps can easily be linked with other data sources, including the decennial census, the number of bars and/or liquor outlets and zoning data. We found, for example, that once the number of housing units had been taken into account through the production of burglary rates, the concentration of residential burglaries into certain blocks became less marked. Similar analyses could determine the importance of subway stops, public housing or schools in predicting crime rates (see Block and Block 1999; Kamber *et al.* 1999; Roncek 1999).

Despite its ease of use and intuitive appeal, the block aggregation technique has several limitations. First, the technique does not handle small amounts of data especially well. In a one-month time period for example, most blocks experience relatively few crimes. The counts of crimes for these areas are subject to all the statistical problems associated with small area data (Diehr 1984). The data for each block have a large random variability from month to month, so that the maps depicting those values may be misleading and inaccurate. On the block-level choropleth maps, increasing the cut-off point by one additional crime may drastically reduce the number of blocks identified in the highest crime category and vice versa. This often results in maps with either too few or too many 'hot areas' to be operationally useful.

The sizes of the blocks may skew the data. Some blocks incorporate malls or parks, while others refer only to small underpass areas. Large blocks, not surprisingly, often have a lot of crime, but may not be especially hot compared with similarly sized areas that are divided into three or four blocks.

The block aggregation technique was included in the CMAA because the advantages outweighed the shortcomings. Block aggregation is a useful tool for studying historic crime patterns, and provides an easy 'first cut' at the data before additional analysis using more sophisticated techniques. It also creates a direct link to demographic and housing data from the census and thus provides a valuable foundation for exploring the associations between crime and socio-economic conditions.

Kernel density estimation

The second tool, kernel density estimation, is a statistical method for determining the density of crimes or other point events at different locations (Bailey and Gatrell 1995). The method is used to generate a continuous crime density surface from crime point data. The analyst begins with a dot map of crime events. Kernel smoothing results in a continuous 'weather map' that shows geographic variation in the density or intensity of crime. Peaks on the map represent areas of high crime (crime hotspots) and valleys represent areas of low crime. Increasingly, crime analysts are employing kernel smoothing to visualise and analyse crime patterns (Williamson *et al.* 1999; Brown and Dalton 1998). A particular benefit of the method is that unlike in block aggregation, the analysis is not limited to some arbitrary geographic boundary, and it is much easier to discern spatial patterns than on a complex point map.

Kernel estimation begins by laying a fine grid across the study area. In most GIS environments, the user can define the grid cell size. Deciding on an appropriate cell size is important for two reasons. First, and less significant, is the output will appear more aesthetically appealing if the cell size is small. With a small cell size, the generated maps will appear less 'choppy', and smoother. Second and far more significant, when comparing the same point distribution, different cell sizes will ultimately lead to different density values. This is apparent when comparing density maps of the same point distribution with different cell sizes. This is also important when analysis between maps is done. Density maps should be created with same cell size if comparisons between point distributions are to be done.

Then, a circular window with a constant radius or bandwidth is moved across the study area, centered at each grid point (see Figure 9.4). The density of events is computed within this circular window. Events within the window are weighted according to their distance from the centre of the window; the point at which density is being estimated (Gatrell *et al.* 1996). Events located near the centre have a greater weight than those further from the centre. The kernel function therefore describes mathematically the weight assigned to points (crime events) within the circle in calculating density. In this way, kernel estimation reflects the underlying geographic locations of events within each circular window. Common mathematical forms for the kernel function include the Gaussian and quartic functions. Research indicates that density estimates are very similar regardless of which function is used (Diggle 1983).

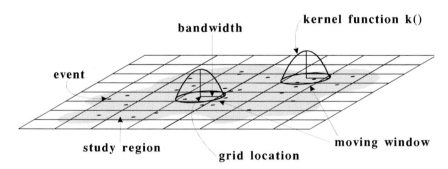

Figure 9.4 Calculating density of events using bandwidth and kernel function.
Source: McLafferty *et al.* 1999.

After computing kernel estimates of crime density for each regularly spaced grid point, one can generate a smooth map of density values. The results may be displayed as a standard contour map, a three-dimensional surface, or as a continuously shaded raster map with grey- or colour-tones representing density levels (see LeBeau 1995).

Figures 9.2 and 9.5 present a point map and a corresponding kernel density map of robberies in the 40th precinct in the borough of the Bronx, New York for a four-week period. By simply examining the point map, it is difficult to discern any clear patterns. Although several clusters of robberies are visible, differences in the numbers and intensity of events are unclear. It is also possible that in the densest areas, some dots may conceal other dots giving a false impression of the true crime density. By comparison, the kernel density map in Figure 9.5 is easier to interpret. Areas with large concentrations of incidents appear as shaded peaks on the map. Geographical variation in crime density is clearly visible on the smooth density map. In addition to its ease of interpretation, kernel smoothing, unlike other traditional methods for identifying crime hotspots, such as STAC (Spatial and Temporal Analysis of Crime), is that the hotspots can

Figure 9.5 Kernel density map of robberies in the 40th precinct of the Bronx, New York.

be irregularly shaped and need not follow regular geometric shapes like circles or ellipses (Block 1995).

Neither MapInfo nor MapX supports kernel estimation, since neither product has the functionality for creating grids or continuous data surfaces, and such grids are an essential output of kernel estimation. Therefore another product was utilised, Vertical Mapper SDK, which is the programming environment for Vertical Mapper. An algorithm to perform kernel density estimation was written in Vertical Mapper SDK and linked to the CMAA through the map window.

Voronoi analysis

The third tool, Voronoi diagrams, is a technique of spatial analysis that has seen wide application across many disciplines. Voronoi diagrams or Theissen polygons, divide a mapped area, into a number of polygons. Each polygon is constructed around a generating point, here the location of a crime incident, in such a way that every other point within the polygon is closer to the enclosed generating point (crime incident) than to any other generating point. The area within the polygon surrounding each generating point is the point's natural neighbourhood or Theissen polygon (see Figure 9.6). As the intensity of crime in a local area rises the Voronoi polygons become smaller and more closely packed. Thus, the Voronoi process can be interpreted as a clustering method.

The Voronoi diagram associated with a crime incident map may be quite helpful to police analysts and managers who are confronted with the problem of choosing the geographical areas to be assigned some special patrol resources. Specifically we present a method for performing what we have termed 'coverage analysis'. Coverage analysis relates the percentage of the total incidents mapped to the percentage of the total map area covered by the sum of the corresponding Voronoi polygons.

The relationship between the percentage of incidents and the percentage of area is based upon two factors. First, each Voronoi polygon is associated with one and only one crime incident, and second, the Voronoi polygons associated with clustered crime incidents are smaller than those associated with widely spaced crime incidents. Given this, we can create a Voronoi diagram that shows the trade-off between the number of crime incidents and the total area that lies within the Voronoi polygons associated with those incidents.

To create the Voronoi diagrams for a set of crime incidents, the generated polygons are ranked from the smallest to largest based upon each polygon's area. The ranked list can then be summed moving from the smallest to largest area row by row giving an accumulation for both incidents and for polygon areas. The cumulative sum in the last row containing the largest polygon and its associated incident will total the sum of all incidents represented in the map and the total area of the map,

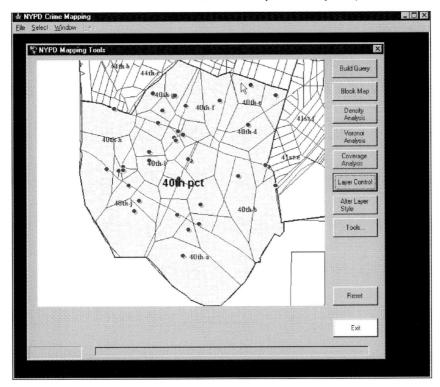

Figure 9.6 Voronoi diagrams of incidents in the 40th precinct.

respectively. The accumulation of each sum can be expressed as a percentage by dividing the cumulative row values by the respective totals. When the row by row percentages of cumulative count and matching cumulative area are plotted against one another in scatter plot format we have constructed the coverage curve.

At each plot point, the coverage curve displays the relationship between the percentage of the total incidents displayed in the specific map and the percentage of the total area covered by the Voronoi polygons generated by those points. By examining the coverage curve, and particularly specific graphic representations of the curve, crime analysts and police managers will be better able to select areas within their jurisdiction requiring special patrol attention. We can therefore envision a crime analysis tool that allows an analyst to move up and down the coverage curve while simultaneously viewing the appropriately shaded group of Voronoi polygons overlaid on a map of the jurisdiction. In this manner, the analyst can gain useful insight into the clustering of incidents within the jurisdiction. The analyst can also be assured that the coverage area at each level includes the most closely packed grouping of incidents that can be assembled (see Figure 9.7).

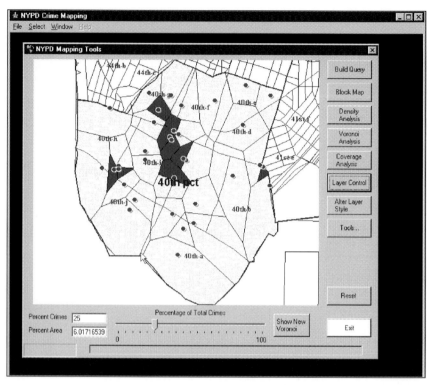

Figure 9.7 High density voroni polygons in the 40th precinct.

As with kernel estimation, neither MapInfo nor MapX supports Voronoi analysis so Vertical Mapper SDK was used to implement the tool. This presented a challenge. Vertical Mapper requires that there be no duplicate points, so two or more crime points cannot occur at the same location. This is significant when dealing with crime, because of the phenomenon of 'repeat' crimes – crimes that take place at the same address. Duplicate points are a major problem in densely populated cities like New York where it is common to find as many as ten crimes at the same address. Some of the crimes occur in different apartments in the same building, creating duplicate points because they are geocoded to the same street address. In developing the Voronoi tool, deleting duplicate points was not an option because it would result in a loss of data, and an underestimate of incidence. To overcome this problem, a script was written in MapBasic for dispersing duplicate points. The script takes a layer of points, checks for duplicates, randomly disperses any duplicates around the initial point and then writes out a new point layer. Therefore, the application must call MapInfo, run the script for dispersing points, return control to the application, then call Vertical Mapper to create the Voronoi polygons. Transferring control was quite tricky, but was finally resolved using OLE (object linking and embedding) which gives programmers the ability to place common applications within another application.

Another challenge was that the functionality of sorting and cumulating Voronoi polygon areas does not exist anywhere in MapInfo or Vertical Mapper. To accomplish this, Microsoft Excel was used. Excel was chosen because of the ease with which many of the tasks could be performed, such as sorting and calculating new values based on values in other cells. A macro was written in Visual Basic for Applications (VBA) which carried out all the necessary tasks. This script takes the resulting layer from the Voronoi analysis and performs all the required Excel functions. Then, based on the percentage of crimes the user wishes to analyse, the specific Voronoi polygons are identified. Once they are identified, MapInfo is called. There the polygons are selected based on percentage of crimes and a new layer is created that contains only those polygons. The new layer is returned to the application, with the associated cumulative area, so that the selected polygons can be shaded and displayed on a map. The user can also choose the desired percentage of crimes to be covered by moving a sliding bar.

Animation

The final tool incorporated in the CMAA is animation. Animated maps are: 'maps characterized by continuous or dynamic change' (Slocum 1999: 222). The maps are displayed dynamically, in sequence, forming a constantly changing image or animation. The field of animation has advanced rapidly in recent years, stimulated by developments in computer hardware and graphics. These advances are fueling changes in map making as cartographers gain access to one of the first effective tools for representing continuous change through space and time. Analysts are just beginning to explore the use of animation in crime mapping. Openshaw *et al.* (1994) were among the first to propose the use of animation for visualising spatial and temporal variation in crime patterns. More recently, crime analysts for the Tempe, Arizona Police Department put an animated map sequence on the web to depict changing patterns of crime density over time.

Creating animated map sequences involves decisions about the timing of maps in the sequence and their rate of change. Duration refers to the length of time each map is in view (Slocum 1999). A short duration means that each image disappears quickly producing a smooth, but constantly changing animation. In contrast, a longer duration gives the viewer more time to study each map, but the animation appears choppy. Rate of change describes the smoothness of the animated map sequence. It is computed as the amount of change between maps divided by the duration. If the positions or attributes of features on the map change substantially during the animation, the animation has a high rate of change. One can reduce rate of change by increasing the duration of each map and thus smoothing the transition from map to map. Similarly, reducing the amount of change between maps gives a lower rate of change and a smoother animation. One way to accomplish this is by using overlapping time intervals for the maps rather than discrete intervals. For example, the first map might show crime incidence for weeks 1–4, the second for weeks 2–5, the third for weeks 3–6 and so on. The one-week overlap means that some of the data on a map is shown on the next map so that the rate of change is more gradual. An innovative discussion of the smoothing and analysis of temporal crime data for small areas can be found in Ratcliffe and McCullagh (1998).

The animation component of the CMAA is designed to provide flexibility in defining duration and rate of change for a particular animated sequence. The crime analyst first selects the time interval for maps in the sequence and then defines the degree of overlap among the maps. This way one can control the smoothness or roughness of change in the animation and the time periods to be displayed. The animation works with crime density maps generated by kernel smoothing, because they are visually appealing and easy to comprehend in the short time interval of the animation. We experimented with animating dot maps of crime, but found them too complex to understand when viewed in sequence.

Animation is an effective way of displaying changes in crime through time and space; however, it is primarily a visual tool. Animated maps clearly show regular patterns, but if events move or vary in intensity unpredictably over time, the animation will be difficult to comprehend. Viewers often have trouble comprehending information on animated maps. The images move by quickly and are difficult to compare. Therefore we expect that the animation tool in the CMAA will primarily be used for visualisation and display, for 'gee-whiz' presentations, and to give the viewer a sense of general space-time trends.

To create the animation, the user is prompted to perform a selection of the crime data based on attributes such as precinct, crime type and date. The user is also asked to define a 'time window' that specifies the duration of time to be represented in each frame of the animation, i.e. five days, seven days, etc.. The user is also prompted for an incrementor that specifies how much each animation frame will be advanced by. The incrementor determines if the animation will show a moving average or not. This is useful because it smoothes the animation to make it less jumpy, as well as displaying more of the actual trend in 'real-time'. For example, if the time window is seven days and the incrementor is one day then there will be six overlapping days in the animation. Once the user specifies all the necessary parameters, the application begins querying the data, creating the maps and exporting the maps as images. A shareware product known as VFD (video for DOS) assembles the frames (images) into one seamless video file. The process can be CPU intensive, as well as memory intensive. The resulting animation can be viewed from the application itself, or by using a standard Windows media player. The final file format of the animation is a Windows video file (.avi).

Conclusion

The Crime Mapping and Analysis Application moves beyond the creation of computerised pin maps to assist decision-makers with visualising, analysing and uncovering patterns in the large spatial databases that law enforcement organisations work with on a daily basis. The application offers a series of technically sophisticated, yet easily used tools to understand when and where crimes are clustered in space, how those clusters change over time, and how a given level of resources might be allocated to cover the largest amount of crimes.

Although the CMAA was designed to be used by decision-makers with little or no training in spatial analysis, it is unclear how these 'non-specialists' will respond to the system and which of its components they will find of greatest value. In the future, we will monitor how different types of user react to the different functionalities of the package. This will enable us to identify and correct any problem areas, as well as to determine whether additional training might help realise the full potential of the application. It will also be important to determine, at some future point, the extent to which this technological innovation has helped in reducing crime and developing better strategies for crime prevention in New York City. The real test of such a system lies in its impact on crime and on the lives of those most affected by criminal activity.

References

Anselin, L. (1995) 'Local indicators of spatial autocorrelation: LISA', *Geographical Analysis* 27(2): 93–115.

Bailey, T. and Gatrell, A. (1995) *Interactive Spatial Data Analysis*, New York: Wiley.

Block, C.R. (1995) 'STAC hotspot areas: a statistical tool for law enforcement decisions', in C. Block, M. Daboub and S. Fregly (eds) *Crime Analysis Through Computer Mapping*, Washington, DC: Police Executive Research Forum, pp. 15–32.

—— (1997) 'The geo-archive: an information foundation for community policing', in D. Weisburd and T. McEwen (eds) *Crime Mapping and Crime Prevention*, Monsey, NY: Criminal Justice Press, pp. 27–82.

Block, C. and Block, R. (1999) 'The Bronx and Chicago: street robbery in the environs of rapid transit stations', in V. Goldsmith, P, McGuire, J. Mollenkopf and T. Ross (eds) *Analyzing Crime Mapping: Frontiers of Practice*, Thousands Oaks, CA: Sage Publications.

Block, C.R., Dabdoub, M. and Fregly, S. (eds) (1995) *Crime Analysis Through Computer Mapping*, Washington, DC: Police Executive Research Forum.

Brown, D. and Dalton, J. (1998) *Regional Crime Analysis Program (RECAP)*, presented at Crime Mapping Specialists Meeting, National Institute of Justice, Washington, DC, February.

Canter, P. (1997) 'Geographic information systems and crime analysis', in D. Weisburd and T. McEwen (eds) *Crime Mapping and Crime Prevention*, Monsey, NY: Criminal Justice Press, pp. 157–92.

Diehr, P. (1984) 'Small area statistics, large statistical problems', *American Journal of Public Health* 74(4): 313–4.

Diggle, P. (1983) *Statistical Analysis of Spatial Point Patterns*, London: Academic Press.

Gatrell, A., Bailey, T., Diggle, P. and Rowlingson, B. (1996) *Spatial Point Pattern Analysis and its Application in Geographical Epidemiology*, Institute of British Geographers, Transactions, NS 21: 256–74.

Hirschfield, A., Yarwood, D. and Bowers, K. (1997) 'Crime pattern analysis, spatial targeting and GIS: the development of new approaches for use in evaluating community safety initiatives', in *Crime and Health Data Analysis Using GIS*, Sheffield: SCGISA.

Kamber, T., Mollenkopf, J. and Ross, T. (1999) 'Crime, space and place', in V. Goldsmith, P. McGuire, J. Mollenkopf and T. Ross (eds) *Analyzing Crime Mapping: Frontiers of Practice*, Thousands Oaks, CA: Sage Publications.

LeBeau, J. (1995) 'The temporal ecology of calls for service', in *Crime Analysis Through Computer Mapping*, Police Executive Research Forum, pp. 111–28.

Levine, N. (1999) *CrimeStat: A Spatial Statistics Program for the Analysis of Crime Incident Locations*, Annandale, VA: Ned Levine and Associates/Washington, DC: National Institute of Justice.

McLafferty S., Williamson D. and McGuire P. (1999) 'Identifying crime hot spots using kernel estimation', in V. Goldsmith, P. McGuire, J. Mollenkopf and T. Ross (eds) *Analyzing Crime Mapping: Frontiers of Practice*, Thousands Oaks, CA: Sage Publications.

Openshaw, S., Waugh, D. and Cross, A. (1994) 'Some ideas about the use of map animation as a spatial analysis tool', in R.A. Earnshaw and D. Watson (eds) *Animation and Scientific Visualization: Tools and Applications*, London: Academic Press.

Ratcliffe, J. and McCullagh, M. (1998) 'Aoristic crime analysis', *International Journal of Geographical Information Science* 12(7): 751–64.

Roncek, D. (1999) 'School and Crime', in V. Goldsmith, P. McGuire, J. Mollenkopf and T. Ross (eds) *Analyzing Crime Mapping: Frontiers of Practice*, Thousands Oaks, CA: Sage Publications.

Slocum, T. (1999) *Thematic Cartography and Visualization*, Upper Saddle River, NJ: Prentice Hall.

Williamson, D., McLafferty, S., McGuire, P., Goldsmith, V. and Mollenkopf, J. (1999) 'A better method to smooth crime incidence data', *ArcUser*, January.

10 The evolution of crime mapping in the United States

From the descriptive to the analytic

Nancy G. La Vigne and Elizabeth R. Groff

Until quite recently, the use of Geographic Information Systems (GIS) for the purpose of mapping crimes in the United States was limited to a small group of geographers with an esoteric knowledge of the mechanics of map digitising and mainframe computer technology. In recent years, however, the marked reduction in the price of personal computer hardware, along with the availability of comparatively more user-friendly desktop mapping programs, has resulted in numerous crime mapping efforts in law enforcement agencies across the country. The academic community in the US has also made significant strides in the spatial analysis of crime. Partnerships between researchers and practitioners have advanced the state of knowledge even further. This chapter traces the growth of spatial and temporal crime analysis, which has evolved from the descriptive to the analytic, and summarises the current state of the field in the United States.

Introduction

Law enforcement officers and civilian crime analysts have been mapping crime virtually since the time that police agencies were established. Historically, however, such mapping was achieved through the use of pushpins and a paper map. The diffusion of GIS into crime analysis has been a slow process primarily because of cost (both hardware and software) and complexity. In the early 1970s, technological advancements in computers made computerised mapping accessible only to the largest and most innovative of police agencies. However, these systems required expensive, high-powered mainframe computers and trained personnel to run them.

It was not until the introduction of client server technology in the late 1980s that GIS became available at a more reasonable cost. At this point, a handful of police departments began to experiment with mapping and Geographic Information System (GIS) programs. These programs automate mapping and allow crime analysts and officers to produce maps with increased speed. However, true affordability did not arrive until the early 1990s, when personal computers powerful enough to handle large databases were coupled with software programs that did not require the disk space, memory and processing speed of a mainframe or workstation

computer. Since the mid-1990s, the use of GIS technology in law enforcement agencies has grown tremendously.[1] Through partnerships with
researchers, crime mapping has evolved from a descriptive exercise of pin
mapping to a more rigorous analytic effort. This chapter will discuss the
growth of spatial and temporal crime analysis and summarise the current
state of the field in the United States, both in terms of practitioner use, as
well as how research has influenced the direction of development.

Tracing the history of crime mapping in the United States

While geographic analyses of crime existed at an earlier date, the emergence of the study of the spatial distribution of crime as a school of
thought is generally considered to have taken place in the 1800s with what
is termed the Cartographic School of Criminology. The Cartographic
School of Criminology initiated in France and soon spread to England and
other European countries. Researchers used maps to assess regional variations in crime rates and particularly urban–rural differences, correlating
crime rates with other indicators of social conditions. Members of the
Cartographic School included Guerry (1833), who analysed crime patterns
in France and found consistent regional differences by socioeconomic
status. Later, in England, Mayhew (1862) examined variations in crime by
population density, concluding that crime is most prevalent in industrial
and urban areas.

For the most part, the Cartographic School analyses examined aggregate
statistics by region, comparing areal crime rates. Despite the limitations of
areal analyses, these early studies set the stage for more detailed examin-
ations of crime in urban settings in the United States. These studies
originated from the Chicago School of Sociology, noted for defining the
term 'human ecology'[2] and applying the general assumptions of ecology to
urban settings (Park and Burgess 1924). Burgess (1925), for example, used
human ecology to develop his concentric zone model, which contends that
urban land uses tend to form concentric zones around the central business
district. Shaw and McKay (1942) applied these assumptions to crime,
borrowing Burgess' concentric zone model and applying it to residences of
juvenile offenders brought before the Cook County (Chicago, Illinois)
court. Their examination of overall rates of crime revealed a decreasing
concentration from the central business district to the city's periphery, a
phenomenon referred to as 'distance decay'. Shaw and McKay's research
was complemented by ecological analyses that correlated variables such as
substandard housing, poverty, foreign-born population and mobility, with
high delinquency areas. These findings led them to formulate the social
disorganisation theory of criminality.

The Chicago School wielded great influence over the criminological
community in the United States, stimulating continued research on the
spatial distribution of crime and criminals during the decades of the 1950s,

1960s, and 1970s. The majority of these studies examined aggregate data and tested sociological explanations for the distribution of crime and criminal behaviour in relation to other social factors embodied in such theories as differential association, differential opportunity, social disorganisation and relative deprivation (Schmid 1960a, b; Schuessler and Slatin 1964; Marlin 1973; Flango and Sherbenou 1976; Strahura and Huff 1979; Worden 1980). For the most part, geographic methods remained elementary during this period of research. Analyses moved away from factorial toward multivariate regression, but these were merely different tools applied to the same data forms used by members of the Cartographic School in the 1800s. While the research of Shaw and McKay and their contemporaries was not without its theoretical merit in terms of providing sociological explanations for the occurrence of crime, 'the theoretic component of the Chicago ecology . . . became lost in a thicket of technique' (Brantingham and Brantingham 1981: 14). Thus, while much information was gained on sociological variables as correlates of crime, little was learned about the manifestation, patterning and distribution of crime until the advent of environmental criminology. Brantingham and Brantingham's (1975, 1977, 1978, 1981, 1984) work in environmental criminology examines how individuals' movements through the course of their daily activities are related to the spatial and temporal distribution of crime. The Brantinghams spearheaded the movement of studying crime as discrete events, analysing the location of crimes to sort out where, when, and how crimes occur. This new focus on criminal events gave rise to microanalyses of crime and criminal behaviour, highlighting studies of offender movement patterns and the ways in which the spatial patterning of crime is associated with the immediate physical environment. These efforts were not without their rewards, but the far-reaching analytic potential of the geography of crime did not manifest itself until researchers in academic settings partnered with crime analysts in law enforcement agencies – partnerships that serendipitously coincided with the advent of more affordable and user-friendly mapping software.

History of practitioner efforts

Despite the long history of academic work on this topic, practical application of crime mapping was still in its infancy in the 1980s. Only a few law enforcement agencies were using mapping, and in those cases, the mapping function was often housed in other local government agencies, such as the Planning or Public Works Department. By the late 1980s, the National Institute of Justice noted the potential of GIS technology and established a grant program called the Drug Market Analysis Program (DMAP). DMAP funded partnerships between researchers and police departments in five US sites to use innovative analytic methods to identify drug markets and track their movements over time in response to police interventions. These were some of the first crime mapping projects funded; their results promoted strong and lasting partnerships, generating great interest in GIS among other law enforcement agencies as well as criminal justice researchers (McEwen and Taxman 1995; Maltz *et al.* 1989).

Examples of the fruits of these DMAP-funded partnerships include those of Rutgers University and the Jersey City Police Department, who together conducted experimental designs testing problem-oriented policing tactics to combat violent crime. In Hartford, a partnership between the police and Abt Associates, a private consulting firm, promoted crime mapping as a means of engaging the community in crime prevention efforts. The San Diego Police Department's partnership with the Police Executive Research Forum to map the incidence and impact of drug markets and police interventions evolved into a system in which crime mapping is fully integrated into the department's problem-oriented policing philosophy. Finally, researchers at Carnegie Mellon University, through a partnership with the Pittsburgh Bureau of Police, developed a system whereby thematic maps were produced to illustrate changes in crime by patrol sector over time. These maps clearly depicted areas that were heating up and enabled proactive targeting of police resources. Overall, these DMAP projects set the stage for many of the crime mapping efforts underway in American policing today.

Crime mapping in practice

Crime mapping in the late 1990s, while increasingly sophisticated, is still in its infancy. A 1997 survey of US law enforcement agencies revealed that only 14 per cent of the nation's law enforcement agencies are engaged in computerised mapping; of those agencies with 100 or more sworn officers, 35 per cent were doing crime mapping (Mamalian and La Vigne 1998). While relatively few in number, these agencies are nonetheless using mapping in a variety of ways to support the following law enforcement functions: operations, command and control decisions, investigations, community policing, cross-jurisdictional analyses, and multi-agency public safety partnerships (Mamalian and La Vigne 1998). The following subsections provide examples of how law enforcement agencies are using GIS to support these and other activities.

Operations

Several standard types of crime analyses have proven helpful to patrol officers: automated pin mapping, 'hotspot' analysis, and radial analysis are a few of the most extensively used. Automated pin mapping is the most rudimentary and in some ways the most flexible of these uses. Law enforcement practitioners have begun to realise the advantages of maps over printouts in enabling officers to visualise spatial patterns of criminal events.

Mapping provides the capability of displaying any subset of events on a map. Not only can the user specify the time period they want to examine, they can also display events of a certain type or that meet specific criteria. By enabling the visualisation of subsets of information, mapping provides an invaluable tool for revealing clusters and patterns of crime that are not readily apparent from a list of crime events in a report. Another important function that mapping enables is the visualisation of the concentration of events at a single address. This is accomplished by tying the size of the symbol at a location to the number of events occurring there: the more events, the larger the symbol. This method for identifying repeat events at a single address supports problem-oriented policing efforts by making locations with several calls easily identifiable. In addition, the use of non-crime data from other city agencies (vacant housing or percentage of tenant- versus landlord-owned residences) can be overlaid with crime events to provide a more holistic view of crime in its environment. It is through the integration of data about a specific geographic area that an exploration of causality can begin.

GIS can also be used to identify the locations of high concentrations of crimes, known as 'hotspots'. Several algorithms are available to calculate the areas of highest density in a point distribution, including the Spatial and Temporal Analysis of Crime program, referred to as STAC. STAC consists of statistical tools for the identification of hotspots of crime and provides other basic spatial crime analysis functions.[3] Once identified, hotspots can be targeted for directed patrol activities and can be examined to determine if they coincide geographically with specific community characteristics that may be contributing to the crime problem. For example, hotspots of violent crime can be mapped with hotspots of substandard housing locations to determine if these two factors are related. Such maps are frequently used by police to encourage the local housing authority to increase inspections in a specific area. Finally, the persistence or displacement of hotspots can be examined by plotting several weeks, months or years of hotspots on the same map (see Figure 10.1). This use of hotspots is increasing, particularly in departments that are instituting results-oriented management.

Another commonly used GIS function that has important applications in policing is radial analysis. Often police are interested in characterising the crime situation around a specific location or locations. GIS makes answering this question an easy task. For example, a convenience store is frequently a magnet for criminal activity occurring both in the store and on or near its grounds. An officer may want to illustrate how a particular convenience store had a greater number of crimes committed within 1,000 metres of it than did other convenience stores in the area. Since the exact location of features is known in a GIS, an analyst can simply select all the crimes that are within the specified distance. Radial analysis also provides the means for complying with notification laws in the US. Many

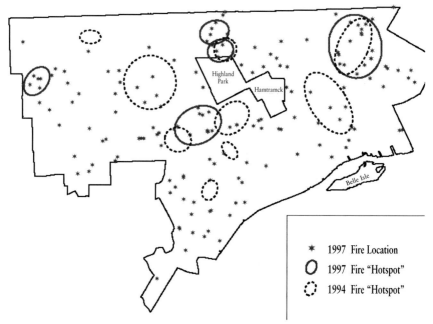

Highland
Park

Hamtramck

Belle Isle

*   1997 Fire Location

○   1997 Fire "Hotspot"

⬭   1994 Fire "Hotspot"

Figure 10.1 Hotspots of arson in Detroit, 1994 and 1997. This map illustrates
         how police in Detroit used mapping to examine the movement of
         arson hotspots over time.

Source: Martin *et al.* 1998.

departments, under 'Megan's Law', have to notify residents within a certain distance that a convicted sex offender has moved into a neighbourhood. Using a GIS, the departments can plot the address of the registered
sex offender and then select all the properties that fall within a specified
radius of that location. Letters are then generated to all of the property
owners notifying them of the sex offender's presence.

    GIS can also be used to integrate digital orthophotography with other
information about an area to give the line officer a more 'fleshed out'
picture. Orthophotographs are those taken from a bird's eye view – photos
shot from above a landscape that are then converted into digital images.
These photos have a fine level of resolution that enables one to identify
building 'footprints' – the physical shapes of buildings – as well as details
such as alleyways and footpaths. Orthophotos provide a more realistic and
detailed picture of the environment and can be linked with GIS to enable
the analysis of crime with more specificity than typical vector representations allow. The greater detail depicted in orthophotos is often used in
tactical situations because officers can 'see' the layout of the terrain before
they even arrive on the scene. Once at the scene, orthophotos enable the
pinpointing of officer's positions, for example on the left corner of a

particular rooftop or behind a specific row of bushes. Orthophotos in conjunction with global positioning systems (GPS) can aid in understanding the characteristics of the physical environment of where a crime occurred. The Baltimore County Police Department is experimenting with the use of orthophotos to enhance crime analysis activities by siting the crime incidents at the specific x, y coordinates where they happened rather than simply placing the events in the centre of the appropriate address polygon (Harries 1999). Use of orthophotos is increasing because of greater availability. As municipalities invest in orthophotography to update their infrastructure data this powerful tool will become routinely available.

Command and control decisions

The ability to keep abreast of crime trends is essential to making informed command decisions. GIS can play an important role at this level. A very recent and successful application of crime mapping to command and control decisions is the New York Police Department's (NYPD) 'CompStat' program (McDonald and Greenberg, forthcoming). GIS is also used to support major operational endeavours such as parades and presidential visits.

News of the success of the New York City Police Department's comprehensive approach to fighting crime, CompStat has spread worldwide. CompStat, which stands for computerised statistics, combines officer accountability with the implementation of GIS to aid officers in strategic and tactical prevention and control efforts. The department's GIS is virtually 'real time', enabling crime analysts to identify an upward trend in crime immediately. Most of the trend identification is achieved through trend mapping or hotspot analysis. When a problem is identified, a meeting is convened during which the precinct commander must explain his or her response to the crime problem. CompStat holds all police officers – from patrol to command level – accountable and responsive to the crime that occurs on their beat. The success of CompStat has prompted many other law enforcement agencies to follow suit, adapting the CompStat approach to their own mission and policing philosophy. A few of the departments that have successfully implemented CompStat-like processes include: Baltimore, Maryland; New Orleans, Louisiana; Philadelphia, Pennsylvania; Durham, North Carolina; and Minneapolis (McDonald and Greenberg, forthcoming).

Another important command and control application of GIS is to support crowd and automobile traffic management. Careful planning using up-to-date street information is essential to maintaining smooth operations during traffic diversions. Many times police are called upon to redirect traffic during parades, street festivals, and presidential visits. GIS plays a vital role during these situations by providing an accurate street base including pertinent community landmarks. The route or affected areas can be plotted on the map, as well as the unit assigned to each traffic diversion point, which makes keeping track of many units in a variety of positions much easier.

Investigations

The use of GIS to support investigations is centred on suspect identification and pattern analysis. GIS can play a significant role in cases in which the victim and perpetrator are strangers. These types of cases are particularly frustrating to investigators since they may only have a partial description of the suspect. However, by linking the location of the crime with databases containing previous offenders, a list of potential suspects can be generated. Examples of databases that may be used to identify potential suspects include: parolees/probationers, arrestees, registered sex offenders and individuals on pre-trial release. Investigators can use any known descriptive factors and map a radius around the crime scene to narrow their search. The list that is generated by the GIS serves as a starting point for the investigators.

In an enhancement to the techniques described above, several law enforcement agencies have been working on developing decision support systems (DSS) capable of ranking potential suspects. These rankings are based on previous arrest history, similarity to the perpetrator description or modus operandi and the distance of an offender's home address from the crime scene (Alexander *et al.* 1997). Typically, the DSS uses existing data-sets of arrestees, probationers/parolees and suspects as inputs and then produces a list of potential suspects by rank.

GIS is also used to examine spatial patterns in the sequence and location of a series of related crime events. This is an invaluable method for examining events by their different characteristics. For example, a robbery investigator may want to analyse the spatial pattern of armed robberies by time periods, day of week, modus operandi and/or victim type. Computer mapping allows the investigator a method to quickly view and compare patterns of crime events. In Seattle, Washington, detectives used the Spatial Crime Analysis System (SCAS[4]) to automatically calculate the first and third standard deviational ellipses around a series of related crime events. Ellipses are calculated using the events in the series and they define the area in which the next event is most likely to occur. Seattle has used this tool to make arrests on a high-profile string of violent robberies (Robbin 1999).

Another innovative police agency use of GIS is that of the Baltimore County Police Department (BCPD) in the State of Maryland, which has linked computerised crime mapping with another technological advancement: the auto-dialer. Traditionally designed for telemarketing purposes, the auto-dialer is used by the department to broadcast messages of recent crime 'rashes' to specific neighbourhoods based on the locations of the crimes. The auto-dialer calls individual households that are identified geographically and issues a recorded message describing the nature of the crime problem, advising residents on appropriate preventive measures, and requesting individuals to report any suspicious behaviour. The GIS component of the auto-dialer initiative is used to identify the neighbourhood afflicted by the crime problem in such a manner as to flood the vicinity with the recorded advice, as well as to analyse potential displacement to neighbouring areas. The auto-dialer, in conjunction with crime mapping technology, has been credited with apprehending serial burglars, thieves and robbers throughout the Baltimore County region (Canter 1998). Police use of maps to investigate crimes and warn citizens is only half the story. The other half of the equation involves using maps to facilitate dialogue with community members.

Community

A relatively recent trend in law enforcement is the use of maps during interactions with community members. Maps provide a forum in which to discuss a neighbourhood's crime problems (both real and perceived). In many jurisdictions, residents have found these maps so useful that they expect officers to bring maps with them to the community meetings. However, the true power of GIS is as a tool for information exchange. Residents of a neighbourhood know the most about an area. If officers can convince them to communicate that wealth of information back to the police, it creates a true dialogue making the possibilities for empowering neighbourhoods limitless.

Hartford, Connecticut provides a prime example of such a positive community–police partnership. Researchers from Abt Associates coordinated with the Hartford Police Department to develop a crime mapping system for use by neighbourhood associations. This user-friendly system was designed for community members to do their own crime mapping in conjunction with the police department's community policing program. For their first project the community members began to map drug calls-for-service. Upon completion of the map they noticed a modest amount of drug activity, a finding that did not match their perceptions of the level of drug activity in the neighbourhood. A quick survey of their neighbours confirmed that drug activity was still high, but that the community had stopped reporting it due to apathy or lack of police response to earlier calls. As a result of this experience, the community became much more aware of its critical role in reporting criminal activity to ensure the accuracy of maps produced (Rich 1998).

Cross-jurisdictional analysis

State and local law enforcement in the United States consists of over 19,000 law enforcement agencies (Bureau of Justice Statistics 1999). Given that each agency operates independently, even the best mapping application provides limited utility when analysing across jurisdictional boundaries is not possible because data are not shared. Data sharing is particularly important given that prior research suggests crime events occur in clusters along major thoroughfares (Brantingham and Brantingham 1984). Because jurisdictional boundaries tend to be drawn along major thoroughfares, the picture of a crime problem is significantly warped when an analyst only has crime data for one side of a street.

In response to this common crime analysis dilemma, the Baltimore County Police Department has launched an effort with over a dozen neighbouring law enforcement agencies to form a consortium by which agencies share a common geographically referenced offence and suspect database. Agencies download crime data to a common database on a regular basis and each agency can map the crime with the mapping software of its preference. The consortium is in the process of implementing the Regional Crime Analysis Geographic Information System (RCAGIS), which will enable agencies to use a common mapping platform for their analyses.[5]

Interagency partnerships and collaborations

Many law enforcement agencies have moved beyond mapping just crime data in an effort to integrate other important data sources representing health, economic and social service data. The purpose behind such expansive mapping efforts is to collaborate with other city and county agencies in an effort to pool resources to address public safety problems in a comprehensive manner. Historically, the biggest hurdle to sharing data among departments was the lack of a common item on which the data could be associated. Since GIS uses location to link data, and given that most data sources have some type of location information, a GIS serves as an ideal data integrator.

While inter-agency collaborations of different scales are occurring all over the United States, there are two major demonstration projects sponsored by the Department of Justice (DOJ) that involve the use of data from a variety of sources to identify problems, create strategies and evaluate interventions. Five cities are using a multi-agency, collaborative approach to problem solving in the Strategic Approaches to Community Safety Initiative (SACSI), and the pilot city in the Community Mapping, Planning, and Analysis for Safety Strategies (COMPASS) project is using a modified SACSI approach. In order to facilitate data sharing, data repositories are being developed that will be accessed using an interface called the Community Safety Information System (CSIS) (Groff 1999; Conley et al. 1999). Since GIS is an integral part of the information system, participants will be able to analyse data both spatially and in tabular form.

Collaborations with courts and corrections

One of the newest applications of GIS in law enforcement involves its use in collaboration with courts and corrections. These partnerships usually take the form of support during court cases or data sharing among agencies to identify suspects. Many police departments routinely provide maps as exhibits in court cases. These visual aids have proven effective at helping juries understand chronology and positioning in complex cases (Cook 1998; Moland 1998). GIS can also be used to enhance inter-agency collaboration between law enforcement and community corrections (Fleury 1999). A partnership between Maricopa County Adult Probation and Arizona State University is experimenting with the integration of police and probation databases to enhance problem-solving efforts and improve the police's ability to identify suspects, as well as to evaluate the impact of the data sharing partnership (Webb 1998).

Increasingly courts and corrections are using GIS to support a variety of criminal justice operations (Fleury 1999). One example of how GIS is being used by probation and parole agencies is to enable the geographic assignment of probationers or parolees to officers (Rich 1995). Geographical assignment cuts down on the amount of time officers spend travelling between visits. Also, by concentrating their travel and interactions in one area, officers are able to develop a more in-depth knowledge of the neighbourhoods in which their clients live and the resources and job opportunities available to them there. One example is the Wisconsin Department of Corrections, which mapped out all the home addresses of probationers and parolees in the region and then prioritised areas for increased resources based on the concentration of clients. Officials believe that the targeting of resources has resulted in improved completion outcomes for clients in these areas (Mixdorf 1999).

Agencies are also using GIS to identify community resources, such as treatment centres and training programmes, that are near probationers' or parolees' homes. Beyond merely identifying where the facilities are located, the GIS can also provide directions to the facility. Strategic planners in the field of offender management are using GIS to identify areas with high concentrations of offenders so that they can plan appropriately. The Delaware Department of Corrections has examined the relationship between offender residences, bus lines and the locations of frequently used services. The results clearly demonstrated a concentration of services in urban areas, leaving rural areas underserved (Harris *et al.* 1998).

While the previously mentioned applications of GIS are useful, for the most part they rely upon the straightforward use of GIS capabilities. These applications will continue to support criminal justice policy and practice even while new, more analytic functions discussed in the next section are explored.

Where research meets practice: the movement toward analytic mapping

The application of research to concrete problems has propelled the use of GIS to new levels of analytic mapping. This section examines those research efforts that have expanded the practical uses of GIS in law enforcement. Three of the most useful and widespread developments in the research community are using GIS to identify causal factors relating to crime patterns, to develop more rigorous hotspot identification methods and analysis tools, and to predict the likely location of crime hotspots before they emerge.

Identifying causal factors: high definition mapping

One common use of crime mapping is to map crime in relation to other causal factors that may be influencing crime. For example, a pin map of drug activity may be combined with a thematic map representing the percentage of vacant houses by census tract. If the concentrations of these two factors coincide, it may lead officers to address the problem of vacant houses, which most likely are being used as shelters by drug dealers and users. Drawing on environmental criminology concepts that emphasise the importance of 'place' in the crime equation, recent research on 'high definition mapping' has increased the sophistication of these types of analyses by mapping information on precisely where crimes are occurring in relation to specific characteristics of the physical environment.

Figure 10.2 provides an example of how high definition mapping is supporting the development of successful crime prevention measures at Temple University in Philadelphia, PA (Henderson and Lowell 2000). On the Temple campus, features such as sidewalks, building footprints, street lights, shrubbery, fences and other physical features are mapped along with crime and victimisation data to provide a detailed picture of the environment. Based on such a mapping exercise and in partnership with university researchers, campus police identified four clusters of assault incidents on campus based on a survey of students, faculty and staff. The clusters appeared to be related to other factors on the map, such as lighting, the location of security kiosks, and points of limited visibility. Police decided upon four intervention strategies: increasing staffing of security kiosks, improving lighting in vulnerable areas, increased foot patrol in and around the four clusters, and increasing provision of an escort service. When a survey was administered a year following this interventions, not one of the four hotspot areas had recurred.

Partnerships for the development of analytic tools

As the numbers of law enforcement agencies adopting crime mapping increases, so too has the demand for more sophisticated tools. Indeed, one

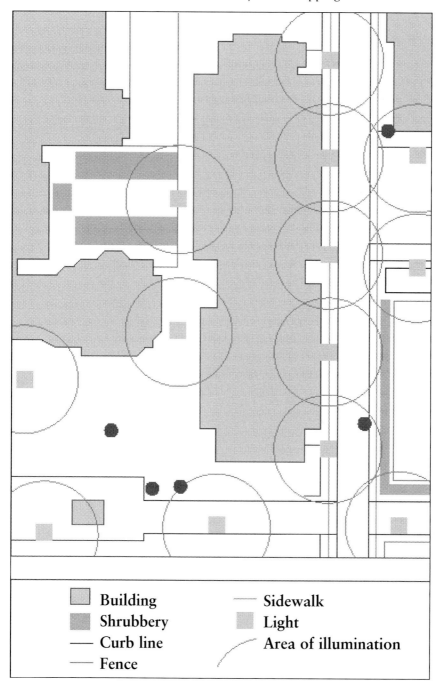

Figure 10.2 High definition GIS at Temple University.
Source: Rengert 1998.

of the chief complaints among crime analysts and criminal justice researchers alike is the dearth of spatial statistical tools available in GIS software packages. Historically, there has been relatively little exploration to identify spatial statistics that are applicable to the study of crime and criminal behaviour. A shift from reactive to proactive policing strategies has only magnified the need for more sophisticated methods and models.

In response to this need, CrimeStat,[6] a new spatial statistical application designed specifically for the analysis of crime and criminal behaviour, was developed (Levine 1999). CrimeStat is a standalone application that contains a variety of spatial statistics, producing outputs that can be exported to a variety of GIS software programs for display. Developed in partnership with the Baltimore County Police Department, which served as the beta test site, CrimeStat includes statistics to describe distributions (e.g. mean centre and standard distance deviation), calculate journey to crime estimates (e.g. trip generation, trip distribution, and network assignment), and conduct cluster analyses (e.g. k-means and nearest neighbour).

The development of more sophisticated analysis tools is necessary not only to increase the proactive nature of policing but also to manage the ever-increasing volume of data that is available to police agencies. The ReCAP (Regional Crime Analysis Program) software is a good example of a program that offers both sophisticated spatial analysis of crime and innovative data mining tools. The ReCAP program was developed through a partnership with three Virginia law enforcement agencies (Albemarle County, Charlottesville and University of Virginia Campus Police) and researchers at the University of Virginia Systems Engineering Department (Brown 1998). The system integrates data from the three participating agencies and allows seamless analysis across jurisdictional boundaries. The system also monitors crime levels and compares them with historical levels. If the current number of crimes exceeds a pre-established threshold of increase, the system automatically notifies the user. ReCAP represents an example of how software can intelligently assist law enforcement personnel to sift through mountains of available data to support decision-making.

Hotspot identification and analysis

As mentioned in the previous section, the identification of hotspot areas is very important both in understanding where concentrations of crime exist and as a starting point for understanding the underlying processes that may have contributed to the formation of that concentration. While hotspot analyses are commonly conducted, practitioners are confused at the array of hotspot identification tools on the market and researchers are frustrated at the lack of statistical rigour of many of these tools. In response to these concerns, the National Institute of Justice's Crime Mapping

Research Center (CMRC) sponsored a research effort to systematically compare current spatial analysis software packages and hotspot identification tools and methods. Using a common set of data and pre-established parameters, participants compared thirteen methods and applications and assessed them on ease of use, reliability, face validity, utility for statistical comparisons, and underlying algorithms (CMRC 1998). While these papers offer a useful evaluation of hotspot identification methods, there remains a need for further research to define what threshold of crime makes a hotspot.

Predictive modelling

Hotspot analyses and other spatial analyses have gained popularity due to the fact that they aid in the identification of causal factors that represent underlying causes of persistent crime problems and help guide the allocation of resources. Yet current hotspot analyses are based on data of past events, merely telling analysts and researchers where hotspots of crime have already occurred. Ideally, early indicators of troubled areas would help to identify future patterns of crimes committed across time and space and inform a more proactive approach to policing. Predictive models that identify 'hotspots' of crime and disorder, as well as areas where crime is abating would guide policing so that preventive measures and interventions could be deployed beforehand. While some early work has been conducted on the predictive modelling of drug markets using neural networks (Olligschlaeger 1997) further explorations are in order.

Drawing on the exploratory neural network mapping conducted by Olligschlaeger (1997), NIJ has launched a predictive modelling research program, awarding five grants to develop models that use spatial and temporal crime information, as well as environmental data, to predict changes in the spatial distribution and intensity of crime incidence.[7] Analytic techniques for these projects range from spatial econometric modelling to artificial neural network analysis. One unique modelling approach is to compute clusters of event features, locations and times on each of three axes (Figure 10.3). These clusters can then be used to identify areas where crimes are likely to occur, an essential piece of information for enabling proactive policing efforts (Liu and Brown 1998).

This group of predictive modelling grants will ultimately equip law enforcement agencies to better identify and proactively engage areas that are likely to evolve into hotspots. Additionally, several of the projects will assess the utility of monitoring lower-order offending as predictive of later, more serious, crime. This will be a particularly valuable contribution to the field in that nearly all previous tests of the underlying 'broken windows' hypothesis were cross-sectional in nature, although the hypothesis is explicitly longitudinal (Taylor 1999).

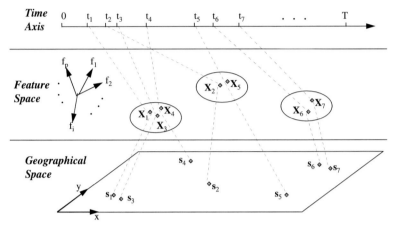

Figure 10.3 Multi-dimensional predictive modelling. Three aspects of a crime incident are incorporated in this multi-dimensional model: time of occurrence, characteristics of the crime and location in space. By considering event characteristics in the model, the authors hope to gain a more robust prediction of future events.

Source: Liu and Brown 1998.

Conclusion

This chapter has attempted to provide an overview of the state of crime mapping in the United States. Undoubtedly, as the diffusion of GIS technology continues, it will touch many more criminal justice researchers and practitioners. As more individuals from a variety of backgrounds begin working with GIS, the potential for innovation can only increase. Concurrently, the technological advances that increased the accessibility and robustness of the desktop GIS will continue and, in doing so, open up new avenues toward the development of more advanced spatial analysis techniques. However, true progress requires the continuation of the partnerships between researchers and practitioners that have already advanced this field of study, as well as the expansion of such partnerships to new agencies and research entities. Exploration and expansion of partnership possibilities will need to take place both outside the discipline of criminology, and outside the boundaries of the United States, if continued advancements are to be achieved.

Notes

1 The expanded use of crime mapping in the United States can be measured by increased attendance at the Crime Mapping Research Center's annual conference, sponsored by the National Institute of Justice, which has grown from 400 attendees at the first conference in 1997, to 750 attendees a year later.

2 'Human ecology' applies the competition model for scarce space, which was originally developed to explain plant and animal relationships, to human interactions.

3 STAC uses standard deviational ellipses to delineate the highest concentration of points in a distribution. The program can be obtained free of charge from its developers, the Illinois Criminal Justice Information Authority at www.icjia.org.

4 SCAS is an ArcView application developed by the Criminal Division GIS staff at the Department of Justice to offer an easy to use front-end with some preprogrammed statistical capabilities. For more information about SCAS please go to the Criminal Division's web page at www.usdoj.gov/criminal/gis/scashome.htm.

5 RCAGIS is being developed by the Criminal Division GIS staff at the Department of Justice, and will be made available free of charge when it is completed.

6 CrimeStat is available free of charge from the CMRC. To download the program, go to www.ojp.usdoj.gov/cmrc/whatsnew/welcome.html#crimestat.

7 Projects funded in this area include: (1) *Detection and Prediction of Geographical Changes in Crime Rates*, NIJ Grant #98–IJ-CX-K008, State University of New York, Buffalo; (2) *Crime Hotspot Forecasting: Modeling and Comparative Evaluation*, NIJ Grant #98–IJ-CX-K005, Carnegie Mellon University; (3) *Evaluation of Drug Markets: An Analysis of the Geography of Susceptibility, Accessibility, Opportunity and Police Action*, NIJ Grant #99–IJ-CX-K005, Temple University; (4) *Predictive Models for Law Enforcement*, NIJ Grant #98–IJ-CX-K010, University of Virginia; and (5) *A GIS Analysis of the Relationship Between Public Order and More Serious Crime*, NIJ Grant #98–IJ-CX-K009, University of Texas at Austin.

References

Alexander, M., Groff, E.R. and Hibdon L. (1997) 'An automated system for the dentification and prioritization of rape suspects', *Proceedings Environmental Systems Research Incorporated User Conference*, www.esri.com, P333.htm.

Brantingham, P.J. and Brantingham, P.L. (1975) 'The spatial patterning of burglary', *Howard Journal of Penology and Crime Prevention* 14: 11–24.

—— (1977) 'Housing patterns and burglary in a medium-sized American city', in J.E. Scott and S. Dinitz (eds) *Criminal Justice Planning*, New York: Praeger, pp. 63–74.

—— (1978) 'A theoretical model of crime site selection', in M. Krohn and R. Akers (eds) *Crime, Law and Sanction*, Beverly Hills, CA: Sage Publications, pp. 105–18.

—— (1981) 'Notes on the geometry of crime', in P.J. Brantingham and P.L. Brantingham (eds) *Environmental Criminology*, Prospect Heights, IL: Waveland Press, pp. 27–54.

—— (1984) *Patterns in Crime*, New York: Macmillan.

Brown, D.E. (1998) 'The regional crime analysis program (ReCAP): a framework for mining data to catch criminals', *IEEE International Conference on Systems, Man, and Cybernetics*, San Diego, CA, 11–14 October, 2848–52.

Bureau of Justice Statistics (1999) State and Local Law Enforcement Statistics, http://www.ojp.usdoj.gov/bjs/sandlle.htm.

Burgess, E.W. (1925) 'The growth of the city', in R.E. Park, E.W. Burgess and R.D. McKenzie (eds) *The City*, Chicago: University of Chicago Press, pp. 47–62.

Canter, P. (1998) 'Baltimore County's autodialer system', in N. La Vigne and J. Wartell (eds) *Crime Mapping Case Studies: Successes in the Field*, Washington, DC: Police Executive Research Forum, pp. 81–92.

Conley, J.B., Groff, E.R. and Lesser, T. (1999) 'Using GIS to support community safety: strategic approaches to community safety initiative in Winston-Salem, NC', *Proceedings of the Environmental Systems Research Institute User Conference*, July, www.esri.com/p523.htm.

Cook, P. (1998) 'Mapping a murderer's path', in N. La Vigne and J. Wartell (eds) *Crime Mapping Case Studies: Successes in the Field*, Washington, DC: Police Executive Research Forum, pp. 123–8.

Crime Mapping Research Center (1998): *Hotspots: An Exploration of Methods*, www.usdoj.gov/cmrc.

Flango, V. and Sherbenou, E. (1976) 'Poverty, urbanization, and crime', *Criminology* 14: 331–46.

Fleury, J. (1999) *National Institute of Justice Mapping in Corrections Resource Group Meeting Summary*, Wasington, DC: Department of Justice, article on Crime Mapping Research Center web site (www.ojp.usdoj.gov/cmrc).

Groff, E.R. (1999) 'Strategic approaches to community safety initiative (SACSI): a project overview, *Proceedings of the Urban and Regional Information Systems Conference*, August.

Guerry, A.M. (1833) *Essai sur la Statistique Morale de la France*, Paris: Crochard.

Harries, K. (1999) 'Data integration, visualization, and community policing', paper read at the Association of American Geographers Meeting.

Harris, R., Huenke, C. and O'Connell, J.P. (1998) 'Using mapping to increase released offenders' access to services', in N. La Vigne and J. Wartell (eds) *Crime Mapping Case Studies: Successes in the Field*, Washington, DC: Police Executive Research Forum, pp. 61–8.

Henderson, K.H. and Lowell, R. (2000) 'Reducing campus crime through high definition mapping', in N. La Vigne and J. Wartell (eds) *Crime Mapping Case Studies: Successes in the Field* (volume 2), Washington, DC: Police Executive Research Forum.

Levine, N. (1999) *CrimeStat: A Spatial Statistics Program for the Analysis of Crime Incident Locations*, Annandale, VA: Ned Levine and Associates/Washington, DC: The National Institute of Justice.

Liu, H. and Brown, D. (1998) 'Spatial-temporal event prediction: a new model', *Proceedings of the IEEE International Conference on System, Man and Cybernetics*, October.

Maltz, M., Gordon, A. and Friedman, W. (1989) *Mapping Crime in Its Community Setting: A Study of Event Geography Analysis*, Washington, DC: National Institute of Justice.

Mamalian, C. and La Vigne, N.G. (1998) *The Use of Computerized Crime Mapping by Law Enforcement: Survey Results*, Washington, DC: National Institute of Justice.

Marlin, J. (1973) 'City crime report of council on municipal performance summary', *Criminal Law Bulletin* 9(7): 557–611.

Martin, D., Barnes, E. and Britt, D. (1998) 'The multiple impacts of mapping it out: police, geographic information systems (GIS) and community mobilization during devil's night in Detroit, Michigan', in N. La Vigne and J. Wartell (eds) *Crime Mapping Case Studies: Successes in the Field*, Washington, DC: Police Executive Research Forum, pp. 3–12.

Mayhew, H. (1968) *London Labour and the London Poor. Vol IV: Those That Will Not Work, Comprising Prostitutes, Thieves, Swindlers and Beggars* (originally published in 1862), New York: Dover Publications.

McDonald, P.P. and Greenberg, S. (forthcoming) *Managing Police Operations: A Guide to Implementation of the NYPD Crime Control Model COMPSTAT*, Belmont, CA: Wadsworth.

McEwen, J.T. and Taxman, F.S. (1995) 'Applications of computerized mapping to police operations', in J.E. Eck and D. Weisburd (eds) *Crime and Place*, Monsey, NY: Willow Tree Press, pp. 259–84.

Mixdorff, W.H. (1999) 'Mapping for probation and parole', presentation at the National Institute of Justice Mapping in Corrections Resource Group Meeting, 22 August, New York.

Moland, R.S. (1998) 'Graphical display of murder trial evidence', in N. La Vigne and J. Wartell (eds) *Crime Mapping Case Studies: Successes in the Field*, Washington, DC: Police Executive Research Forum, pp. 69–80.

Olligschlaeger, A.M., (1997) 'Artificial neural networks and crime mapping', in D. Weisburd and T. McEwen (eds) *Crime Mapping and Crime Prevention*, Monsey, NY: Criminal Justice Press.

Park R.E. and Burgess, E.W. (1924) *Introduction to the Science of Sociology*, Chicago, IL: University of Chicago Press.

Rengert, G. (1998) 'Micro-level GIS: zooming in on campus crime', presented at the Crime Mapping Research Conference, December.

Rich, T.F. (1995) *The Use of Computerized Mapping in Crime Control and Prevention Programs*, Washington, DC: US Department of Justice, Office of Justice Programs, National Institute of Justice.

—— (1998) 'Crime mapping by community organizations: initial successes in Hartford's Blue Hills neighborhood', in N. La Vigne and J. Wartell (eds) *Crime Mapping Case Studies: Successes in the Field*, Washington, DC: Police Executive Research Forum, pp. 35–44.

Robbin, C.R. (1999) 'Apprehending violent robbers through a crime series analysis', in N. La Vigne and J. Wartell (eds) *Crime Mapping Case Studies: Successes in the Field* (volume 2), Washington, DC: Police Executive Research Forum.

Schmid, C.F. (1960a) 'Urban crime areas: part 1', *American Sociological Review* 25: 527–42.

Schmid, C.F. (1960b) 'Urban crime areas: part 2', *American Sociological Review* 25: 655–78.

Schuessler, K. and Slatin, G., (1964) 'Sources of variation in U.S. city crime, 1950 and 1960', *Journal of Research in Crime and Delinquency* 1: 127–48.

Shaw, C.R. and McKay, H.D. (1942) *Juvenile Delinquency and Urban Areas*, Chicago: University of Chicago Press, pp. 60–8.

Strahura, J.M. and Huff, C.R. (1979) 'The new "zones of transition": gradients of crime in Metropolitan areas', *Review of Public Data Use* 7: 41–8.

Taylor, R.B. (1999) Crime, Grime, Fear and Decline: A Longitudinal Look, Washington, DC: National Institute of Justice.

Webb, V. (1998) '*Combining Police and Probation Research to Reduce Burglary: Testing a Crime Analysis Problem-Solving Approach, Grant #98–IJ-CX-0059*, Washington, DC: National Institute of Justice.

Worden, M.A. (1980) 'Criminogenic correlates of intermetropolitan crime rates, 1960 and 1970', in D.E. Geogres-Abeyie and K. Harries (eds) *Crime: A Spatial Perspective*, New York: McGraw Hill, pp. 109–22.

Part V

Practical considerations: what can we expect of GIS?

11 What to do about it? Let's turn off our minds and GIS[1]

Ken Pease

The vogue for crime mapping is implicitly based upon the presumption of the unique usefulness of spatial location in identifying people, places and spaces highly liable to crime victimisation. While applauding investment in the mapping enterprise, the writer argues that concentration on the mapping of spatial location to the exclusion, or relegation to secondary roles, of other variables associated with crime hazard is unnecessarily limiting. While this is clearly not the intention of crime mappers, the promulgation of mapping by Government and academics creates the clear danger that this will be a consequence of current priorities in local crime analysis. Concern with spatial location in the crime reduction community owes more to the mind-set of police officers, whose responsibility is territorially defined, than to evidence that crime concentration is primarily spatial in nature. A simple modelling approach is advocated whereby a small number of variables (where that information which is both readily accessible by agents of crime control and most predictive of victimisation), used in allocating crime reduction effort are identified. This may or may not include spatial location. If it does not, this does not remove the value of spatial mapping for activities such as the quicker completion of crime reports and identification of offender residence–offence location linkages.

Introduction

The writer brings to the topic of mapping crime data a history of disillusionment. Some thirteen years ago he used a mapping product of the Home Office Crime Prevention Centre, then at Stafford. It was called the Crime Analysis Package (CAPGEN/CAP_V3 in its mature version to its friends). It was based on a Lotus 123 spreadsheet of crime events, to which measurements of northings and eastings were assigned. It was desperately slow, but it worked. His research team succeeded, with massive effort in assigning location information to calls for police service, in mapping events of crime and disorder in the Norris Green area of Liverpool. The mapping told interesting stories. No pubs existed in the area, and incidents of violence occurred on the road from the corner of the area nearest to the available pubs back into Norris Green. The time for assaultive crime on the streets was late evening and early morning. Youths causing annoyance were concentrated on a few streets and in late afternoon and evenings. Domestic incidents were spread throughout the area. Output from the analysis helped the police, for some offences, to know where to be and when to be there.

Brian Gresty was a senior police officer from Merseyside seconded to the Home Office Crime Prevention Centre in 1989–91, and the dissemination of CAPGEN was among his responsibilities. Interested in the uses to which it was being put, the writer asked him for stories of how and where it had informed policing practice. There were few such stories. One came from a south coast town. Upon further enquiry, it transpired that the mapping facility there had never been enabled, and that the good effects achieved were a result simply of scrutiny of the data in spreadsheet form and its sharing amongst police officers. The virtues ascribed to mapping were in fact attributable to the more effective sharing of information in text form. Thus alerted to the mis-ascription of CAPGEN's benefits, the writer sought to find out where the mapping facility itself had been used. Neither he nor Brian Gresty ever found any police force which did enable the mapping facility of CAP_V3. Everywhere the writer saw the software demonstrated, it displayed the same map of part of Stafford which had been placed there by the developers, and the same data points on that map. Either the system was not sufficiently user-friendly, or the enterprise itself was flawed.

Signs of the times

By the early 1990s, CAP_V3 had clunked its way into oblivion, remembered with qualified affection by only a few of those who had known it. However, the seductiveness of the GIS enterprise meant that work on the spatial distribution of crime had advanced apace, and has continued to do so since. Using the keyword 'mapping' on the holdings of Rutgers University library up to 1998, over half of the sixty-seven publications appeared in 1993 or later. Only six appeared before 1980.[2] 1996 was the modal year.

The Spatial and Temporal Analysis of Crime (STAC) project (Illinois Criminal Justice Information Authority 1987) deserves mention as the most sophisticated early example of an attempt to develop clearer, more efficient ways of analysing and representing the kind of crime data traditionally shown on pin maps. The US Department of Justice in Washington DC has now established its own Crime Mapping Research Centre (CMRC), with a staff of eleven.[3] Interestingly, the pin map analogy is still being used.

The goal of CMRC is the promotion, research, evaluation, development and dissemination of GIS (Geographic Information Systems) technology and the spatial analysis of crime. On the day of writing this, the home page prominently displays a 'Free Crime Mapping Tool' to download. To the writer's knowledge there is no similar centre devoted to other means of analysing crime vulnerabilities. The centre hosts annual International Crime Mapping Research Conferences, of which the third took place in December 1999. The same month saw the publication of *Mapping Crime: Principle and Practice*, a glossy 193-page volume dedicated to the emerging science and its application. This is an impressive work, well-written and thoughtful. Its author, Keith Harries, is to be congratulated. What might appear as criticism of it in what follows is, rather, criticism of the absence of non-spatial analysis to complement it. In the foreword, we read: 'Today about 13 per cent of law enforcement agencies are using GIS regularly to analyse their crime problems, and we are certain to see this number increase significantly as more and more agencies begin using computerised crime mapping to identify and solve their crime problems. We hope this guide will help get them started' (Harries 1999).

Meanwhile, the Police Executive Research Forum's website[4] headlines the publication in 2000 of the second volume of 'successes' of mapping in police work, describing it as a 'must-read' for practitioners.

In the United Kingdom, the work of Alex Hirschfield and his colleagues at Liverpool (see for example Hirschfield and Bowers 1997), and that of Spencer Chainey, formerly of Brent and Hackney Councils, both reflect current interest and activity in mapping crime. Jerry Ratcliffe and colleagues address the integration of mapping into an intelligence environment (see Ratcliffe, in press). The appointment of Paul Wiles to the most powerful position in British criminology (Director of Research, Development and Statistics at the Home Office) places a mapping enthusiast in a job from which the dissemination of GIS can be advocated and substantially implemented. Bob Barr provides sophisticated and visually compelling animations of maps to incorporate temporal variation.

Perhaps the most basic reason for the recent emergence of interest in crime mapping is that it has only been quite recently that it has become possible to generate and print detailed maps quickly. For example, map resolution was hitherto constrained by character size when using line printers. Perhaps it is simply that mapping has started to happen because it is easy. Is there anything more to it? Eck and Weisburd (1995) plausibly link the interest in crime places to a change in the focus of criminology from interest in the development of criminal offenders to interest in the development of crime events. If that which is to be explained is the crime act, it is attributes of the act, notably its location, which can aid analysis. They write: 'While the larger worlds of community and neighbourhood have been the primary focus of crime prevention theory and research in the past, there is a growing recognition of the importance of shifting that focus to the small worlds in which the attributes of place and its routine activities combine to develop crime events' (Eck and Weisburd 1995: 21).

This is consistent with two facts:

- The classic early criminological mapping study (Shaw and McKay 1942) plotted delinquent residences rather than crime events.
- Recent mapping studies, even when they include offender residence, also enter crime location, typically as a way of looking for offender ranges and characteristic target selection (Rossmo 1993).

A final component of the attraction of mapping is that responsibility for policing is spatially divided. This argument is developed more fully later in the chapter.

In brief, mapping is a hot topic in criminology. So it should be, although it seems paradoxical but true that some of the most interesting interventions in which location is a key variable do not use mapping to reveal the patterns of interest. What follows is not a plea for less mapping, but for the placement of spatial mapping alongside other dimensions in terms of which crime risks and offender attributes vary. Thoughtful spatial mappers would doubtless agree. The danger is that spatial mapping develops on a wave of visual beauty and technophilia, with complementary ways of thinking suffering from relative neglect. The recent history of criminology suggests this to be a real danger. This chapter is more than a plea for a place in the sun for non-spatial ways of thought, but is based on the certainty that the crime control enterprise would be hobbled by the pre-eminence of spatial measurement.

Limits to spatial measurement

Writing in 1995, Tim Read and Dick Oldfield note that: 'In the past, there has been a tendency for police forces to become seduced by the appeal of GIS. Currently there are innumerable commercial concerns offering GIS systems to the police for the purpose of 'crime pattern analysis'. Often these systems have been developed in a non-police environment, but are offered on the basis that they can be 'tweaked' to meet police requirements. Bearing in mind the likely cost of a GIS system it is important that police forces plan how the GIS component will be used in analysis, and what its benefits are likely to be, before investing in such a system' (p. 29).

This chimes with experience. Observing divisional commanders and crime managers getting crime maps from their analysts, one senses immediate appreciation of the attractiveness of many such maps, genuine interest in what they can do, followed by an unspoken 'Is that all?' after demonstration or (less frequently) use. Added to this liminal sense of disappointment is concern that depiction as a map may be misleading. For example:

- Mapping in linear distance may make sparsely settled areas look relatively untroubled by crime even when rates of victimisation are high. There are techniques for mapping relative to population or settlement density, but these both make the area unrecognisable from its map, and are unhelpful for deployment decisions. Where is the officer who will increase patrolling in a high crime rate area in preference to an area with a greater number of crimes?

- The distribution of certain crimes is substantially a product of the distribution of police activity (e.g. cannabis possession).
- The distribution of certain crimes will be misleading. For example to allow the charge of unlawfully taking a motor vehicle rather than theft, an offender will lie about the location from which it was taken. Cyber-crime is a special case of a location-free offence type.

More subtly, mapping fails to reflect the victimisation experiences of 'virtual communities', people and households with characteristics other than location in common, which characteristics make them prone to crime (Tilley *et al.* 1999). For example, students live in accommodation spread across several parts of a city. Insofar as they are vulnerable to crime, this will not be well reflected spatially. Unpublished data from North Wales strongly suggests a similar situation as regards to small clusters of sheltered housing. While spread throughout Flintshire, such homes share high risks of victimisation. Those moving home, likewise, bear high risks of property crime (Budd 1999; Ellingworth and Pease 1998).

That much victimisation is not primarily structured on spatial lines is perhaps the reason why GIS so often lead to, if not tears, then at least vague disappointment. Frankly speculating, this is because GIS is adequate to deployment decisions, but largely irrelevant to other kinds of proaction. Location is almost never a sufficient basis for, and seldom a necessary element in, prevention or detection. Let us take as our first example domestic violence, whose distribution in Norris Green, as noted above, was not spatially determined. The unique British Crime Survey's attempt to establish the prevalence of this kind of violence allows us to identify how it is structured (Mirlees-Black 1999). Domestic violence is a notoriously difficult offence to count accurately, but this was a careful and rigorous study. Putting aside any counting reservations for the present analysis, what kind of woman is most likely to experience such violence? Table 11.1 lists characteristics reflecting a risk at least 50 per cent above the national average. The figures indicate the ratio of that group's victimisation relative to the national average.

While many of the covariates may either anticipate or result from domestic violence (alcohol use may be a reaction to despair, for example), for many purposes this does not matter. This may sound heretical, but insofar as the policing problem is to dispense effort where the problem is to be found, the listed variables may be useful. They will allow the location of sub-populations on which to concentrate – and the basis for checklists by, for example, general practitioners and hospital accident and emergency departments to prioritise investigations into injuries suffered.

Table 11.1 Prevalence of domestic violence (assault or threat) among women aged 16–59, by socio-demographic characteristics, relative to national average

Characteristic of person or household	Rate relative to national average
Aged 16–24	2.15
Separated	4.97
Divorced	1.86
Never married	1.86
Council/housing assn tenant	1.90
Household income <£5k	2.25
Financial difficulties	2.32
Health very/fairly bad	1.61
Heavy alcohol use	1.76
Illegal drug use in last year	3.24
Council estate/low income Acorn area	1.51

Domestic assault is one of those crimes which mapping showed not to generate 'hotspots'. Even where hotspots are calculable, there may be non-spatial variables which yield discrimination of risk to complement that achieved by spatial analysis.

Table 11.2 illustrates the point in relation to domestic burglary, the data (derived from Budd 1999) being treated in exactly the same way as was that in Table 11.1. It will be seen that, for example, homes occupied by the young, those of Asian origin, and the recently moved, are more liable to be burgled.

A further example from experience comes from work with repeat victimisation (see, for example, Pease 1998). Unless adequate locational information is available, it requires some time to set geocoding in place before useful maps will be generated. Alternatively, a major enterprise of (inevitably incomplete) back record conversion would be necessary. Either way, usable crime mapping takes some time to put in place. In many forces, the writer has suggested that an adequate proxy for mapping crime hotspots, at least until an adequate GIS system is established, could be found by centring attention upon repeat victims. Repeat victims are disproportionately found in crime hotspots (Johnson *et al.* 1997). In the absence of a functioning GIS, rather than wait for one to be functional, deploying resources at and around the sites of repeat victimisation would be an adequate alternative, and would dispense effort immediately and roughly appropriately. This suggestion never seemed to find favour. GIS had to be used, not other variables (even those we know to be associated with hot spots). Whether the map serves as the source of unique information, comfort blanket or pretty toy is a matter for conjecture.

Table 11.2 Risk of domestic burglary by household type (calculated from Budd 1999)

Household	Relative risk
Head of household 16–24 years	2.71
One adult living with children	2.00
Head of household is single	1.73
Head of household is separated	1.63
Respondent is Asian	1.77
Head of household is unemployed	1.80
Head of household is economically inactive	1.70
Home is privately rented	1.73
Respondent resident for less than one year	1.75
Home has no security measures	2.71
Home in inner city	1.52
Home in an area with high levels of physical disorder	2.14

The tyranny of geography and its consequences

In the NIJ volume (Harries 1999) maps are described as follows: 'Maps:

- are pictures of information about areas and places
- help us *visualise* data
- are like the proverbial pictures worth a thousand words
- enable information to be seen at a glance' (p. 3).

Accepting that the tone of the passage is intended to be light and accessible, nonetheless the second, third and fourth points are all debatable.

Maps help us visualise data: This is true only in the trivial sense that the distribution of data is visible. Visualisation is the preserve of virtual reality depictions or an understanding of the data (e.g. the cluster of assaults is outside the Poco a Poco night club; the cluster of 'youths causing annoyance' is on a small green patch used for soccer).

Maps are worth a thousand words: Their meaning, and hence their memorability and their usefulness, depends on extra knowledge of that which is depicted. A map of player positions on a soccer pitch is informative only if one is aware of the laws and tactics of the game. For example, clustering of twenty of the total twenty-two players within a few metres of the centre line makes sense only if one understands the off-side rule. Clustering of players on one side of a goal with a single player in one corner of the pitch is only interpretable as a corner kick (or a throw-in near the corner flag if the cluster of players is on the same side of the goal as the lone player) with knowledge of how the game works.

Enable information to be seen at a glance: But not understood at a glance, certainly not in a way which informs problem solution.

The notion that maps are of real but limited use, and that non-spatial variables can yield information about crime risk distributed across noncontiguous locations seems so uncontentious as to be banal, indeed scarcely worth saying. However, do we behave as though it were true? Harries (1999) writes: 'Maps are but one way of representing information, and they are not always the most appropriate mode. If information about places is being represented, maps may be the best format. However, if no geographic (place-to-place) information is present, such as when all the data for a city are combined into one table, there is nothing to map. The whole jurisdiction is represented by one number . . . so the map too, could portray only one number. In this situation, a bar chart simply showing the relative levels of each crime category would be the best choice' (p. 7).

The Harries example is instructive in two ways. First, the alternative to mapping is represented by a situation where mapping is impossible, not where it is inappropriate, leaving the impression that where mapping is possible, it is likely to be useful. Second, it neglects the scenario where the distribution of crime is predictable in terms of non-spatial variables. Mapping the problem,[5] rather than mapping the space, is the purpose.

Later we read in Harries (1999), 'Crimes have distinctive geographic patterns for two underlying reasons that often overlap

- First, crimes must have victims and those victims (or their property) have definite geographic coordinates at any given moment.
- Second, some areas in cities, suburbs and rural areas have persistently high rates of crime' (p. 26).

What is again omitted from this is the possibility that non-spatial variables will also generate distinctive patterns of concentration, which may suggest non-geographic allocation of resources.

The phrasing of the chapter so far has been careful to avoid giving the impression that GIS is of little value. Clearly it is of great value. Proactive patrolling, for example, is only possible given adequate information about spatial distribution of crime. Non-spatial analysis should complement, and cannot substitute for, spatial analysis. The problem, rather, is that GIS comes to assume an inappropriately prominent place among techniques of crime analysis. The wider term 'crime pattern analysis' is preferred among many commentators (e.g. Audit Commission 1993; Read and Oldfield 1995), where the term includes the identification of crimes with similar characteristics, crime trends and comparative case analysis. Despite this, prominence is still given to spatial analysis – as is reflected in the title of this volume for example, where mapping comes before analysis. What are the reasons for mapping to assume pre-eminence in the consciousness of many analysts?

Policing is organised spatially. A police force area is divided into basic command units, and into beats within them. The Home Office chooses to present its criminal statistics categorising crimes by police force area. Funding, responsibility for action and crime counting are all locked in to a spatial framework. This is also true of community safety responsibilities amongst local authorities. To discern the primacy of spatial thought one only has to look at the text in the Crime and Disorder Act 1998 devoted to arrangements when local authority and policing areas are not co-terminous, and the debates which that has provoked. It may be convenient for organisations to have their own bailiwicks, but it is no more logical than other means of segmenting the population for the purposes of service delivery. Gas and electricity supply, insurance service and Internet access are dispensed and accounted for along lines of provider, rather than primarily of geography. Policing could in principle be distributed according to victim group, wherever they are to be found. Indeed some policing specialisms, such as child protection, do work that way.

The cast of mind which gives geography primacy is embedded in official thinking about crime. In the first round of the Crime Prevention Programme's burglary reduction initiative, to be eligible for Home Office funding, the area to be covered had to be between 3,000 and 5,000 house-holds in size, and have a burglary rate at least double the national rate. This way of slicing the world up has a number of implications:

- It defines the problem in geographical terms.
- It neglects households highly liable to burglary which fall outside the designated area.
- It invites the inclusion of areas with modest burglary rates to make up the numbers to get the critical area size, thereby diluting areas with acute problems by the inclusion of areas with less pressing problems.
- More subtly, it invites one to think of crime reduction in terms of those activities, centrally police patrolling, which are geographically coherent.

It was as a result of dissatisfaction with 'the tyranny of geography' that the second round of the same programme removed the limits on community size of the first round, and allowed the inclusion of 'virtual communities', i.e. groups of dwellings characterised by commonalities other than geographic contiguity. Instrumental in this were the efforts of the North Wales officers DI Mark Owen and DS Mark Radcliffe, who set out to identify groups of dwellings within North Wales which met the criteria for inclusion (at least double the national burglary rate) but were not geographically defined. No police beat in the force met the criteria, so this was an enterprise undertaken in an area which would not have been eligible for funding had a geographical definition been used.

Two points about the enterprise of Owen and Radcliffe are noteworthy. First, it was difficult, because location is better recorded than any other variable. Second, it did yield a pattern. Small (not large) settlements of sheltered accommodation for the elderly at a variety of sites in Flintshire were consistently heavily victimised by burglars. This enabled a preventive programme to be put in motion. When analysed geographically, the settlements were too small to yield anything like a visible hotspot. When the data were looked at non-geographically, the problem was clear. At the time of writing, proposals such as that from North Wales are coming to the Crime Reduction Unit within the Home Office. A series of seminars addressed by the two officers from North Wales proved fruitful in spawning work of this kind.

There is a case for saying that much of what is valuable in the mapping movement comes from non-spatial adjuncts to the mapping enterprise which bring it closer to the North Wales analysis set out above. For example, Eck (1995) distinguishes open and closed drug markets, and the characteristics of places used in each kind of market. The kinds of variable with which they link market type include type of apartment block and changes in property value since purchase. No maps are used. The result is a model of drug market location which yields a set of suggestions about the disruption of such markets. Likewise Spelman (1995) identifies the consistency of hotspots over time, concluding that '. . . crime, disturbances and other calls for service can be reduced by something like 50 per cent in the most dangerous locations, simply by focusing on the unique characteristics of those locations that create opportunities for crime and disorder' (p. 142).

What really to do?

The challenge is to determine the parameters of crime risk which allow location to take its proper place, whether measured by coordinates or location attributes (bar, school, etc.), without the presumption that conventional spatial mapping is the tool of first resort. The question is how to incorporate location variables within the same modelling process alongside attributes of other kinds. Before doing this, a rehearsal of what the purposes of local crime analysis might be seems overdue. They are:

• Identifying people, households, public or commercial buildings, or spaces in which crime may occur, for the purpose of deploying resources to diminish the crime hazard. These resources may take the form of police patrolling, target hardening or other physical improvements. This enterprise takes no account of offender identity.

• Identifying characteristics of offences, which change the probabilities of their commission by different offenders. This may be achieved by distinctive characteristics of method, by geographic range or by forensic examination of crime scenes. This may be aided by extant databases of fingerprints, DNA, distribution of typical offender range, victim selection, and the like.

For ease, let us concentrate on the first purpose and on the offence of domestic burglary. We can roughly say that the probability of a repeat burglary against a home within one year will be four times an expected rate. We could calculate that, say, the probability of any household within a calculated 'hotspot' might be three times the expected rate.[6] We already know (see Table 11.2 above) that where the householder is under 25, the rate is some 2.7 times that expected.

Taking just those three variables, and operating a single variable selection process for intervention, we would prioritise those already victimised. Dwellings within a hotspot, on the hypothetical figures set out, would be the second option, with young householders the third. The next question would be how the effects combine. If the factors were additive, prior victims in hotspots would be prioritised, followed by prior victims who are young householders, followed by young householders in hotspots, and so on. Following this path simply involves modelling crime hazard. Spatial location may or may not feature among the variables in terms of which resources should be allocated.

Two issues complicate the matter. The more elaborate the modelling of risk, the more difficult and messy resource allocation will become. It is probable that a limited number of hazard factors will be all that could be reflected in resource allocation. Police routines could easily cope with the protection of the recently burgled, or those in a particular area. However, protecting all 'young householder, recently burgled, Asian people who have moved within the last year' before moving on to 'hotspot, separated, residents with no security devices installed in privately rented accommodation' invites chaos. Resource allocation is most realistically based on relatively few variables.

The second problem is thornier. It is the slippery notion of the hotspot. Householder age is usually clear, as is the fact of a prior burglary. By contrast, hotspots are abstractions from data. A very large number of alternative hotspots could be generated, by varying the allowable size of the spot and the hazard relativities of the spots and their surround. As a limiting case, the smallest hotspots would be drawn around each of those dwellings with the highest hazard, and would have hazards equivalent to the highest hazard level derivable from non-spatial variables. This means that the hotspot can take a range of hazard values and be more or less central to the allocation of resources. Here is not the place to develop how to hit the 'right' spot. Some factors will always be relevant, such as the need not to over-fit the ellipse to data from a short period. Others will depend on the deployment options discerned. The central point which should be made is that there are disadvantages in incorporating a location variable among those which determine resource allocation. It may turn out that spatial location is a relatively unhelpful variable in proaction. Such a conclusion must be seriously entertained. It will not mean that investment in GIS was a waste. Technology will advance to the point where patrolling officers use touch screens to record crime location quickly and accurately. Saved time in completion of incident reporting may turn out to be the major benefit of the current vogue for mapping.

Notes

1 The title should be sung to the tune of 'Two Sleepy People'. Sub-poetic licence is used to justify the use of GIS as a verb.

2 Typically, Leslie Wilkins (1968) got in first.
3 http://www.ojp.usdoj.gov/cmrc/
4 http://www.PoliceForum.org/
5 I owe the phrase to Norman Davidson.
6 It is interesting that this is not conventionally the way in which hotspots are depicted, although a strong case could be made for saying that it should be.

References

Audit Commission (1993) *Helping with Enquiries: Tackling Crime Effectively*, Police Paper 12, London: HMSO.

Budd, T. (1999) *Burglary of Domestic Dwellings: Findings from the British Crime Survey*, Home Office Statistical Bulletin 4/99, London: Home Office.

Eck, J.E. (1995) 'The geography of illicit retail marketplaces.', in J.E. Eck and D. Weisburd (eds) *Crime and Place*, Monsey, NY: Willow Tree Press.

Eck, J.E. and Weisburd, D. (1995) 'Crime places in crime theory', in J.E. Eck and D. Weisburd (eds) *Crime and Place*, Monsey, NY: Willow Tree Press.

Ellingworth, D.E. and Pease, K. (1998) 'Movers and breakers', *International Journal of Risk, Crime and Deliquency* 3(1).

Harries, K. (1999) *Mapping Crime: Principle and Practice*, Washington, DC: National Institute of Justice.

Hirschfield, A. and Bowers, K. (1997) 'The development of a social, demographic and land use profiler for areas of high crime', *British Journal of Criminology* 37: 103–20.

Illinois Criminal Justice Information Authority (1987) *Spatial and Temporal Analysis of Crime*, Chicago Ill.: Criminal Justice Information Authority.

Johnson, S.D., Bowers, K. and Hirschfield, A. (1997) 'New insights into the spatial and temporal distribution of repeat victimisation', *British Journal of Criminology* 37: 224–41.

Mirlees-Black, C. (1999) *Domestic Violence: Findings from a New British Crime Survey Self-Completion Questionnaire*, Home Office Research Study 191, London: Home Office.

Pease, K. (1998) *Repeat Victimisation: Taking Stock*, PRG Crime Detection and Prevention Series Paper 90, London: Home Office.

Ratcliffe, J.H. (in press) 'Implementing and integrating crime mapping into a police intelligence environment', *International Journal of Police Science and Management*.

Read, T. and D. Oldfield (1995) *Local Crime Analysis*, PRG Crime Detection and Prevention Series Paper 65, London: Home Office.

Rossmo, D.K. (1993) 'Target patterns of serial murderers: a methodological model', *American Journal of Criminal Justice* 17: 1–21.

Shaw, C.R. and McKay, H.D. (1942) *Juvenile Delinquency and Urban Areas*, Chicago: University of Chicago Press.

Spelman, W. (1995) 'Criminal careers of public places', in J.E. Eck and D. Weisburd (eds) *Crime and Place*, Monsey NY: Willow Tree Press.

Tilley, N., Pease, K., Hough, M. and Brown, R. (1999) *Burglary Prevention: Early Lessons from the Crime Reduction Programme*, Crime Reduction Research Paper 1, London: Home Office.

Wilkins, L.T. (1968) 'The concept of cause in criminology', *Issues in Criminology* 3: 147–65.

12 Decision support in crime prevention

Data analysis, policy evaluation and GIS

Alex Hirschfield

The mapping and analysis of crime data is of interest to a wide range of people. They include police officers interested in where to target patrols, local authority community safety officers tasked with producing crime and disorder audits, policy evaluators, academics, potential inward investors and local communities. Each will have a different reason for studying crime and disorder patterns in their areas. The types of information and evidence that they will need will also vary. For example, for operational policing purposes, information on the distribution of offences will need to be up to date and sufficiently detailed in order to plan operations. The academic will be interested in some of the risk factors that explain the location and timing of criminal incidents. Inward investors will want to know how safe an area is for setting up businesses.

This chapter examines how information and evidence varies according to the needs of different stakeholders. It then considers how the different interests groups approach the analysis of such data. Particular attention is paid to the notion of targeting resources and examples are given of case studies in north-west England. The chapter also examines the need for training in these areas particularly that required for the production of crime and disorder audits and outlines the contents of a national curriculum for community safety.

Introduction

Interest in the analysis and mapping of crime data is not restricted to any one group of practitioners or individuals. In fact, there is potentially a very widespread interest in identifying social and spatial patterns of crime, in documenting how these change over time and in assessing the extent to which such changes are influenced by crime prevention measures. Those who share this concern include the police (e.g. for planning operations against crime), community safety co-ordinators and regeneration partnerships (e.g. for designing and implementing programmes to reduce the fear of crime and to improve the image of unpopular areas) as well as the business community, the public, policy evaluators and academics.

In Britain, the awareness of crime and disorder problems within local communities and what can be done to reduce them has been given a considerable boost through the passing of the Crime and Disorder Act in

1998. The Act made the production of local crime and disorder audits and the formulation of three-year crime and disorder strategies a shared statutory duty between local authorities and police constabularies in England and Wales. Making the production of crime and disorder audits a statutory requirement and one which had to be met within a relatively short period of time has undoubtedly focused minds. In so doing it has brought into sharp focus issues such as the availability and sharing of relevant data, confidentiality and data protection and a plethora of other factors to consider including, the design of the audit, the range of crime and disorder incident categories to include, the amount of background and contextual information required (for example, on land use, demographics and levels of deprivation) and how best to incorporate the views and priorities of local communities. The fact that the audits and strategies were to be produced without additional resources from the government has also led to some hard thinking both within the police service and local authorities on how best to deploy staff and resources to meet the challenge.

The need to construct baselines and position statements on crime and disorder in the UK is also being driven by the priority given by government through the Home Office's Crime Reduction Initiative (CRI) to reduce specific types of crime through the implementation of targeted policing initiatives, funding competitions for closed circuit television equipment (CCTV), and innovative burglary reduction schemes (the so-called 'Strategic Development Projects') which use various combinations of interventions to reduce crime.

Running concurrently with the CRI are a number of government-funded programmes concerned with area regeneration, poverty and social exclusion and the reduction of health inequalities, all of which are designed to improve the quality of life of disadvantaged communities. Many of these (for example, Single Regeneration Budget-funded partnerships and the New Deal for Communities initiative) have strategic objectives which aim to reduce the fear of crime and to improve community safety. The extent to which such programmes have been effective in achieving these goals inevitably relies upon monitoring changes in levels of victimisation and the fear of crime and in being able to attribute some of these shifts to the action which has been taken. This places the analysis of changes in the social and spatial distribution of crime and disorder firmly on the social exclusion/regeneration agenda and, in so doing, extends the field of crime data analysis to a far larger group of stakeholders.

Given the variety of 'interest groups' who share a concern in the changing manifestations of crime and disorder, there is a clear need to explore the similarities and points of departure in the types of data required, in their level of detail and in the analytical methods which are applied to meet their needs. In short, there is a need to establish how far the 'evidence base' on crime and disorder varies for different interest groups and the implications of this for the mapping and analysis of crime data.

The remainder of this chapter investigates these questions by exploring the nature of the evidence base in crime prevention and how different forms of crime data analysis and mapping can be used to meet the varying requirements of different stakeholders. These points are then illustrated using examples of specific applications from north-west England. The chapter concludes with an examination of requisite skills and training needs for those involved in analysing and mapping crime data.

Data, information and evidence in crime prevention

A wide range of data-sets can be identified which are relevant to the analysis and mapping of crime and to the formulation, implementation and evaluation of crime prevention measures. Two of the most widely used sources of data from police information systems include recorded crime information and telephone calls for service (command and control records). Recorded crime suffers from problems of under-reporting and is also highly variable in its accuracy and quality, in particular, in the way in which addresses and locations are geographically referenced. Some police districts have more structured address referencing systems for offence locations than others. Systems that ask for locational information in a fixed format, so that there are fields for the number of the property, the road, the subtown area, the town and the postcode, often facilitate geocoding since they can be compared with each other and to other data-sets more easily. Systems in which locations are entered in a freefield format without consistent naming conventions make the geocoding process more difficult, and there will be a higher proportion of records that cannot be used in spatial analysis.

Command and control data are useful as a barometer of public anxiety and concern about crime and anti-social behaviour (especially in relation to juvenile disturbances, neighbour disputes and other forms of minor disorder), but often suffer from problems of over-reporting where several telephone calls reporting the same incident appear in the data (Warner and Pierce 1993).

A fair proportion of the data from police information systems is amenable to mapping but the coverage and precision of the locational reference is highly dependent upon the crime category. Pinpointing the location of residential burglaries is, for example, in theory, easier than identifying burglaries affecting corner shops, pharmacies and small businesses with twenty-five or fewer employees. This is primarily because non-residential properties are not coded consistently by their function, use and number of employees in police data (Bowers and Hirschfield 1998). But there are also problems with inconsistencies in the way in which residential addresses are entered on computer systems by police officers and civilians. Although seemingly a straightforward exercise, the identification of repeat burglary is in practice quite hard to achieve because each time a burglary occurs at an address it appears as a separate record on the database. In police information systems, incidents of recorded crime are stored as single independent records. These systems are not structured in a way that will identify a single address with a frequency count alongside it denoting the number of burglaries occurring at that address within a 12-month period. To do so involves searching the relevant recorded crime database to determine if offences occur at any addresses on more than one occasion, and then creating a new database that reflects the results of these analyses. Although this may appear to be a straightforward task, it is not. For example, for recorded crime data, there is considerable potential for inconsistency in the recording of addresses, particularly in the case of flats, which makes the task of address matching (i.e. counting the number of times an address reappears over time) difficult, although, a number of innovative and effective approaches have been developed to overcome these problems (Johnson *et al.* 1997; Bowers *et al.* 1998; see also Spencer Chainey's chapter in this volume).

Crimes against the person, in particular, robbery, theft and assault are more difficult to map because of the often high degree of uncertainty about where they occur. In many information systems their location is assigned to the nearest land mark or street intersection, but in many cases it is difficult to obtain a reliable spatial reference for them. These problems are compounded when it comes to pinpointing the location of crime and anti-social behaviour on public transport.

Victimisation surveys are undertaken to overcome problems of under-reporting of crime. The results from them cannot be mapped at the very detailed micro-level because of confidentiality and the fact the number of responses are usually too small to support it.

Although the volume of recorded crimes and command and control incidents provide an indication of the overall size of the problem in an area and enable some analysis of where clusters of crime occur and how they vary over time, they need to be related to appropriate denominators in order to construct crime rates.

Three separate measures of the crime rate can be distinguished, namely, incidence, prevalence and concentration. Incidence expresses the number of crimes committed in relation to the number of residents or households in the area (for example the number of domestic burglaries per 1,000 households). Prevalence relates the number of victimised households to the total number of households (for example, burgled households per 1,000 households) and concentration measures the number of incidents per victim. In short, incidence counts crimes, prevalence counts victims and concentration counts the number of crimes per victim (Farrell and Pease 1993). The phenomenon of repeat victimisation explains why the number of crimes will often exceed the number of victims.

Prevalence rates therefore provide the investigator with an idea of how widespread crime is within the local community. It is also often useful to broaden the range of relevant data-sets to include information about the population at risk and the demographic composition and land use of areas of interest and areas which border them. The spatial manifestation of crime is the result of a complex web of inter-relationships between demographic, social, cultural, lifestyle and land use characteristics. Research has shown, for example, that there are strong links between the distribution of crime and the levels of deprivation and social cohesion found in different areas (Hirschfield and Bowers 1997). It is also important that spatial patterns of crime are not viewed in isolation to the functions of different areas. Wikstrom (1991) stresses how particular areas may be devoted to different types of land use (residential development, retailing, industry, leisure, open space) and how the activities and population profile of an area may vary according to the day or time of day (e.g. city centres on weekday mornings and Saturday nights).

Geodemographic classifications provide a useful means for contextualising residential areas. These identify similar types of residential neighbourhood in terms of their demographic, socio-economic, ethnic and housing composition. It has been long recognised that certain types of residential neighbourhood are more criminogenic than others. The British Crime Survey (BCS), using the Acorn geodemographic classification showed that the areas of highest risk for residential burglary included the poorest council estates, multi-racial areas and areas with a mixed social status and an over-representation of single people. Burglary rates in these areas were between two and three times the national average (Mirlees-Black *et al.* 1998). In short, area classifications provide a better spatial framework than purely administrative units (e.g. electoral wards, census tracts) which are unlikely to contain socially homogeneous populations.

Two difficulties arise in relating contextual information to crime data; one is obtaining demographic and contextual information for crime hotspots and for territorial units such as police beats which are not coterminous with standard statistical reporting units (e.g. enumeration districts and electoral wards). The other is the difficulty in acquiring population denominators (e.g. total population, households and dwellings) that match the time period for which crime data are being assembled. Very often there is little alternative other than to use population data from the decennial population census which rapidly becomes out of date.

Assembling evidence to understand the manifestation of the problems (for example, anti-social behaviour, disorder, crime) is a first step in the identification of appropriate solutions. Yet there is much which needs to be learnt about how to identify problems, how to explain them and how to measure and evaluate their impact. Relevant questions in this context would include:

- How do problems of crime and disorder manifest themselves socially, spatially and temporally?
- What are the underlying social and environmental risk factors that account for them?

- What impact do they have on the communities who experience them and on those responsible for ameliorating them?

Crime data (whether from police sources, victimisation surveys or both) and contextual demographic and land use information is only a partial list of the 'intelligence' and evidence required to support the formulation and implementation of crime prevention measures. Other data are required to generate a holistic picture of what is happening. These include information about the current deployment of situational and social crime prevention measures. This might include the location of CCTV cameras, the identification of dwellings which have been target hardened or the individuals enrolled on a youth diversion programme together with the resource inputs which are being expended on them.

The decision to deploy crime prevention measures, in common with that for any other resource, is not taken as evidence of effectiveness alone. Cost is a crucial part of the equation. A measure might be effective but if it is too expensive in terms of equipment and/or personnel, it might not be cost-effective. Two types of cost are involved. One is the economic cost of crime in terms of damage to property, loss of revenue, loss of employment, value of goods stolen and cost to the criminal justice system including police time. The other, is the cost of crime prevention measures which might include resource inputs for staff, equipment, buildings, training, travel and so on. Cost-effectiveness analysis requires input of both types of data. However, gathering this type of evidence is far from straightforward, although progress is being made in the United Kingdom in developing methods for collecting information about the inputs required to operationalise crime prevention measures, particularly those which would be deemed necessary to replicate successful crime prevention schemes in other areas.

It is often also relevant to identify facilities and resources other than crime prevention measures which are available to local communities and which could have a bearing on changing patterns of crime and on displacement. For example, when attempting to identify and understand changes in 'hotspots' for juvenile disturbances, information on the availability of facilities for young people within the community (for example youth clubs and leisure facilities) and the extent to which levels of provision have changed over time (for example reductions in the number of facilities, hours of operation, capacity) might be essential in interpreting changing patterns of crime and disorder. In short, the evidence base for crime prevention has to be broader than just information on the manifestation of crime and disorder. The supply-side (that is, existing resources and facilities within communities together with existing crime prevention measures) needs to be analysed in conjunction with the need/demand for crime prevention (for example, existing levels of crime and disorder) so that the mismatch between the two can be identified. Once this is achieved any changes or gaps in the existing deployment of resources to combat or prevent crime can be defined. This might involve repositioning CCTV cameras, changing the opening hours and/or location of facilities for young people, increasing guardianship in public places and so on. Identifying need without recourse to the current deployment of resources provides only half the picture. The two need to be analysed in combination to appreciate what needs to change in order to maximise opportunities for reducing crime.

Any position statement which is generated should include projects and programmes implemented by all agencies operating within the area of interest so that situations where there is unnecessary duplication of effort and those where there is synergy can be identified. Targeting crime prevention measures solely on the basis of an analysis of crime patterns in the absence of an evidence base on existing provision runs the risk of delivering responses to problems which are inappropriate and which fail to capitalise upon and add value to existing efforts.

Decision support, targeting and the role of (GIS) information

Decision support

The types of information which practitioners and others use as raw material to inform their decisions have been reviewed above. The types of decision that need to be made and the reasons for wanting to scrutinise problems of crime and disorder will vary according to the needs of the different interest groups. At least eight groups can be identified. They include:

- police officers responsible for identifying strategic priorities and for making operational decisions about the deployment of patrols
- practitioners in local authorities and the police service responsible for producing Crime and Disorder Audits and Strategies for their areas
- community safety coordinators and regeneration project managers developing partnership approaches to achieve sustainable reductions in crime and disorder
- evaluators seeking to measure the impact, efficiency and cost effectiveness of crime prevention programmes
- criminologists and other academics interested in the analysis of crime data and in the development of theories about the causes and prevention of crime
- residents tracking the changing fortunes of their neighbourhoods
- business managers monitoring conditions in their areas of operation
- migrants and business managers appraising alternative locations as places in which to live and invest.

A number of applications involving the mapping and analysis of crime and associated data-sets stem from the needs of these interest groups. All groups would have an interest in identifying the scale and distribution of crime and disorder in their areas.

Key questions of interest here would include:

- Is crime generally a small or a big problem?
- Where do crimes occur?
- When do crimes occur?
- How prevalent are they?
- How concentrated are they?
- How costly?
- Are crimes decreasing or increasing?
- Are crimes diffusing or concentrating?
- Are crimes affecting the same areas or new areas?

Specific applications might include:

- exploring relationships between crime and the environment (physical and social)
- identifying levels of crime in and around selected sites
- identifying mismatches between resources and needs
- providing information that will allow for the improved planning and allocation of resources for community safety and crime prevention work (targeting)
- enabling the better co-ordination of services
- facilitating data sharing between relevant organisations
- evaluating the impact of specific crime prevention measures
- searching for evidence of spatial and temporal displacement of crime
- informing police operations against crime
- relating offence locations to those of previous offenders and known suspects
- communicating with and engaging local communities
- supporting bids for extra resources from central government
- crowd control and traffic management
- developing early warning systems of emerging problems.

Targeting crime prevention

A key area where evidence is needed to inform policy and decision-making is in the targeting of resources. Given the inevitable time and resource constraints experienced by the police, local authorities and community safety partnerships there will always be a need to ration the resources available for crime prevention. Targeting is the means through which such rationing is implemented on the ground. It is perhaps surprising that despite the widespread use of the term targeting among politicians and practitioners there does not appear to be a clear definition of it in the literature. The following definition goes some way towards filling this gap. Targeting is: 'The identification and directing of attention/resources to declared recipient(s)'. The target or 'declared recipient', may be a person (e.g. an actual or potential victim of crime), a household or family unit, a social/client group (e.g. elderly people, lone parent families, ethnic groups), a building (e.g. a repeatedly burgled house), or item of property (electrical equipment, a vehicle), an area (e.g. a deprived area, a policy zone, a public place) or an organisation/service delivery outlet (e.g. a small business, a school). The channelling of resources for crime prevention to any one or more of these 'recipients' becomes clearer when different types of offence and crime prevention measure are matched. This is attempted in Table 12.1 which links type of crime, scale used for identifying recipients and crime prevention measures. For example, the types of crime affecting these recipients might include assault, robbery or rape (in the case of indi-

Table 12.1 Targeting crime prevention

Crimes	Scale	Measures
Assault, robbery, rape	Individuals: Likely victims Actual victims Likely perpetrators Actual perpetrators	Personal attack alarms Crime prevention advice
Domestic violence, neighbour disputes	Households and families: Likely victims Actual victims Likely perpetrators Actual perpetrators	Mediation programmes
Racial harassment, bogus officials	Social/ client groups: Likely victims Actual victims Likely perpetrators Actual perpetrators	Racial harassment units
Burglary, arson criminal damage	Properties: Likely victims Actual victims Likely perpetrators Actual perpetrators	Target hardening/ surveillance, target prolific burglars
Fraud, white collar 'victimless' crime	Organisations: Likely victims Actual victims Likely perpetrators Actual perpetrators	Sting operations, undercover investigations
Disorder, juvenile disturbances	Public places: Likely victims Actual victims Likely/actual perpetrators	CCTV, town centre wardens

viduals), domestic violence (at the household, family level), racial hatred and offences committed by bogus officials (affecting ethnic groups and client groups such as pensioners), burglary, arson and car crime (at the property level), fraud, theft and 'white collar crime' (affecting organisations and institutions) and disorder, anti-social behaviour and juvenile disturbances (affecting specific residential areas and public places). Similarly, crime prevention measures aimed at reducing the vulnerability of actual/potential targets may be directed at individuals (e.g. personal attack alarms), households and family units (mediation programmes), social and ethnic groups (e.g. racial harassment units), properties and property (target hardening, property marking) institutions and organisations (e.g. sting operations) or 'dangerous places' (e.g. CCTV, town centre wardens).

The decision to target persons or households who have previously been victims of crime (actual victims) or to concentrate on those at risk who have not yet become victims (likely victims) has implications, not only in terms of the data-sets needed to identify the target groups, but also, in respect of the types of measures which are provided. Repeat burglary strategies which seek to prevent the further victimisation of existing victims require information about the initial burglary and when it occurred so that appropriate steps can be taken at the right time. This is usually a few weeks after the first burglary when the risk of re-victimisation is at its height. This type of targeting requires data which identifies both the location of previously burgled property and the date and time on which the incident occurred. Ideally, there would also be information on the modus operandi. Typical measures might include the fitting of windows locks, door locks, alarms and the provision of crime prevention advice. The fact that a burglary has taken place is a sufficient indicator of vulnerability or predisposition to future victimisation.

By contrast, strategies which seeks to prevent an initial victimisation have to be based on some assessment of the 'risk' of victimisation so that likely victims can be identified and targeted for assistance. This brings into the analysis the whole question of which criteria to use to measure and assess victimisation risk. For domestic burglary, such factors might include the design and layout of dwellings, levels of social cohesion, guardianship and natural surveillance, and existing crime prevention measures within the area. Other relevant factors in assessing risk would include land use, burglary trends and crime prevention measures in neighbouring areas, and the residential location of known offenders. Any scoring system calculating risk on the basis of these criteria would need to have available data at the individual property level, at the level of the street or block, for the immediate neighbourhood and for areas beyond. In practice, all that may be available to inform the targeting decision is the burglary rate in the police beat and the extent to which this exceeds the national or regional average.

The use of prior victimisation, or in the case of non-victims, the risk of victimisation, to guide targeting decisions applies not only to the selection of properties, but also to the identification of vulnerable individuals (for example, in the case of crimes against the person), vulnerable organisations and hazardous public places.

The same distinction applies to the targeting of actual perpetrators and those at risk of offending. Strategies aimed at reducing recidivism and re-offending will target those with a criminal record whilst those aimed at preventing the onset of a criminal career will target those at risk of anti-social and criminal behaviour. Youth diversion programmes occupy this territory. Once again, relevant data for use in targeting resources will vary.

Two additional factors which affect the logistics of targeting are the temporal dimension (i.e. when to target or intervene) and the dynamics of target selection (i.e. whether to stick to the same area, the same properties, the same individuals over time or to switch to new targets).

Each level and type of targeting requires appropriate data in order to identify the recipients, to deliver the necessary crime prevention measure and to keep track of progress over time so that effectiveness can be evaluated.

In attempting to explain the social and spatial manifestation of crime, there is also a need to understand the mechanisms that underpin the targeting decisions of a wide range of actors not just those of practitioners (police, community safety coordinators) but also those of offenders who commit crime. A clearer understanding of who targets, what is being targeted, for what reason and how, is the starting point for identifying the different types of data needed to analyse crime patterns and to begin to understand why certain individuals, properties and places might be at greater risk than others. Table 12.2 sets out some of these parameters.

The police target criminals to improve clear up rates and to take prolific offenders out of circulation but they also target actual and potential victims (e.g. vulnerable individuals, communities, businesses) to offer crime prevention advice and protection. The information that they use includes intelligence on criminal activities through surveillance and informants, as

Table 12.2 The 'who', 'what', 'why 'and 'how' of targeting

Who is doing it?	What are they targeting?	Why?	How?
Police	Criminals Citizens	Detections/arrests Crime prevention	Criminal intelligence Crime data analysis
Criminals	Vulnerable persons/property	Economic gain personal satisfaction	Environmental cues/ offender networks
Community safety partnerships	High crime areas	Crime reduction Improvements in the quality of life Promotion of regeneration	Community consultation Crime audits/data analysis

well as the analysis of crime patterns and trends. They respond to crime reactively, but also use information proactively to plan and implement operations against crime. Criminals identify suitable targets (vulnerable persons and property) using a combination of environment cues and information gathered by liaising with other criminals. Factors influencing the choice of targets, even for the opportunist criminal, include the routine activities of the potential victims and the level of surveillance and security surrounding buildings and items of property. Motivation varies but usually includes personal satisfaction and/or economic gain.

Community safety partnerships and local authorities typically adopt a more strategic form of targeting. They are not in the business of operational policing but they are concerned with the impact of crime and the fear of crime on the quality of life of residents in high crime communities and on the image and future prospects of such areas. Partnerships usually have a multidisciplinary view of the problems that confront disadvantaged communities, one which reflects the perspectives of the various stakeholders which comprise them.

Awareness of the inter-relatedness and cross-cutting nature of many of the problems that affect high crime communities is reflected in the British government's approach to tackling social exclusion, anti-social behaviour and crime through 'joined-up policy-making'. The implication of this approach for evidence gathering is that more broadly based, eclectic methodologies will be required, not only in terms of where to search (situational crime prevention, for example, crosses several disciplines including geography, planning, sociology, psychology and social policy), but also, in terms of the types of evidence required. The latter would include information on people, places and organisations assembled through the use of both quantitative and qualitative techniques. It would also require evidence on how different policies interact, often referred to now as 'whole systems approaches'.

Community safety partnerships often target clearly defined priority areas and seek to improve community safety, build social cohesion and reduce the fear of crime within them, although, they may also pursue thematic programmes that are local authority-wide or direct their attention to 'virtual communities'. A key feature of their method of targeting is to canvass the views of the community and to ensure that their priorities are reflected in their community safety strategies.

Each of these 'interest groups' requires information to inform their targeting decisions. But because these decisions are made for very different reasons and involve defining different types of 'target' they vary markedly in terms of the time period over which they are taken, in the frequency with which they are made and in the data-sets needed to support them (Table 12.3). A continuum in the scale of the targeting decision can be identified where, at one extreme, decisions need to be made very quickly to respond to rapidly changing circumstances (e.g. the deployment of patrols

Table 12.3 Targeting: scale and review period

Scale	Type of targeting	Review period	Data
Macro	Strategic	1–3 years	Crime rate changes league tables
Meso		Monthly/ quarterly	
Micro	Operational	Weekly, daily, hourly	Individual records point maps

as part of operational policing). Updates of data for 'operational targeting' might be needed daily or even hourly to inform the deployment of police officers under these circumstances. The types of data involved are more likely to be reports of individual incidents perhaps presented as 'pin maps' or images showing the location of offences or offenders updated at regular intervals. At the other extreme are the longer-term more strategic decisions taken by community safety partnerships about what type of crime prevention measures are required and where within the local authority or priority area these need to be concentrated. These targeting decisions are more likely to be influenced by league tables depicting crime rates for different parts of the authority (usually electoral wards) appearing alongside other evidence in the Crime and Disorder Audit. This information would normally be updated in part on an annual basis and more comprehensively every three years. The latter is the interval used for the production of Crime and Disorder Strategies in England and Wales. The review period is substantially longer than that required for operational policing purposes.

The role of GIS

Geographical Information Systems can make significant contributions in the identification of hotspots and high crime areas, in the analysis of displacement, in the targeting of resources and in the monitoring and evaluation of crime prevention programmes. They can also place spatial clusters of crime or high crime neighbourhoods into a social, demographic and land use context through the superimposition and intersection of relevant geographically referenced data-sets. The main uses of GIS in crime data analysis include the following:

- Mapping the distribution of individual and repeat incidents (offence, victim, offender locations)
- Putting contextual information on to the map
- Identifying clusters/'hotspots' from points
- Identifying 'hotspot' demographics and land use

- Calculating and mapping crime rates for administrative policy areas and neighbourhood types
- Conducting specific site and RADIAL analyses
- Identifying buffer zones
- Identifying comparison areas
- Tracking displacement.

The processing and mapping of disaggregate crime data is particularly useful at the micro level and site-specific analyses of crime patterns. For example, when individual level crime data are mapped in relation to operational boundaries (for example, of a target hardening initiative) valuable insights can be gained into the possible impacts of interventions on the timing and location of offences.

The visualisation of disaggregate crime data can be further enhanced by the superimposition of land use maps and digital aerial photographs. These provide valuable information about the presence of factors that can significantly increase or significantly decrease the risk of victimisation. For example, the picture gained by using a GIS to plot domestic burglaries for individual properties by time of occurrence and modus operandi can be enhanced considerably if land use maps and aerial photographs identify those dwellings that back on to the open space or situations where the presence of trees and shrubs are blocking the natural surveillance of properties. Similarly, if the target hardening scheme focused on installing gates to restrict access to alleyways to the rear of terraced houses, superimposing disaggregate burglary data on to detailed site maps which showed the location of the gates, would facilitate the search for crime displacement. However, this level of analysis would not be possible if access to individual records was restricted and only aggregate crime data for police beats were available because any shifts in crime within the target area would not be identifiable.

The superimposition, on a crime map, of ecological data for small areas, for example, census indicators or residential neighbourhood classification data (geodemographics) can add to the evidence base and point the way to possible causal processes underpinning crime patterns in and around specific sites. For example, knowledge of the social composition of target areas selected for crime prevention measures might provide some indication of guardianship, social cohesion and victimisation risk. Knowing what surrounds a target area (for example, deprived council estates, or affluent neighbourhoods with low levels of victimisation) may also help in explaining any displacement and that may occur from within the area to adjacent areas or vice versa.

Bringing together data on crime and disorder with boundary information, land use maps, aerial photography and geodemographic and social indicators will also facilitate the definition of 'buffer zones' surrounding crime prevention projects and that of comparison areas used in the evaluation of the impacts of crime prevention projects on levels of crime.

A GIS makes it possible to define concentric buffer zones surrounding a target area that can be used to search for evidence of displacement. These can be designed to mimic the shape of the target area and to contain a population of similar size in order to maximise the chances of being able to detect displacement. If buffer zones are too large (as is often the case when entire police beats are used as building blocks), there is a danger that any displacement into them from the target area goes undetected because it is disguised in the far higher frequency of incidents recorded in a significantly larger area. This is more of a problem when analyses are undertaken using aggregate crime records in place of disaggregate data.

Defining comparison areas requires knowledge of the social and land use characteristics of the target area and a capability to search for non-adjacent areas, without a comparable crime prevention project, but with a similar population profile and similar levels of victimisation. The search for comparison areas can be facilitated greatly by using a GIS equipped with socio-demographic and land use data that cover a wide area. In the British context, population census small area statistics, geodemographic classific-ations such as Super Profiles and Ordnance Survey 10:000 scanned raster images have nationwide coverage and would be appropriate data-sets for undertaking such an exercise using GIS.

Other roles of GIS include its use as a visual front end to programmes which identify spatial crime clusters and hotspots from disaggregate point data and as a means of producing aggregate crime statistics for catchment areas and radii surrounding selected buildings and landmarks (for example, schools, public houses, transport terminals). Examples of such applications have been covered extensively elsewhere in this book.

An important use of the technology is in the estimation of population denominators for non-standard areas for use in constructing crime rates. In Britain, crime statistics are routinely generated for police beats by local constabularies but population data and social indicators are generally not available for these areas. A GIS can be used to apportion population and social data recorded for one set of boundaries (for example, for enumer-ation districts) to another set of boundaries (e.g. police beats). These apportionments can take into consideration the amount of built up area common to both sets of zones and exclude any population which falls outside the zone of intersection between two sets of boundaries. These methods can also be used to reconstitute crime and population data from redundant police beats to new beats which emerge following the often frequent re-organisation of police administrative boundaries.

Examples of applications from practice

The ways in which information on crime and disorder, land use and socio-demographic context can be brought together to answer questions of relevance to different interest groups is best illustrated through some examples. These are presented below drawing on evaluation research carried out by the author for the Safer Merseyside Partnership (SMP), a seven-year community safety initiative funded through the Single Regeneration Budget. The SMP is a collaboration between local authority-based community safety practitioners, the police, the fire brigade, the transport authority (Merseytravel), voluntary organisations and private sector companies. A number of crime prevention programmes have been implemented over the past five years including initiatives aimed at preventing repeat burglary (both of domestic dwellings and small businesses), fire safety programmes, strategies to reduce criminal and anti-social behaviour on public transport and a Youth Action Programme targeting vulnerable young people. Discussions of the evaluation work undertaken in respect of some of these schemes appears elsewhere (Hirschfield and Bowers 1998).

Crime and disorder on public transport

The principal aim of the SMP's Travel Safe Programme is to reduce vandalism, assault and anti-social behaviour on Merseyside's public transport system. The strategy is seeking to reduce, not only the fear of crime among the travelling public, but also attacks and verbal abuse directed at staff. The perception of crime on public transport can have a significant impact upon patronage and can deter people from visiting city centre areas in the evenings and at weekends. This, in turn, can have an impact on the night-time economy of such areas. The British government's White Paper on the future of transport, published in July 1998 (DETR 1998), suggested that over 10 per cent extra patronage of public transport could be generated, mainly in off-peak times, if travellers, particularly women, felt safer in making their journeys.

Several interventions are being used by Travel Safe to tackle these problems. They include improving radio communications between drivers and depots; training staff in how best to deal with difficult customers; deploying plain clothes police officers to travel on selected highly victimised bus routes (so the 'bobbies on buses' campaign) and supporting rapid response teams established by some of the private bus companies. A detached youth work project (the 'Youth on the Move' initiative) is also being funded to raise awareness among young people of the importance of public transport and to divert them from possible anti-social and criminal behaviour.

The lack of information on incidents occurring on public transport is a major obstacle to producing strategic intelligence that can be used to target crime prevention measures. Following the deregulation of bus services in the 1980s a number of bus companies now provide services on Merseyside. Each company has a different approach to the monitoring and recording of incidents on the routes that they operate. A consistent county-wide database does not exist and there is substantial under-reporting of such incidents through the police command and control and recorded crime systems.

The need to develop a consistent approach towards recording incidents on the bus network has been recognised by the Travel Safe Initiative and as a result Merseytravel, the transport authority, has funded a three-year PhD studentship at the University of Liverpool to take matters forward. The priorities for the research include:

- capturing consistent contemporary digital representations of local bus and rail networks
- generating a consistent set of geographically referenced baseline statistics on crime and disorder incidents on the public transport system serving Merseyside
- identifying hotspots and peak times for the occurrence of particular types of incident and highlighting the most affected routes and locations
- establishing whether relationships exist between the patterns of incidents on public transport and those displayed by juvenile disturbances and other crimes in communities served by these routes, stops and stations
- accounting for discrepancies found between reports of incidents from public transport operators and police command and control records so that steps to reduce the scale of under-reporting can be identified.

One of the early research tasks has been to identify data-sets already held by Merseytravel and to determine whether or not these are being exploited to their full potential. A database already exists on damage to bus shelters, signs and street furniture which is geographically referenced to an accuracy of one metre. However, this information has only been used to generate aggregate statistics on the volume of incidents for reporting purposes. The challenge and indeed, opportunity, is to process existing data-sets such as these in new ways so as to build up an evidence base that can be used to help target crime prevention resources more effectively.

A pilot study was undertaken on the Wirral, one of Merseyside county's five local authority districts, to identify the location of repeat incidents of criminal damage at bus stops and to calculate the financial implications of such damage in terms of repair costs. The volume of incidents affecting each bus stop between February and October 1999 was calculated together with repair costs. These were then plotted, using a GIS, and displayed in relation to the bus routes, the street network and the distribution of different types of residential neighbourhood using the Super Profiles geodemographic classification. Plate 7 shows the number of reported incidents of criminal damage per bus stop on the Wirral over the period in question. The volume of incidents is depicted using proportional circles.

The largest circles show bus stops that were damaged between nine and thirteen times. The information in Plate 7 provides an indication of where the volume of incidents was greatest and shows clear evidence of spatial clustering in the centre and towards the north-east of the borough. However, the map does not inform the observer of the extent to which the incidents were concentrated into particular bus stops and areas. In order to identify this, it was necessary to produce a resource targeting table (RTT). The latter ranks the bus stops in descending order of the frequency of incidents at each site, expresses those occurring at each bus stop as a percentage of all incidents in the area and identifies the cumulative percentage of bus stops alongside the cumulative percentage of incidents. The RRT for the volume of criminal damage incidents appears as Table 12.4.

One hundred bus stops, 6.6 per cent of the total, experienced two or more incidents of criminal damage. Some were very highly victimised. One bus stop, for example, accumulated thirteen incidents over the 18 months period accounting for 2.75 per cent of all cases of criminal damage to bus stops on the Wirral. In terms of volumes of cases, just over one-fifth of all incidents (20.97 per cent) were concentrated in just under 1 per cent of all bus stops which translated into fourteen of the 1,507 bus stops in the borough. These could then be readily identified through maps and tables providing precise locations. The RTT would provide useful information for targeting crime prevention measures on the basis of the volume of incidents.

A different picture emerges when the cost of criminal damage is analysed. The RTT for costs appears in Table 12.5.

This table shows that over half of the cost of criminal damage to Wirral bus stops was concentrated in thirty-seven of the 1,507 bus stops; just 2.4 per cent of the total. The total cost of this damage was £32,650. Plate 8 shows the location of victimised bus stops according to the costs of their damage in relation to the distribution of different types of residential area. The correlation in terms of the costs of damage and the most deprived areas (the 'have nots') is unmistakable.

Table 12.4 Resource targeting table for volume of criminal damage incidents: Wirral bus stops

Incidents per bus stop	Number of bus stops affected	Cumulative number of bus stops	Cumulative number of incidents	Cumulative percentage of bus stops	Cumulative percentage of incidents
13	1	1	13	0.06	2.75
8	2	3	29	0.19	6.14
7	4	7	57	0.46	12.07
6	7	14	99	0.92	20.97
5	6	20	129	1.32	27.33
4	11	31	173	2.05	36.65
3	20	51	233	3.38	49.36
2	49	100	331	6.63	70.12
1	141	241	472	15.99	100.0
0	1265	1507	n/a	100.0	n/a

Table 12.5 Resource targeting table for cost of criminal damage incidents: Wirral bus stops

Cost of incidents per bus stop	Number of bus stops affected	Cumulative number of bus stops	Cumulative percentage of bus stops	Cumulative percentage of cost	Cumulative cost
£1,600	2	2	0.13	4.98	£3,200
£1,400	2	4	0.26	9.34	£6,000
£1,350	1	5	0.33	11.44	£7,350
£1,300	1	6	0.39	13.46	£8,650
£1,250	1	7	0.46	15.41	£9,900
£1,200	2	9	0.59	19.15	£12,300
£1,100	1	10	0.66	20.86	£13,400
£1,000	3	13	0.86	25.53	£16,400
£925	1	14	0.92	26.97	£17,325
£900	3	17	1.12	31.17	£20,025
£800	1	18	1.19	32.42	£20,820
£750	3	21	1.39	35.92	£23,075
£700	4	25	1.65	40.28	£25,875
£650	1	26	1.72	41.30	£26,525
£600	5	31	2.05	45.97	£29,525
£550	2	33	2.18	47.68	£30,625
£525	1	34	2.25	48.50	£31,150
£500	3	37	2.45	50.83	£32,650
£450	3	40	2.65	52.93	£34,000
£425	1	41	2.72	53.60	£34,425
£400	10	51	3.38	59.82	£38,425
£350	4	55	3.64	62.00	£39,825
£300	10	65	4.31	66.66	£42,825
£275	2	67	4.44	67.53	£43,375
£250	13	80	5.30	72.59	£46,625
£225	1	81	5.37	72.94	£46,850
£200	33	114	7.56	83.22	£53,450
£150	13	127	8.42	86.25	£55,400
£125	1	128	8.49	86.45	£55,525
£100	60	188	12.47	95.79	£61,525
£75	2	190	12.60	96.02	£61,674
£50	51	241	15.99	100.0	£64,225
0	1,266	1,507	100.0	n/a	n/a

The cross-referencing of these different data-sets in a GIS enables additional analyses to be conducted. These include the production of tables showing the costs of crime by bus route, by distance travelled, by levels of deprivation or by the crime and disorder rates of the areas through which the bus routes pass.

The analysis of crime patterns on public transport poses a number of technical challenges but also raises several theoretical issues. On the technical front, there is the problem of being able to pinpoint, with accuracy, where along a bus route, incidents of crime and anti-social behaviour occur. Ideally, incidents would be recorded using geographical positioning systems so that the timing and location of events can be logged accurately. In practice, however, bus companies are still a long way from achieving this.

Theoretically there are many new and exciting research questions, which can be studied using GIS approaches. These include investigating:

- How far the presence of capable guardians against crime is affected by the fact that such crimes are mobile
- How far the configuration of bus routes affects the risk of victimisation
- The extent to which public transport aids crime displacement.

There are also a number of practical crime prevention questions such as:

- Should transport planners avoid setting bus routes that go through high crime areas?
- Should routes be planned so that they only go through areas of high natural surveillance?
- Should incidents be contained and dealt with on the vehicles which are affected?

The application of the RTTs to highlight the volume, cost and location of crimes against transport infrastructure has certainly focused minds. However, the true value of this approach lies in its applicability to other types of victimisation including repeat burglary of domestic and non-domestic premises.

The Youth Action Programme

The second example concerns applied evaluation research undertaken for the SMP's Youth Action Programme. The programme has funded eleven youth projects located in some of the more deprived areas of Merseyside. The overall aim has been to contact some of the most vulnerable young people in these areas through approaching them on the streets and encouraging them to become involved in programmes of activities aimed at raising their self-esteem. These include group activities around specific issues (for example, sexual health, violence and crime) and out of area activities involving overnight stays, referred to as 'residentials'. The majority of projects operate in well-defined target areas.

A wide range of methods and techniques has been used by the University of Liverpool to evaluate the impact of the schemes on the young people themselves and on the wider community. These include:

- Analyses of calls to the police reporting juvenile disturbances
- Examination of the number of contacts made by youth workers with young people for each project

- Analysis of results from a self- assessment questionnaire completed by young people
- Direct observation of schemes
- Interviews with young people, project managers, youth workers and police officers.

Some of the analyses have involved the collection of primary data. Examples include information on contacts made between youth workers and young people and data on the lifestyles, aspirations, needs and concerns of young people collected by means of the self-assessment questionnaire.

Of particular concern to police officers and to the SMP, was the rising number of calls to the police from the public reporting juvenile disturbances. These had been increasing within Merseyside at a rate of 10 per cent per annum throughout most of the 1990s. Although such calls are not reporting the committing of crimes per se, they are, nevertheless, a good barometer of the public's concern over what it perceives is anti-social behaviour by young people. The key issue here is the perception and the discomfort or fear that such a perception brings even if in practice all that young people are doing is socialising on the streets for want of alternative venues.

Prior to the evaluation, there was no systematic way of being able to map and analyse changes in the volume and spatial distribution of juvenile disturbance incidents. However, the number of cases within the county (circa 40,000 per annum) and the structure of the data make this feasible to achieve.

Each call logged on the command and control system, contained a 100 metre grid reference for the location of the incident, the time and the date of the incident and three classification codes denoting the nature of the incident. An application was developed in MapInfo by the evaluation team to enable the volume of calls to be displayed, not only within each youth project patch, but also in two concentric buffer zones surrounding each target area. The application, which was programmed in MapBasic, enables the evaluator to specify, for each of the digitized youth project areas, a start date and end date as well as a time interval. Up to four maps can be specified in any one run. Thus, it is possible to match the dates and times of day to activities taking place in the projects or to changes in the volume of contacts made with young people by youth workers.

An example of a map produced for the Arundel Project in Liverpool appears in Figure 12.1. The output from the program comprises a map with circles proportional to the volume of juvenile disturbance calls covering the project area; the first buffer zone is a 0.25 kilometre cordon surrounding the project area boundary and the second buffer extends out by a further 0.25 kilometres. A table of frequencies is also generated showing the volume of calls in the project area and each of the two buffer zones for each set of dates. In addition, a full matrix giving the frequency

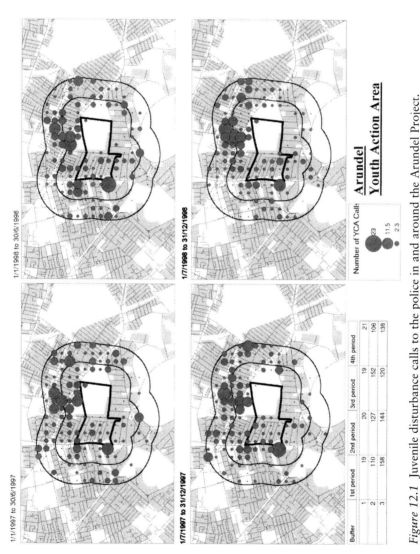

Figure 12.1 Juvenile disturbance calls to the police in and around the Arundel Project.
Source: University of Liverpool, Department of Civic Design

of calls on a monthly basis for each of the three zones for every year from 1992 to the end of 1999 is produced by the program on each run.

The maps are a useful starting point for investigating the possible displacement of juvenile disturbances from the youth work projects to adjacent areas. Table 12.6 shows the results of such an analysis for all projects. Possible signs of target area/ peripheral displacement emerged in four of the eleven projects, but there were also cases where both the target area and each of the buffer zones saw either increases or reductions in the number of calls over the relevant time periods.

The maps can also show how effective targeting has been by individual projects through their choice of operational areas. Figure 12.1 suggests that the Arundel Project in Liverpool may not have identified the most sizeable hotspot for juvenile disturbances which on these maps appeared to be to the north-east of the actual project area.

The GIS processing of the calls to the police data also facilitates the analysis of temporal changes in call rates per 1,000 population at the broader strategic level. Figure 12.2 compares rates in the nine Youth Action areas that had fixed boundaries to those in the most deprived areas

Table 12.6 Changes in youths causing annoyance within and beyond each area

Youth Action area	Percentage change in YCA between 1995/96 and 1997/98			Merseyside
	Target area	Hinterland buffer 2 ≤0.25 km	Hinterland buffer 3 0.26–0.50 km	
Reductions all areas				
Abercromby	−24.5	−12.4	−5.5	9.8
Target area, periphery displacement				
Dovecot	−13.4	19.8	33.4	9.8
Shining out	−10.5	25.6	8.8	9.8
Youth on move, Sefton	−0.3	13.9	7.2	9.8
Birkenhead	−3.3	12.9	39.2	9.8
Increases, most areas				
Croxteth	42.7	-1.8	−11.5	9.8
Arundel	25.4	21.0	−1.7	9.8
Increases, all areas				
Travel Safe	6.9	33.4	27.1	9.8
Broadway	16.5	10.1	6.1	9.8
Fender	**112.6**	**50.2**	**11.9**	**9.8**
Halewood	**24.4**	**10.0**	**4.6**	**9.8**

Note: Rows in bold denote areas with significantly higher than expected calls in 1997 and 1998.

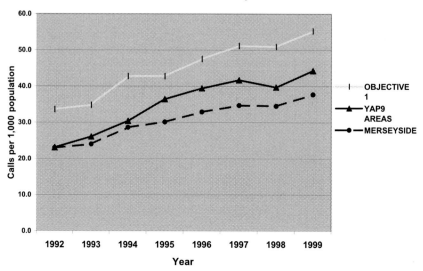

Figure 12.2 Changes in juvenile disturbance call rates for selected areas.

on Merseyside (the European Union Objective One areas) and to the Merseyside average.

Between 1997 and 1998, when all SMP projects were fully operational, the Youth Action Programme areas showed a modest downward shift in the juvenile disturbance rates. This was in contrast to the position in Merseyside generally and to that in the most deprived areas, the EU Objective One areas where little change occurred in juvenile disturbance rates during the period 1997 to 1998. However, most projects wound down after April 1999 when the SMP funding came to end. This is also the period that saw an increase once again in call rates in the Youth Action project areas. The reductions observed during the Youth Action Programme's main phase between 1997 and the end of 1998 had not been sustained.

Finally, the types of residential neighbourhood from which young people participating in the projects were drawn were identified by linking post code to census geographies. Over 230 self-assessment questionnaires were returned to the evaluation team and a sizeable proportion of these contained the full post code of the young person's residential address. These were used to identify the 1991 Population Census enumeration district within which each young person lived. Since each census enumeration district had been assigned a Super Profiles Lifestyle code (that is, denoting the 'type' of residential area it comprised), it was possible to produce a demographic profile for those participating in the youth projects. The percentage of project beneficiaries in each Super Profile Lifestyle are shown in Figure 12.3 alongside the Merseyside county distribution.

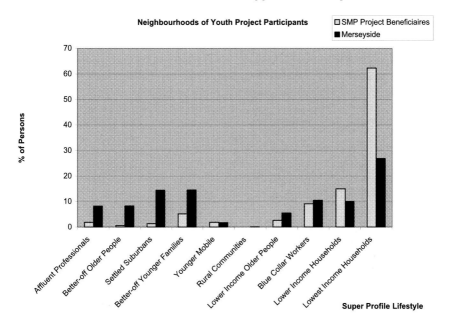

Figure 12.3 Neighbourhood type of youth project beneficiaries on Merseyside.

The results for the SMP project beneficiaries clearly indicate that targeting had been effective in that vulnerable young people from the most disadvantaged areas had, indeed, been reached by the projects. A common problem affecting some regeneration projects is that many of those who benefit are neither those most in need nor those from deprived areas. This appears not to have happened in this case.

The applications, described above, were undertaken by researchers and evaluators at the University of Liverpool for the SMP. With the passing of the Crime and Disorder Act and the emerging culture of evaluation within organisations, practitioners in local authorities, the police service and regeneration partnerships are increasingly going to have to develop mapping and data analysis capabilities in-house. The next section explores levels of skills and competence among practitioners and discusses the role which higher education institutions can play to facilitate skills and technology transfer.

Requisite skills and training needs

The analysis and mapping of crime data to support decision-making in crime prevention and evaluation exercises requires access to appropriate data and software but also competence and skills in a number of key areas. These include:

- An awareness of sources of spatially referenced data on crime, disorder, land use and socio-demographic conditions
- An awareness of data quality and data protection issues
- Expertise in the manipulation, processing and handling of large data sets
- Familiarity with and competence in the use of GIS
- Knowledge of appropriate denominators for use in deriving crime rates
- Basic skills in data analysis
- Skills in map design and in the presentation of data as tables and graphs
- An ability to interpret the results from data analysis
- Writing skills.

Other areas of competence relevant to some of the functions described earlier in this chapter include:

- Expertise in identifying crime clusters and hotspots from disaggregate data
- An ability to identify repeat crimes using police data and other sources
- Knowledge of crime displacement and how to detect it
- Competence in designing and executing crime victimisation surveys
- Expertise in consulting with local communities.

There may well be a division of labour in terms of these core skills in that crime analysts and police local research and intelligence officers may be better equipped to undertake some tasks (e.g. identifying repeat crimes) than local authority community safety officers.

The statutory duty to produce Crime and Disorder Audits placed upon police forces and local authorities by the 1998 Crime and Disorder Act has meant that the possession of many of these skills has become essential to fulfil their roles effectively. In practice, the picture across England and Wales is a very mixed one with some local authorities being far better prepared than others.

In the period between the passing of the Act and the deadline for publishing the first round of audits, the Universities of Liverpool and Huddersfield undertook a postal survey aimed at all local authorities and police constabularies in the country to identify how well prepared these organisations were for the production of the audits. The survey sought to establish, not only the levels of skills and competence in each organisation, but also the extent to which the required infrastructure (e.g. software, data-sets, management arrangements) was in place.

The issues that were examined included arrangements for and experience in data sharing, the availability of GIS software and the availability, in-house, of computing and GIS skills. Other questions enquired about the different types of crime and disorder problems likely to feature as priorities in the forthcoming strategies and the extent to which there had been liaison and consultation with other agencies (Hirschfield *et al.* 1998).

Over 50 per cent of all local authorities that were approached and 80 per cent of police constabularies responded to the survey. The results that emerged showed significant differences in levels of expertise in some of the key areas, not only between the police forces and local authorities, but also between different types of local authority. London boroughs and metropolitan districts were far better equipped and prepared to produce the audits than the largely rural 'shire' counties and the new unitary authorities.

Some of the findings from the survey are shown in Table 12.7 below.

Only 30 per cent of local authorities had access to software that could be used to map crime data compared with 64 per cent of police constabularies. However, local authorities claimed to be more skilled than the police in project management (5.9 per cent of local authorities lacked skills compared with 23.5 per cent of police forces), in monitoring and evaluation techniques (14.8 per cent and 35.3 per cent, respectively, lacking skills), in partnership development (6.9 per cent compared with 20.5 per cent) and in community consultation (9.6 per cent and 17.6 per cent, respectively).

The police claimed to be more skilled compared with the local authorities in the identification of repeat crimes (5.9 per cent lacking skills compared with 49.7 per cent of all local authorities), in the statistical analysis of crime data (11.8 per lacking skills compared with 44.2 per cent of local authorities) and in the design of victimisation surveys (23.5 per cent lacking skills compared with 62.8 per cent of local authorities).

Significantly, a high proportion of both police forces (45.5 per cent) and local authorities (61 per cent) felt that they lacked skills in crime mapping and GIS.

Table 12.7 Local authorities and police forces lacking key skills

Skill/area of expertise	% Lacking skills or poorly skilled: local authorities	% Lacking skills or poorly skilled: police forces
Training for audits	41.6	35.3
Victimisation survey design	62.8	23.5
Priority area selection	36.8	20
Identifying repeat crime	49.7	5.9
Crime data analysis	44.2	11.8
Crime mapping and GIS	61	45.5
Implementation of strategies	22.9	20.5
Project management	5.9	23.5
Partnership development	6.9	20.5
Monitoring and evaluation	14.8	35.3
Community consultation	9.6	17.6

Source: Liverpool and Huddersfield Universities survey, 1998.

Nearly all local authorities (99 per cent) acknowledged the need for external training to help them through the auditing process and 84 per cent were willing to send staff on training programmes if costs were deemed to be 'reasonable'. The equivalent statistic for police forces was 74 per cent.

A detailed breakdown of the demand for external training on the eve of the crime and disorder audit process appears in Figure 12.4.

A similar proportion (just under half) of both the police forces and the local authorities expressed a need for external training in crime mapping and GIS. There was also very little difference in the percentage of police forces and local authorities eager to be trained in crime data analysis (Figure 12.4).

The national curriculum for community safety

Shortly after the survey, the Home Office established a small working party to design an outline National Continuing Professional Development and Higher Educational Curriculum in Community Safety and Crime Prevention (Edwards *et al.* 2000). The aim of the exercise was to identify the role that higher education establishments might play in Britain in running courses to train practitioners in the skills needed to manage and to run community safety programmes.

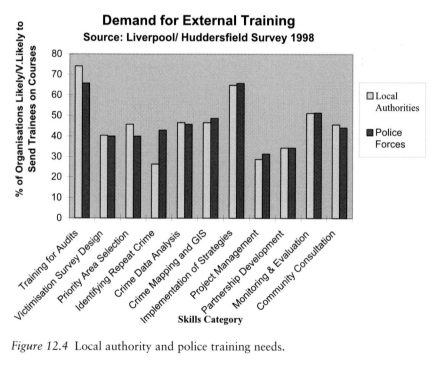

Figure 12.4 Local authority and police training needs.

Among the objectives was a desire:

- To offer a coherent national framework for training and education in community safety
- To publicise details of modules and courses that would meet the requirements of the national curriculum
- To identify the types of occupational groups, professionals and activists that could benefit from the curriculum.

Six key areas of competence were identified which should embrace the range of skills required by community safety and crime prevention practitioners. These were:

- Policy analysis, inter-agency collaboration and synergy maximisation (joined-up policy-making)
- Strategic tasks (including crime and disorder audits, strategy formulation and development)
- Project implementation, management, monitoring and evaluation
- Criminality prevention (working with offenders and those 'at risk' – understanding and curtailing criminal careers; development of inter-personal skills)
- Working with victims and preventing victimisation (understanding patterns of victimisation and managing their differential impacts)
- Community engagement (inter-personal skills and techniques to facilitate community participation, capacity building and development).

The most relevant skills with regard to the mapping and analysis of crime data were the strategic tasks. These were divided into the following three sub-categories; practice in strategic community safety, theories of strategic practice in community safety and research on strategic practice in community safety. Recommended training in the practice of community safety included:

- The design of surveys, including gathering of data on: crime, disorder, social conditions, land use, infrastructure, costs of crime
- The identification of repeat victimisation
- Crime mapping and the use of Geographical Information Systems
- Bench marking and the identification of crime reduction targets
- Data quality, best practice and consistency in the recording of crime and disorder incidents
- Data sharing and data protection issues
- Formulation of crime and disorder reduction strategies
- The potential of policy on education, health, housing, urban planning, leisure and employment to reduce crime opportunities and dispositions
- Safety in public spaces and town centres

- Security technology and management: strengths and weaknesses of surveillance technologies (CCTV), private security, police patrolling, and 'Watch' scheme
- Potential contribution of town planning and management to public safety (including extension/restriction of entertainment licences; development of entertainment zones and '24 hr cities'; use of late-night public transport schemes; street lighting experiments, etc.)
- Management of neighbourhoods (including policing, housing management, wardens, concierges, caretakers, rangers and patrols).

Additional instruction was recommended on criminological theories, particularly those most relevant to situational crime prevention. These included:

- Applied criminology (what theories of crime, criminality and deterrence can tell us about how best to prevent crime)
- Applied social science (what sociological, social geography, political etc.., theories of crime and disorder can tell us about: (1) patterns of crime and 'anti-social behaviour'/ 'incivilities'; and (2) implications for 'opportunity reduction')
- Community decline, crime and incivilities (including 'broken windows thesis'; zero tolerance, etc.) and community organisation, defence and development (including 'routine activities theory' and 'lifestyle' theory)
- Strategic approaches to community safety through situational crime prevention (crime events, rational choice theory, routine activity theory, environmental criminology), design, planning and crime – Crime Prevention Through Environmental Design (CPTED).

The National Curriculum for Community Safety and Crime Prevention is the first attempt in Britain to bring together into a single coherent framework, the whole range of skills needed to fulfil the role of the community safety practitioner. Defining the core competencies has been, in itself, a valuable exercise. However, there remains an urgent need to translate the ideas in the curriculum into deliverable training packages which can be of benefit to practitioners preparing for the publication of the second round of audits in April 2002. This is particularly true of those engaged in the mapping and analysis of crime data.

Conclusion

This chapter began by exploring the nature of information and the evidence base in crime prevention and went on to examine the meaning of targeting and the range of data-sets required to inform resource allocation decisions. Particular attention was focused on the wide range of stake holders who have an interest in crime data analysis and mapping and the reasons why they need to conduct such exercises. Some examples of applications followed where GIS approaches were used in one case to quantify the extent of criminal damage to bus stops, and in the other, to monitor changes in the volume, timing and spatial distribution of juvenile disturbances.

The need for training in the 'strategic tasks' associated with crime data analysis and, in particular, the production of crime and disorder audits was explored in the previous section. Selected details were presented of an outline national curriculum for community safety to be delivered by higher educational institutions.

This chapter has demonstrated, above all, that community safety and crime prevention are particularly diverse fields. There is diversity not only in terms of the actors involved, but also, in terms of the topics and themes that can be investigated, the types of analyses that can be performed and the range of data-sets that can be harnessed. The police officer will often be working to tight deadlines and will be driven by the need to take action to respond to existing and emerging problems. The academic is often interested in explaining why crime occurs and may be more interested in pinning down some of the environmental and social risk factors associated with crime and disorder. The community safety practitioner, a relative newcomer, will be driven by the need to formulate community safety strategies and to oversee their implementation. He or she will also be thinking ahead to the next round of crime and disorder audits and strategies and will be focusing on data sharing and the forging of partnerships with local agencies. Methods of bringing on board local communities will also be given high priority.

The diversity of approaches in crime prevention means that nobody has a monopoly on knowledge and expertise. Each of the stakeholders can learn from each other. The way forward must be one of dialogue and exchanges of views, of experiences, of ideas and of learning as well as the pooling of data.

Acknowledgements

The author would like to thank the staff at the Safer Merseyside Partnership, the youth workers and the young people who participated in the youth action questionnaires. Thanks also to Andrew Newton the PhD student researching safety on public transport at the Department of Civic Design, University of Liverpool for his assistance with the maps and tables.

References

Bowers, K.J., Hirschfield, A. and Johnson, S.D. (1998) 'Victimisation revisited: a case study of non-residential repeat burglary on Merseyside', *British Journal of Criminology* 38(3): 429–52.

Bowers, K. and Hirschfield, A. (1998) 'High risk, low risk: the use of data in the identification of potential targets of commercial crime offenders', in M. Gill (ed.) *Crime at Work: Increasing the Risk for Offenders*, vol. 2, Lyme Regis, Dorset: Perpetuity Press: pp. 35–49.

Department of Environment, Transport and Regions (1998) *A New Deal for Transport: Better for Everyone*, Transport White Paper, DETR.

Edwards, A., Shaftoe, H., Hirschfield, A. and Chenery, S. (2000) *Draft Indicative Framework for a National Continuing Professional Development and Higher Education Curriculum in Community Safety and Crime Prevention*, Scarman Centre, University of Leicester.

Farrell, G. and Pease, K. (1993) *Once Bitten, Twice Bitten: Repeat Victimisation and Its Implications for Crime Prevention*, PRG Crime Prevention Unit Series Paper 46, London: Home Office.

Hirschfield, A. and Bowers, K.J. (1997) 'The effect of social cohesion on levels of recorded crime in disadvantaged areas', *Urban Studies* 34(8): 1275–95.

—— (1998) 'Monitoring, measuring and mapping community safety', in A. Marlow and J. Pitts (eds) *Planning Safer Communities*, Leicester: Russell House Publishing, pp. 189–212.

Hirschfield, A., Bowers, K., Pease, K. and Grundy, M. (1998) 'Counting on crime, results from a national survey of local authorities and police', *Forces Municipal Journal*, 4 December: 18–9.

Mirlees-Black, C., Budd, T., Partridge, S. and Mayhew, P. (1998) *The 1998 British Crime Survey for England and Wales*, Home Office Statistical Bulletin Issue 21/98, Government Statistical Service.

Johnson, S.D., Bowers, K. and Hirschfield, A. (1997) 'New insights into the spatial and temporal distribution of repeat victimisation', *British Journal of Criminology* 37(2): 224–41.

Warner, B.D. and Pierce, G.L. (1993) 'Re-examining social disorganisation theory sing calls to the police as a measure of crime', *Criminology* 31(4): 493–517.

Wikstrom, P.-O. H (1991): *Urban Crime, Criminals and Victims: The Swedish Experience in an Anglo-American Comparative Perspective*, New York: Springer-Verlag.

Index

Note: Page numbers in *italics* refer to figures; those in **bold** refer to Tables